FERMENTED FOODS

FOODS

A Practical Guide

FERMENTED FOODS

A Practical Guide

Dr Caroline Gilmartin

THE CROWOOD PRESS

First published in 2020 by
The Crowood Press Ltd
Ramsbury, Marlborough
Wiltshire SN8 2HR

enquiries@crowood.com

www.crowood.com

British Library Cataloguing-in-Publication Data
A catalogue record for this book is available from the British Library.

ISBN 978 1 78500 757 6

Typeset by Jean Cussons Typesetting, Diss, Norfolk

Printed and bound in India by Parksons Graphics

CONTENTS

A fermenter's shelf.

PREFACE

As a human it is tough to come to terms with the fact that we aren't nearly as important as we think we are. We have always looked at the evolution from simple unicellular organism to complex multicellular being as progress; but what if it's just bigger, not better?

The nineteenth-century microbiologist Louis Pasteur was on the right track, when he said, 'C'est les microbes qui auront le dernier mot' ('the microbes will have the last word'). From the first sighting of tiny 'animalcules' by Antonie Van Leeuwenhoek in the 1680s, it has taken us 300 years to learn how to study them by examining their genetic code. We now know that microbes not only occupy every domain on earth, from the top of Everest to the bottom of the Mariana trench, but that there are probably billions of different species. So far, we have identified just a few thousand. We also know that our lives and theirs are closely, symbiotically intertwined – we are covered in them from head to toe and we have a trillion inside each of our gut microbiota.

And before we even knew of their existence, as far back as the Neolithic era, humans were unwittingly benefiting from microbial activity, as the first fermented drinks and foods were created. Fast forward several thousand years and, despite the seemingly endless development of convenience and ultra-processed foods, the tradition of consuming fermented drinks and foods still endures in many cultures, as an integral part of everyday life. Perhaps it is possible to combine progress with the past, by making some of our own food, enjoying the process and appreciating the results.

This book will explore two different mechanisms: cultured fermentation and wild fermentation. In cultured fermentation, the process is carried out by tangible sources of bacteria and yeast, such as kefir grains, yoghurt starters and kombucha SCOBYs (symbiotic cultures of bacteria and yeasts). Wild fermentation involves nothing more than the naturally occurring microbes on fruit and vegetables, using certain techniques to promote the growth of those that are most helpful to us. To put the use of the mechanisms into context, it will also examine current knowledge about both the gut microbiota and fermentation principles. Although this is not a recipe book as such, some recipes will be followed to show how the methods may be put into action. Then it will be up to you.

ACKNOWLEDGEMENTS

It is not every day that someone is asked to write down everything they know about their favourite subject, but this is what happened to me. It has been an honour, a privilege and at times a nightmare, and it could not have been achieved without the help and support of a lot of people. As this is a method book I shall start with my parents for having me in the first place, and my husband and children for being perfect. I must then thank Xanthe Clay for kicking me into action one day a few years ago when she insisted that I knew enough to do a fermentation demo, and Katie Venner, who kindly put my name forward as a potential author. A whole host of the UK's growing band of fermenters shared their ideas, and gave me help and encouragement, most notably Rose Whitehouse, Alana at Fermented by LAB, Katie Venner, Jo Webster, Tara Clist, Lisa Cadd and Beth Osbourne.

I have to mention all my workshoppers who have attended Kefir School, Kimchi College and Kombucha Class, because I have learned so much by teaching this subject to such interested and inquisitive people. EveryGoodThing's Instagram and Facebook friends everywhere deserve a mention too.

Thanks to Markas Gilmartin and Nicola Armstrong for making sure the chemical/nutritional bits were right, and the two Joannas – House and Webster – for helping me to get all the information I needed. A great deal of fun was had working with Eliza Moreland taking the photos (all the best ones are hers!) – thank you to Hugo the greengrocer, Lizzy Skirton and Sally for being very photogenic.

AWAKE! for morning in the bowl of night
has flung the stone that puts the stars to flight.
Rubiyat of Omar Kayam

CHAPTER 1

INTRODUCTION TO THE MICROBIOTA AND GUT HEALTH

FERMENTED FOODS

A Potted History of Fermentation

Imagine how excited our Anthropocene ancestors must have been when they discovered fermentation in action for the first time. Getting that warm fuzzy feeling from eating over-ripened fruit might have been where it all started. Recent investigations have identified what may have been the world's first brewery, with 13,000-year-old residues of beer having been discovered in a cave near Haifa, Israel. The consumption of yoghurt may date back as far as 10,000 years, when the action of thermophilic bacteria in raw milk kept in goatskin bags produced a soured, thickened, creamy foodstuff, the heat of the African climate providing the perfect temperature for it to set. It must have been a revelation – a way of both preserving and extending the diet. Over subsequent years, sauerkraut, kimchi, kombucha, kefir and water kefir have all have had their moments of discovery.

Interestingly, these foods have endured for thousands of years, probably because they could be preserved for many months, and were also found to be beneficial to human health. It is even possible that these early diets influenced the formation of the human gut microbiota.

What is 'Fermentation'?

The word 'fermentation' means different things to different people. To the microbiologist or biochemist, it is the utilization of carbohydrates by microbes in the absence of oxygen. To the wine or beer maker, it is the action of, specifically, yeast upon sugar to make alcohol. For someone who is interested in fermented foods, however, the definition becomes much wider; it is not restricted to precise biochemical pathways

Residues of alcohol have been found in 13,000-year-old pot fragments. ADOBE STOCK

The heat of the desert – a perfect temperature for yoghurt to form in goatskins. ADOBE STOCK

A plain white cabbage: decomposition on the left and fermentation on the right. E MORELAND

and can include any food that is pleasantly or usefully altered by microbes:

> Fermentation is a controlled process where microbes use carbohydrates to produce a range of useful end products, including lactic acid, alcohol and acetic acid, which can also preserve and enhance food and make new flavours.

One of the most curious things about fermentation is how it differs from decomposition – the process by which food rots. Both are carried out by microbes, but the two outcomes are poles apart. Consider a cabbage that has been left sitting in the vegetable basket for some time; the leaves start to yellow, bacteria and fungi start to feed upon it and after three or four weeks it will be a pile of black-brown mush. However, by removing the oxygen and adding a little salt – that is to say, controlling the conditions in which it finds itself – it is possible to supress the growth of the microbes associated with decay, while encouraging others to produce lactic acid. The result will be a perfectly preserved, nutritiously enhanced vegetable, sitting in a delicious tangy brine.

Doing It Yourself

Changing the humble cabbage into sauerkraut (and, indeed, milk into yoghurt or tea into kombucha) involves science, alchemy and a little magic, but it is essentially a simple process. However, making your own kimchi, fermented chilli sauce or preserved lemons will introduce you to a whole new range of flavours that you never knew existed. And you will have created them all on your own – well, you and just a few billion microbes!

Of course, you could just pop to the shops for your kefir and sauerkraut, so what are the benefits of doing it yourself? First, when processes are industrialized, corners are cut, natural variation is eliminated, and products change. For example, many brands of shop kefir are made by reconstituting acid whey waste from commercial Greek yoghurt production with isolated milk proteins to make a base. Individual bacterial cultures are then added to the mix and a short fermentation conducted. This is a far cry from the kefiran-rich symbiosis of home-made milk kefir. Similarly, much commercially produced sauerkraut is pasteurized, so that it remains stable for transportation and storage. Often, starter cultures are introduced for reproducibility purposes, reducing the natural variety of strains involved.

Second, home fermentation is extremely economical. While artisanal fermented foods are comparatively expensive to purchase, because the processes are difficult to scale up, they are easy to do yourself in small quantities.

Fermentation can also be great as a collaborative experience – large-scale vegetable prep is best done with friends, with chatter and sharing of expertise and ideas. It is often better to be shown how to do something than to read about it, which is probably why fermentation workshops are so popular. Hopefully you will have the confidence to be one of the expertise sharers after using this book.

Fermentation is even better with friends.

THE HUMAN GUT

There is a growing body of evidence around the health benefits of fermented foods, but why exactly are they good for human health, both prebiotic and probiotic? During fermentation, microbes synthesize vitamins and minerals, increase the digestibility of proteins and carbohydrates, increase the bioavailability of phytochemicals (plant compounds) and produce bio-active compounds that have important health benefits. Many of the microbes involved are probiotic, probably leading to the prevention and improvement of many chronic and metabolic conditions.

From a scientific perspective, it is an exciting time to be a human. Over the past 30 years, it has become clear that the human being as an 'individual' does not really exist. Within every large intestine resides the microbiota – an enormous 2kg population of about 40,000,000,000,000 (40 trillion) microbes, including around 400

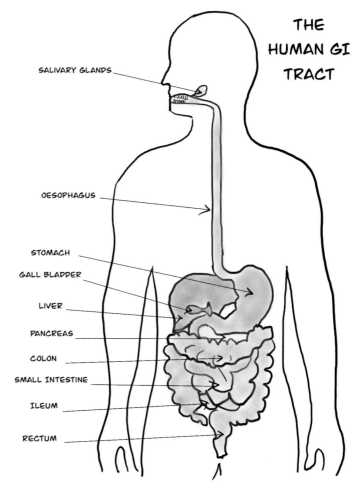

THE HUMAN GI TRACT

SALIVARY GLANDS
OESOPHAGUS
STOMACH
GALL BLADDER
LIVER
PANCREAS
COLON
SMALL INTESTINE
ILEUM
RECTUM

The human gastrointestinal tract.

MICROBIOTA

40,000,000,000,000 MICROBES
400-500 DIFFERENT SPECIES

↓
WITH

MICROBIOME

↓

3,000,000 GENES

↓
PRODUCING

METABOLOME

↓

114,158 METABOLITES
.....SO FAR!

The microbes in the microbiota contain many more genes than a human does, which make hundreds of thousands of metabolites. To date, over 100,000 different human metabolites have been listed on the Human Metabolome Database.

known species of bacteria, plus fungi, protozoa, viruses and bacteriophages. They work together to play an essential role in almost all of the body's daily functions. The microbiota is so integral to the body's survival and development that it is considered a virtual organ, or sometimes even the second brain.[1]

If it were stretched out, the gatrointestinal (GI) tract would be about 9 metres or 30 feet long. It extracts nutrients from the food you eat, while leaving the waste products behind and protecting the internal environment of the body. As the lining of your gut is first-line defence against invasion from unwanted microbes and particles, 70% of your immune system can be found in its walls.

The gut microbiota resides in the colon and constitutes about 80% of your body's microbes; the rest occupy your skin, mouth, urogenital and upper GI tracts. It does not sit there like an enormous lump: microbes occupy the inner folds of the lumen, are mixed up in the digesta (the mass of fibre that passes through your intestine) and also in the colon's double mucous layer.[2]

The human body has just 23,000 genes that make proteins involved in growth and development. This may seem a low number for something as

complex as a human – in fact, tomatoes have more genes than a human – but the microbes in the microbiota contain over 3,000,000 genes. (These genes in the gut are referred to as the 'microbiome' rather than the 'microbiota', which refers to the microbes themselves.) Humans have outsourced production of thousands of important compounds to the gut microbes. These 'metabolites' (products of metabolism) make up the 'metabolome'. Some metabolites are produced by several different bacterial species, and it does not matter which makes it as long as you have the product. Others are made by specialized bacteria; these metabolites cannot be replaced if the microbes are lost.

It seems that the microbiota has shaped the development of *Homo sapiens*, gradually gaining additional advantages from the colonization of the gut by these 'external' yet essential microbes. One clue to this theory is the discovery, for example, that Japanese people can easily digest seaweed, because their microbiota have specific enzymes from marine bacteria.[3] Another is that the microbiotal production of equol, which can reduce hot flushes in menopausal women, is produced in twice as many women in countries with high soy consumption.[4]

Just a few of the most well-studied functions of the microbiota. There seems to be an axis with every organ: gut–brain, gut–kidney, gut–heart, and so on.

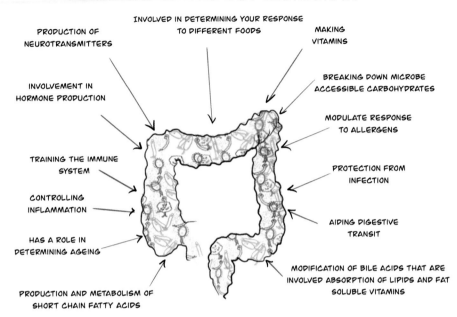

FUNCTIONS OF THE GUT MICROBIOTA

PRODUCTION OF NEUROTRANSMITTERS

INVOLVED IN DETERMINING YOUR RESPONSE TO DIFFERENT FOODS

MAKING VITAMINS

INVOLVEMENT IN HORMONE PRODUCTION

BREAKING DOWN MICROBE ACCESSIBLE CARBOHYDRATES

MODULATE RESPONSE TO ALLERGENS

TRAINING THE IMMUNE SYSTEM

PROTECTION FROM INFECTION

CONTROLLING INFLAMMATION

HAS A ROLE IN DETERMINING AGEING

AIDING DIGESTIVE TRANSIT

PRODUCTION AND METABOLISM OF SHORT CHAIN FATTY ACIDS

MODIFICATION OF BILE ACIDS THAT ARE INVOLVED ABSORPTION OF LIPIDS AND FAT SOLUBLE VITAMINS

THE MICROBIOTA

The functions and role of the microbiota are immensely complex and diverse, but, at the top level, they break down plant fibres that the body cannot digest itself, and make vital metabolites.

Microbiota Development
Early Years

Colonization of the gut might begin even before birth, as it seems that the placenta and umbilical cord are not as sterile as first thought. However, for a normally delivered baby, it all starts upon contact with the

FACTORS INFLUENCING MICROBIOTA DEVELOPMENT FROM 0-3 YRS

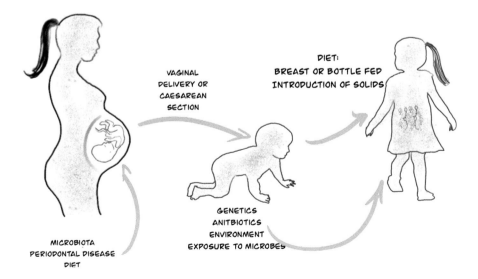

VAGINAL DELIVERY OR CAESAREAN SECTION

DIET: BREAST OR BOTTLE FED INTRODUCTION OF SOLIDS

Factors influencing the development of the gut microbiota from conception to age 3.

MICROBIOTA PERIODONTAL DISEASE DIET

GENETICS ANITBIOTICS ENVIRONMENT EXPOSURE TO MICROBES

vaginal microbiota and associated faecal organisms. Caesarean-born children have microbiotal differences, which are evident for some years afterwards.

Breast milk plays the next crucial role, with *Bifidobacterium infantis* bacteria in the infant gut breaking down the oligosaccharides (sugars) it contains. Bottle-feeding can also affect microbiotal development.[5]

Infancy is the 'window of opportunity' that can shape the microbiota and also affect future susceptibility to conditions including allergies and asthma. By the age of 3, it is pretty stable (with good health/lifestyle) and remains so until old age, when some of the species are lost.

Genetics

Many of a person's characteristics are determined by their genes. 99.9% of human DNA is the same in everyone but the 0.1% difference is what creates individuals. Some of the genes probably influence the types of bacteria that are in the microbiota. For example, more lactase-producing bacteria exist in the gut of some people who have a problem with the lactase-making gene.[6] However, as even identical twins can have very different microbiota, the role of genetics is not clear-cut. Within families there does seems to be a 'core' microbiota[7], although separating this as a genetic issue from the effects of cohabiting is tricky. There is gender-specific variance too, which might be because of disparities in male/female immune systems, which may allow different microbes to colonize the gut.[8]

Other Factors

Geographical location – city or countryside, island or inland – and lifestyle (westernized or hunter-gatherer, for example), all have an influence. The administration of antibiotics is also significant. Their over-use is not just bad for creating resistant microbes, it can also have a long-term effect on the microbiota, especially in early childhood.

Colonization

The adult microbiota consists of hundreds of species that exist nowhere else in nature. Other than via birth/breastfeeding, they need other routes of entry. Some microbes are strict anaerobes, which cannot survive in the presence of oxygen, so they have elaborate strategies for survival. Faecal transmission plays a role in this: organisms leave the host in faecal matter and survive in an environment – people, food, animals, objects, surroundings, especially bathrooms – until ingested by a new host. They then need a colonization strategy to avoid host defences and to survive in the gut.

The immune system is so highly specialized it can tell the difference between pathogens and these useful bacteria. People who live in the same house share more species than non-cohabiters; shaking hands, hugging, kissing and having sex are all ways of transmitting microbes. Other routes for less specialized species that can survive outside of the gut include raw fruit and vegetables, water, the environment and animals, especially pets.

The Perfect Microbiota?

The perfect microbiota probably does not exist. It is believed that there are about 5,000 microbiotal species in total, but many have not yet been characterized. Although there is a core of microbes present in most people, there is no single optimal gut composition; each one is as individual to its host as a fingerprint. A healthy microbiota is 'highly diverse', with between 600,000 and 3 million bacterial genes and probably at least 400 different species.

Once established, the microbiota can vary, but the same core species endure. Some types of bacteria are particularly associated with good health, for example, *Christensenella* and *Akkermansia* sp. are rare in overweight people, yet common in the lean and/or physically fit. More microbial diversity is better for health and wellbeing, and that diversity is heavily influenced by diet.

DYSBIOSIS

The microbiota can adapt to a degree of change, but sometimes things go too far. This is called dysbiosis (the opposite of the usual symbiotic relationship a body has with its microbiota) and is linked to a huge list of about 70 health problems, including bowel disorders,

Examples of dysbiosis include loss of beneficial bacteria (people who are deficient in *Coprococcus* sp. and *Dialister* sp. have been found to be more susceptible to depression[9]), and overgrowth of pathobionts (in which bacteria that are not usually harmful can take over and have negative effects; this may be a factor in colorectal cancer[10]).

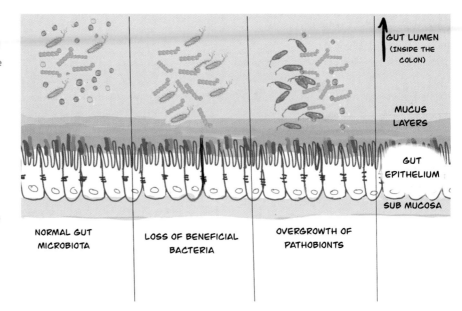

NORMAL GUT MICROBIOTA

LOSS OF BENEFICIAL BACTERIA

OVERGROWTH OF PATHOBIONTS

GUT LUMEN (INSIDE THE COLON)

MUCUS LAYERS

GUT EPITHELIUM

SUB MUCOSA

inflammatory bowel disease, allergies, coeliac disease, obesity and diabetes, neurodegenerative conditions and several types of cancer. It is not clear which comes first, the disease or the dysbiosis. In fact, it probably varies, or one may exacerbate the other. There are several different ways in which the microbiota can be off balance.

General Symptoms

Dysbiosis as an underlying cause for illness is generally not yet recognized by the medical profession; it is always seen as a symptom of something else. Because it could be cause or effect and there is an enormous range of symptoms, including bloating, abdominal cramping, unusual bowel behaviour, indigestion, food intolerances, fatigue, moodiness, depression, joint pain, skin conditions, it can be hard to identify. Alternatively, a patient might present with specific symptoms of one of the conditions mentioned. Faecal sample analysis is likely to be used more commonly in the future to see whether there is an issue.

Leaky Gut

One of the internal effects of dysbiosis is increased intestinal permeability or 'leaky' gut. Although a little leakiness is normal, if the microbiota is not making the right components for the gut lining, it can become severe. Gaps can appear between the cells forming the gut wall, and tiny fragments of food or microbes can end up in the tissue outside the gut. This can trigger an

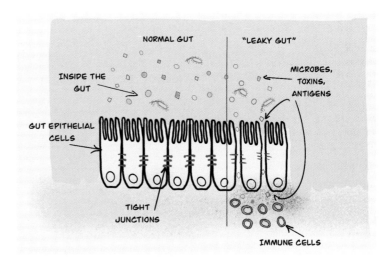

NORMAL GUT

"LEAKY GUT"

INSIDE THE GUT

MICROBES, TOXINS, ANTIGENS

GUT EPITHELIAL CELLS

TIGHT JUNCTIONS

IMMUNE CELLS

The cells lining the gut are linked together by tight junctions. Failing to make the right components to maintain these junctions can cause the gut to become 'leaky'. Channels can open up, and tiny particles may reach the lower layers of the gut lining, setting off inflammation.

immune response, leading to inflammation of the gut lining. Maintenance of the mucous layer and the tight junctions between cells is pivotal to gut health.

When the microbiota ferments the fibre in the colon that the body cannot process, some of the most important end products are short chain fatty acids (SCFAs). (They may also be referred to by their specific names, such as butyrate, acetate or propionate.) They are extremely important in strengthening the gut barrier and regulating the immune system, in order to keep inflammation at bay.

EATING FOR GUT HEALTH

Everybody has a fair amount of control over the state of their microbiota, as lifestyle choices can impact gut, physical and mental health. With every mouthful, you never eat alone – what you eat, your microbiota eats. Changes to the microbiota can happen extremely quickly. Just a couple of weeks of 'holiday eating' – burgers and chips with a few glasses of wine, puddings and ice creams – are enough to cause loss of diversity

and alterations to immunological and metabolic functions.

The good news is that, if you have a healthy microbiota, and the diet change is temporary, bacteria hidden in the crypts of your guts, and your appendix if you have one, are able to restore the balance. The bad news is that no one really knows how long it is possible to eat like that before dysbiosis begins to play a role in the development of a metabolic disorder. It is probably best to switch to a healthy diet as soon as possible.

Prebiotics

Simply put, prebiotics are foods for the microbiota. The better nourished the gut microbes are, the greater diversity there will be and the more useful end products of metabolism will be produced.

Fibre

Dietary fibre is found only in plant-based foods. One of the major roles of gut microbes is to digest it for the body, as it cannot be assimilated otherwise, unlike the proteins, fats and sugars, for which the body has the enzymes. There are different types of fibre. Some act as bulking agents for the stool, while others, such as inulin, resistant starch and fermentable oligosaccharides, provide energy for the microbiota. These are usually referred to as 'microbe available carbohydrates', or MACs.

When MACs reach the large intestine, the microbes ferment them (just like in sauerkraut!), producing SCFAs. In the presence of a low-fibre diet, or a very high-fat one, the microbes are under-nourished. The result is that they eat too much of the top mucus layer, and work their way into the lower layer, where they should

Positive influences upon gut health	Negative influences upon gut health
High-fibre diet, rich in microbe-accessible carbohydrates	Low-fibre diet
Great variety of plant-based foods	High carb/fat/protein diet in the absence of fibre
Exercise	Sedentary lifestyle
Eating at sensible times in line with circadian rhythms	Irregular eating patterns / late eating / continuous grazing / bingeing
Avoiding stress	Stress
Eating fermented foods	Over consumption of ultra-processed foods
Avoiding ultra processed foods	Artificial sweeteners
Regular sleep pattern	Irregular sleep pattern
Moderation in all things including alcohol, ultra processed foods	Excessive alcohol consumption
Appropriate use (as opposed to over-use) of medication	Antibiotics and other medication

You are how you live: there are many factors that may have a negative influence upon the diversity of the microbiota. Smoking and the contraceptive pill have also been implicated.

not be. They start making the wrong sort of products from their metabolism, which can be harmful. When the microbes or products get this far, they are sensed by the immune system, which can cause an immune, inflammatory response.

The Hadza tribe in Tanzania: as near as possible to a perfect microbiota?
ADOBE STOCK

Polyphenols

Polyphenols are a huge class of phytochemicals that contain the compounds that colour fruit and vegetables. They are also found in dark chocolate, coffee and red wine, which is why these seemingly indulgent products can be included in a healthy diet. Most polyphenols reach the colon where they become a delicious nutrient source for the microbiota, which releases beneficial metabolites from them. Polyphenols also help to maintain microbiota balance, inhibiting potential pathogens and stimulating proliferation of beneficial species with their breakdown products.

Thirty Plants a Week

The Hadza tribe of hunter-gatherers in Tanzania have the most diverse microbiota in the world today. Their ancient and largely unaltered diet comprises a huge range of foraged plant-based foods, with occasional helpings of meat. They regularly eat over 30 varieties of plant each week, providing their microbiota with many different types of MACs and polyphenols. After just three days of eating with the tribe, professor of genetics Tim Spector saw his microbiota increase in detectable species by 20% (shown by stool sample analysis). Unfortunately, however, this change was not sustainable and within days of the professor returning home it had returned to its former state.[9]

Spector's research has led a team at King's College London to propose that one of the best ways of improving gut heath is to consistently eat an extremely varied diet, based on 30 different plant-based foods a week. The reasons for this are that each of the different types of microbe in the microbiota (there may be as many as 400) have slightly different nutritional requirements, which can be met by eating a vast range of foods all containing slightly different MACs and phytonutrients. This does not imply a need to become vegan or vegetarian; it is not necessary to exclude either dairy or a modest amount of meat.

As unachievable as this may sound on paper, a 30-a-week plan does not require fixed portion sizes, and includes herbs, spices, seeds, nuts, pulses, whole grains, fruit and vegetables. Easy wins are buying ready-mixed dried rice/grain mixtures for cooking, mixed bags of salad, and mixed nuts and seeds to sprinkle on top of things.

Probiotics

Probiotics are 'live bacteria and yeasts that, when administrated in adequate amounts, are beneficial to human health'. The word 'probiotic' meaning 'for life' is derived from Greek – the opposite to 'antibiotic' in fact. The first inkling that certain bacteria were beneficial was reported by microbiologist Eli Metchnikov over 100 years ago, in his text *Studies on Optimism*: 'With various foods undergoing lactic acid fermentation and consumed raw (sour milk, kefir, sauerkraut, pickles) humans introduced huge amounts of proliferating lactic acid bacteria to their alimentary tracts.'[10]

These days, in order to be designated as probiotic, a microbe must have passed rigorous lab tests, and have been shown to be non-pathogenic, able to survive the GI-tract journey to the colon, and to have a proven effect. Probiotics are available in liquid capsule form and as dried supplements, but it is also possible to take a more natural approach, as exactly the same kind of microbes are found in fermented foods. Some examples of known probiotics include:

- *Lactobacillus rhamnosus GG*
- *Lactobacillus acidophilus CL1285*
- *Saccharomyces boulardii CNCM 1-745*
- *Bifidobacterium bifidum W23*

Some might say that the advantage of having supplements with probiotics is that it is easy to identify exactly what you are consuming. I would counter that with a list of why functional foods can beat a capsule:

- **Variety.** Functional foods contain myriad species of LAB and also functional yeasts, which can all have positive effects on the microbiota. In some cases, this could be more beneficial than a huge influx of a very limited number of species.
- **Health.** Functional foods are so much more than a capsule. They are nutrient-rich sources of vitamins, minerals, short chain peptides, phytonutrients, organic acids, fibre. Food is not just for nutrition. It also protects the microbes from conditions in the GI tract, increasing their chances of arriving unscathed.
- **Prebiotic.** Fermented vegetables are prebiotic too, containing a range of phytonutrients such as polyphenols and MACs.
- **Sustainable.** Probiotic capsules are big business, produced in large quantities in busy factories. On the other hand, fermented foods are economical and sustainable, with no ultra-processing required.
- **Functional.** It is possible that the natural symbiosis of strains that grow together is more beneficial than those artificially grouped in probiotic capsules.

Although probiotics seem to be mentioned in the general media almost daily, the mechanisms for their action are not well understood. It seems that they communicate with the existing gut microbiota by some kind of 'cross-talk', sending chemical messengers using complex pathways. In the most basic sense, they kick the gut microbiota into action, and fight off the pathogens, via some of the following actions:

- Attaching to sites on the gut mucosa, preventing pathogens from adhering.
- Stimulating the immune system, by sending chemical messengers across the membranes.
- Fermenting MACs to produce the ever-helpful SCFAs.[11]
- Altering patterns of gene expression for immune and mucosal genes (turning them up, a bit like a dimmer switch).
- Encouraging the proliferation of beneficial species perhaps by the production of growth factors, or substrates for commensals to use.

There is some debate about whether probiotic organisms 'colonize' – become permanent residents of – the gut or not. The answer in most cases is generally not, or certainly not permanently. They are rather like tourists, who come to visit a city, stay for a couple of weeks, buoy up the local economy and then go home!

There are various complicated mechanisms involving surface molecules, by which they could attach, but one thing is certain – they are not recognized as pathogens and the body does not raise an immune response against them. They are not competitively excluded from attaching to the mucosal surface by the existing microbiota either.

THE PERSONALIZED DIET

As each person's microbiota is as individual as that person, researchers have been studying the body's individual responses to food. The 'Predict' study has looked at the responses of identical twins to the same foods. Even identical twins have different microbiota, and they do not have the same response to food; their glucose, insulin and dietary fat levels (which may be used as metabolic markers) were found to vary significantly after the consumption of the same foods.[12] Another study has shown the same sort of results with people's individual responses to bread.[13] However, even with this knowledge, the next step – what to do with it, in order to give personalized dietary advice – is complicated. It is thought that only a fraction of the responses were due to the fat, sugar or protein content of the food. The rest was probably to do with the micronutrients, or even additives from ultra-processed food.

HOW TO EAT FERMENTED FOODS

Can fermented foods change your life? Possibly, especially if you have previously been a sickly person, seemingly susceptible to every passing germ. Although not everyone will see immediate benefits, as it depends on the status of their own particular gut, in preventive terms, the impact of fermented foods could be significant. There is a possibility that metabolic and autoimmune disorders or even cancers could be avoided by maintenance of good gut health, but a major retrospective cohort study will be required before this can be asserted.

All fermented foods are extremely nutrient dense and the additive effects of too much of a good thing are unknown. Apart from purchased yoghurt cultures, it is not possible to know what probiotic microbes they contain or what microbes are in your own microbiota and how they might interact. As a result, it is necessary to start eating fermented foods in small quantities – a spoonful of sauerkraut, a couple of sips of kefir – and then see how you feel. Any gastrointestinal gurgling is likely to pass as

the microbes are usually transient gut visitors. The amount can then be increased gradually over a few days. This is especially important if you have IBS/IBD, as individual responses can differ hugely.

Fermented foods are suitable for almost everyone, but there are caveats. You should start eating them when you are well, not when you are in the middle of any kind of serious illness, especially any form of cancer, or any other condition where you may be immuno-compromised. If you have had recent gastric, hepatic or dental surgery, you must check with your consultant first. Occasional infections have arisen post-surgery in chronically ill patients; almost all caused by large doses of just one type of microbe from probiotic capsules. In this regard, the natural symbiotic interactions of fermented foods may be preferable to capsule monocultures. Some researchers are concerned that antibiotic resistance genes present in the environment could transfer to probiotic bacteria. To be honest, they probably already have, and into lots of your gut microbes.

Fermented vegetables have a 2% salt content, so you should be aware of this if you need to watch your intake. All fermented foods also contain the biogenic amine histamine to varying degrees, which can cause allergic reactions in intolerant individuals. Remember, though, even if you cannot tolerate fermented foods, you can still improve your gut health through the prebiotics route: diet, fibre intake and exercise.

Eat fermented foods little and often; they are nutrient-dense, and fermented vegetables have always been salted. Aim for diversity, with several different types on the go at the same time!

CHAPTER 2

FERMENTATION: THE BASICS

FOOD-FERMENTING MICROBES

Microbes are organisms that are so small they are only visible (singly) under a microscope. However, although they may be small, they are not simple! Consisting of just a single cell, they are like a factory with everything in one place – electrical wiring, gas supply, windows and doors, a sewage system, machinery

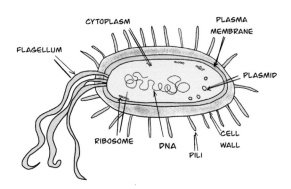

The basic structure of a prokaryotic bacterium. The colours are imagined; it can only be seen at this level with an electron microscope.

The unwitting father of microbiology, Antonie Van Leeuwenhoek (1632–1723), was a textile manufacturer in the Netherlands. He was the first person to see microbes, when he developed lenses used for the inspection of fabric fibres to create a microscope. ADOBE STOCK

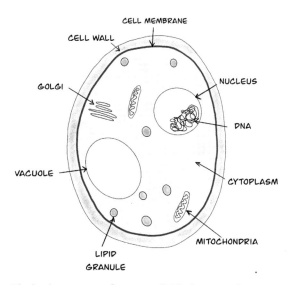

The basic structure of a yeast cell. Like humans, they are eukaryotes, sharing features such as mitochondria and a nucleus.

for manufacturing, food and water. In reality, this translates to a cell envelope that allows transport in and out, which contains cytoplasm, where a mixture of water, genetic material, nutrients, protein synthesizing machinery and enzymes are all suspended.

The number of different microbial species on the planet is the subject of much hot debate, but there may be as many as a few trillion. So far, just a few thousand have been identified and named.

There are two types of food-fermenting microbes: bacteria and yeasts. They are fundamentally very different. Yeasts are eukaryotes with their DNA inside a cell nucleus – just like humans, in fact. In prokaryotic bacteria, the DNA floats around the cytoplasm in a clump. What unites the two types is that they are all unicellular and contain all the machinery they require for growth and reproduction within their own selves. Their ability to ferment food is not deliberate, but comes as a by-product of their metabolism, which is then harnessed to produce the beneficial foodstuffs.

The microbes use different fermenting pathways: lactic acid fermentation, acetic acid and alcohol fermentation.

Lactic Acid Fermentation

Lactic acid is an organic acid with the formula $CH_3CH(OH)CO_2H$. It is similar to acetic acid or vinegar, although actually volume for volume it is about

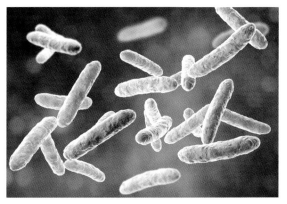

Electron micrograph showing the rod shape of *Lactobacillus plantarum*, a type of LAB. ADOBE

10 times more acidic. It acts as a preservative for fermented foods.

Lactic acid bacteria (LAB) produce lactic acid (among other things) from carbohydrates including glucose, fructose or galactose. Many different types of bacteria have this property, including *Lactobacillus*, *Lactococcus*, *Streptococcus*, *Weisella*, *Leuconostoc* and *Enterococcus* species, but they may be referred to collectively as LAB. They are not just important in home fermentation; they are also major players in the food and biotechnology industries, used for the natural processing of chocolate, vanilla, olives, coffee and honey, and for the production of food additives such as dextran, and also now in the production of probiotics.

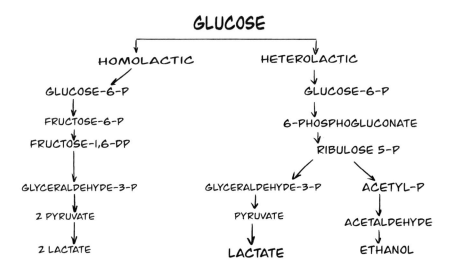

The different pathways for heterolactic and homolactic fermentation by LAB.

LAB can be divided into two main groups, depending upon which pathway they use to make lactic acid, for which they need a lot of sugar and little oxygen:

1. **Homofermenters** produce just lactic acid. Examples include *Streptococcus thermophilus*, *Streptococcus lactis*, *Lactobacillus lactis*, *Lactobacillus bulgarius*. Many of these are yoghurt cultures as their production of just this with a few additional flavour compounds gives the characteristic tang.

2. **Heterofermenters** produce lactic acid and, in addition, carbon dioxide and ethanol or acetate. Examples include species of *Leuconostoc mesenteroides*, *Leuconostoc lactis* and *Weisella* sp. This is why one of the first signs of activity in vegetable fermentation is the formation of bubbles of carbon dioxide by heterofermentative *L. mesenteroides*.

WHAT HAPPENS IN A MICROBE: HOW LACTIC ACID FERMENTATION OCCURS

Imagine a lone lactobacillus sitting in a jar of milk. Transporters in its cell wall recognize the lactose molecule and selectively let it in, acting like doormen. Once inside, the lactose molecule is recognized by beta-galactosidase, an enzyme that splits it into its component glucose and galactose parts. Some LAB can utilize the galactose but if they cannot, it is excreted back outside the cell (or thrown out by the doorman!).

Next, the glucose enters a complex cycle of reactions that extract its energy, resulting in the production of lactic acid. If the acid concentration is too high, it will become toxic to the cell, so it is excreted into the medium – in this example, milk kefir – where it acidifies it. This is just one of many simultaneous mechanisms in one microbe of billions in milk kefir.

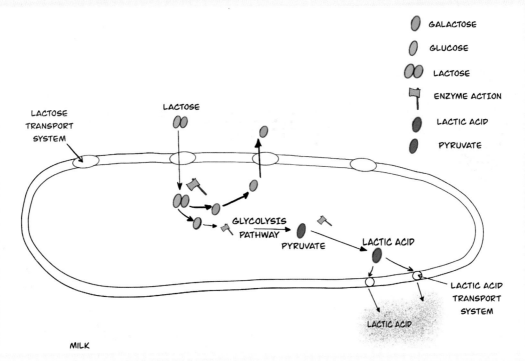

Inside an LAB.

Of course, nothing is that simple in science, so some microbes can be both homo- and heterofermenters, depending on their environment, including *Lactobacillus casei*, *Lactobacillus rhamnosus* and *Lactococcus lactis*.

LAB also contain enzymes that can break down proteins (via proteolysis) into smaller peptides and free amino acids. The amino acids can be further converted into flavour compounds including the various alcohols, acid and aldehydes that give fermented foods their distinctive flavours.

Some strains of LAB, such as *L. delbrueckii*, *L. bulgaricus*. *L. casei*, and *L. plantarum*, are able to break down fats (via lipolysis) if present, for example, in milk. This releases free fatty acids, glycerol and mono and di-acylglycerides. These compounds naturally emulsify other food components, which aid in the texture development of the final product.[14]

Acetic Acid Fermentation

Acetic acid bacteria (AAB) produce acetic acid from alcohol. This group includes *Acetobacter*, *Gluconobacter* and the inconveniently named *Komagataeibacter* sp. As well as having important roles in fermented foods, especially kombucha, vinegar and to a lesser extent milk and water kefir, they are used industrially for the production of vinegar. All are strict aerobes.

Alcoholic Fermentation

Louis Pasteur first identified yeasts as the agents of fermentation in 1875, realizing that alcohol was produced anaerobically in the absence of oxygen. It is now known that many species of yeast also carry out the process in the presence of oxygen, as long as there is lots of sugar present. Examples include *Saccharomyces* sp., *Brettanomyces* sp., *Candida* sp. and *Kluyveromyces* sp.

Yeasts also produce invertase, an enzyme that breaks down complex sugars (for example, sucrose) into simple sugars such as glucose and fructose, which it can use to make alcohol. In water kefir and kombucha, these sugars also become available to LAB. Some bacteria, such as *Zymomonas* sp., can also produce alcohol from sugars, using a slightly different pathway. These bacteria may be present in water kefir grains or kombucha.

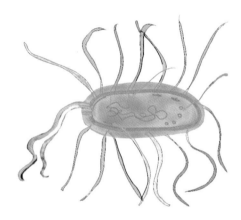

Acetic acid bacteria have peritrichous flagella – they are covered in them. These structures make them motile.

OXIDATION OF ETHANOL TO ACETIC ACID

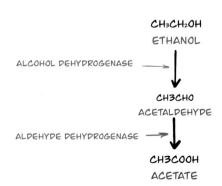

CH_3CH_2OH
ETHANOL

ALCOHOL DEHYDROGENASE →

CH_3CHO
ACETALDEHYDE

ALDEHYDE DEHYDROGENASE →

CH_3COOH
ACETATE

The enzymes required and the pathway that changes alcohol into acetic acid. This is performed by AAB.

SAFETY IN HOME FERMENTATION: THE RUMOURS

Many people fear microbes – not entirely unreasonably, since there are some nasty ones out there – and find it difficult to accept that consuming foods deliberately laden with them, left to fester on the side awhile, is acceptable. However, during fermentation, a series of fortunate events occurs that means that, if the guidelines given here are followed, the food will be safe. Considering the world-wide popularity of the practice, its microbiological safety record is excellent, and the evidence in its favour is clear.

One of the most common concerns is the fear of contracting botulism. The cause of this illness, *Clostridium botulinum*, which is sometimes fatal, is a spore-forming anaerobe that commonly exists in nature, but is inhibited by salt and acidity. If you follow the instructions in this book, you most certainly will not be at risk, but there are three commonly cited examples that are worth noting. Two cases of botulism arose in the USA in 2012, from the fermentation of shop-bought tofu of dubious origin (which had been sitting in open, water-filled vats before purchase), without salt. Two things are clear from this: first, the importance of salt in fermented foods, and second, the importance of starting with good-quality ingredients of reliable provenance.[15]

Home canning is a common method of preservation in the USA. Low-acid vegetables must be canned under pressure, to ensure that spore-forming microbes are destroyed. If the wrong procedure is used, there is a risk of spores surviving and germinating in the can. The canning of vegetables is not the same as fermentation; it is merely a method for heating and storing vegetables.

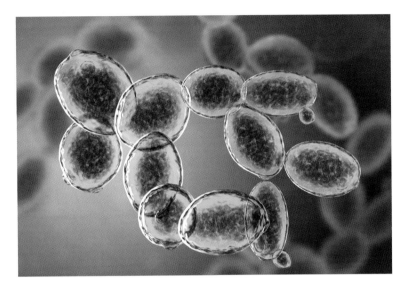

Electron micrograph of a yeast, *Saccharomyces cerevisiae*, showing the buds that will split off to make new cells. ADOBE

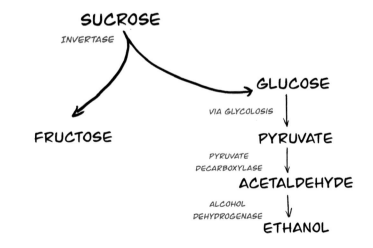

The fermentation pathway to produce alcohol used by yeasts, as long as carbohydrates are in good supply.

HOW MICROBES GROW (USING BACTERIA AS AN EXAMPLE)

After a lag phase to get used to their environment, bacteria enter a growth phase where they multiply by binary fission (or by budding in yeasts); effectively, one bacterium divides to make two. The doubling time varies according to the bacterium in question.

For our LAB, let us assume 90 minutes in optimal conditions (2–3 days in the gut). This happens exponentially, so one bacterium becomes 2, 2 become 4, 4 become 8, and so on. The bacteria carry on in this phase until one of three things happens: nutrient availability is compromised; toxic compounds begin to accumulate; or they just run out of space. Eventually if no changes to the system are made, they will enter a death phase.

Let's apply this to kefir: we make some sweeping assumptions along the way, but it will give us an idea of the potential probiotic content. Kefir grains contain about 110 million microbes per gram, so in 3g of kefir grains, there will be 330 million microbes. Let's put them in 500ml of milk at room temperature, in a clip-top jar, and leave the culture for 24 hours.

Assuming a lag phase of 4 hours and then doubling every 90 minutes over the next 20 hours, that's 13 generations: we could have 330,000,000 x 2^{13} = about 2.70 trillion microbes in our 500ml jar. In a 150ml serving that would be about 900 billion cfu/ml. Some of them will survive the GI tract; according to some research, viability is not essential.

In 1989 there was a popular fad for popping raw garlic cloves into oil and leaving it on the side to infuse. Garlic can have *C. botulinum* spores on. Unfortunately, without any salt to stop them, the spores were able to germinate in the oxygen, salt and acid-free environment, and several people became very ill.[16]

There have been a few commercial instances of contamination, but usually in a situation that is most unlikely to be encountered at home. One example was in Korea in 2013, when cabbages were washed with norovirus-contaminated water. In 2014, an unknown source of *E. coli* contamination occurred in the same country.

SAFETY IN HOME FERMENTATION: THE FACTS

The factors that make fermentation safe are salt, acidity, oxygen availability, bacterial competition, basic hygiene and common sense. These will collectively ensure that *C. botulinum* and other bacteria associated with food poisoning, including *Salmonella* sp., *E. coli* sp., *Staphylococcus aureus*, *Listeria monocytogenes* and moulds, are not able to grow.

Salt

Salt is an essential addition in vegetable fermentation. It has a long history of use in preservation, because of its antibacterial and dehydrating properties. To understand why, it is important to have some knowledge about the physical concepts relating to the microbial requirement of water for growth.

Water activity is a little-known concept, but it underpins the safety of fermentation. The moisture content of a food is simply the water it contains, which can be calculated by working out the difference between fresh and dehydrated samples. For example, the moisture content of fresh red peppers is about 93%, while in dried peppers it is about 6%. In the 1950s, the concept of water activity (a_w) was introduced by William James Scott to describe the 'boundness' of water in food. He defined it as being present in two ways:

- **Chemically bound water** is bound so tightly that it cannot be utilized by microbes, enzymes, and so on.
- **Free water** is bound through weak bonds. It can be utilized by microbes and can exchange with the environment.

SALT

As with all other ingredients, there are choices to be made when it comes to salt. Ordinary refined table salt is easily available and cheap, but it is not ideal. It has a stronger taste than artisan varieties, which can taint a ferment. This may be due to the anti-caking agents used, usually sodium or potassium ferrocyanide; generally, it will contain about 99% salt and 1% additives. However, if it is the only type available, you can still go ahead with it. Iodized salt should not be used, as the presence of iodine could inhibit the growth of beneficial bacteria; again, if it is all you have, it is worth a try.

Other varieties of salt that are more gentle on the palate include Maldon sea salt (98% salt); Himalayan salt, a type of mined rock salt from the Punjab in Pakistan (96% salt); and Fleur de sel (97% salt), which comes from a thin layer that forms in salt marshes.

Broadly speaking, even though salts are not pure (including table salt, which has additives instead of additional mineral content) and contain about 97–99% salt, it is not necessary to compensate for this when adding salt to a ferment. It is unlikely that domestic scales would be accurate enough to be able to do so anyway.

When following a recipe that talks in terms of teaspoons or tablespoons of salt, it is important to remember that, because of the grain size, a tablespoon of table salt will weigh more than a tablespoon of Maldon salt with its large crystals. Approximate comparisons are shown here, but you will need to weigh out the quantities to be sure:

- 1 tablespoon Maldon salt 11g;
- 1 tablespoon of table salt 15g;
- 1 tablespoon of rock salt 13g.

Maldon sea salt crystals dissolve easily and are ideal for fermentation.

Calculating water activity is tricky. Generally speaking, pure water has an a_w of 1, while honey, which is both viscous and complex, has an a_w of about 0.6. When salt is added to normal water, the sodium and the chloride interact with the water molecules making them less 'free' and the water activity is lowered – also, there will be other impurities that will have an additional effect. It is sufficient to know that adding 2% salt to a fermentation system is enough to make the a_w too low for pathogens. Fortunately, the LAB are more tolerant. Some non-pathogenic yeasts can survive in honey at much lower water activities.

Osmosis and Osmotic Pressure

The salt that is lowering the a_w is also causing osmotic stress for the bacterial cells in a fermentation system. Osmosis is the movement of water through a semi-permeable membrane from a less concentrated solution (for example, salt or sugar) into a more concentrated one. It is a passive process, which happens naturally. Both bacteria and plant cells are affected by it; both contain water, and both will respond to external osmotic pressure. One of three things can happen:

- If the concentration of salts/sugars is the same both inside and outside the cell, it will be in isotonic balance with the solution.
- If the concentration of salts/sugars outside is lower, then water will move from the environment into the bacterium, and it will swell up.

OSMOSIS – THREE SCENARIOS

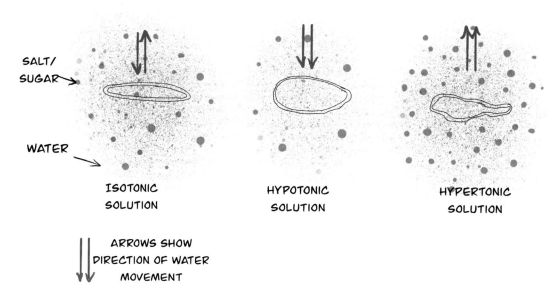

SALT/
SUGAR

WATER

ISOTONIC
SOLUTION

HYPOTONIC
SOLUTION

HYPERTONIC
SOLUTION

ARROWS SHOW
DIRECTION OF WATER
MOVEMENT

The effects of osmosis on cells, plant, animal and bacterial.

- If the concentration of salts/sugars outside is higher, then water will come out of the cytoplasm through the bacterial membrane to try to dilute the solution, shrinking the cells.

Just as with the a_w, LABs have features that make them more tolerant to osmotic stress than most pathogens – another fortunate event that makes fermentation more robust.

Taste and Texture
There are other reasons for adding salt, the most obvious of which is taste. A mouthful of fermented vegetables should be tangy, crunchy and crisp, and that texture is determined by several factors: the osmotic state of the cell, the pH, and the amount of strengthening pectins of various vegetable cell walls and how they stick together.

After salting cabbage, osmosis reduces the water inside the cells, increasing the amount of plant material relative to the amount of water present. This is thought to be one of the reasons for the crispness, but it is not sufficient explanation, because mere loss of water to plant cells causes a vegetable to go floppy (like that bendy carrot dying in the fridge). Osmotic pressure from salt is thought to be involved – researchers have found that low-salt sauerkraut is soggy.[17] Also while osmosis is responsible for drawing water out, various products of fermentation and sodium ions will enter the plant cells via channels in the cell walls. Once inside, some of these may bind with pectins to give greater stability[18] or inhibit some cell processes that might lead to softening. pH may also play a role, as the incredibly complicated structure of pectin changes in acidic conditions.

Some might suggest that it is possible to ferment without salt, perhaps for dietary reasons, but it is not advisable. Salt is crucial to safe and successful fermentation. Ferment with salt, and then soak your fermented vegetables to remove some of the salt before you eat them, or resist adding any extra salt to your meal.

The amount of salt can affect the rate of fermentation. If it is too high, at about 10% salt concentration, the osmotic stress will overpower the LAB. The advice in this book is to use 2% pretty consistently – with a couple of exceptions.

Acidity

The second parameter for safe fermentation is the production of lactic acid. It allows LAB to thrive while preventing germination and/or proliferation of potential pathogens, which are naturally present in the soil and on vegetables in low numbers, as well as being critical for maintaining your kombucha cultures. pH is a crucial element in the production of fermented foods. Eventually, the LAB produce so much lactic acid and lower the pH to such an extent that they can even inhibit their own growth!

Before fermentation begins, vegetables in salt water will have a pH of about 5–7. This will fall rapidly as the process begins. The holy grail for 'safe' fermentation is pH 4.5, the level at which *Clostridium botulinum* is unable to survive and produce its lethal toxin, and at which another potential pathogen, *Listeria monocytogenes*, is also inhibited. Almost all of the ferments in this book will reach this level – if not ph 3.7 – within three to four days, and fermentation will be seen to be actively happening, with the production of vast amounts of carbon dioxide. Occasionally, dark green vegetables fermented alone will struggle to reach this pH, so this is not recommended. For a list of vegetables and any likely difficulties with each, *see* page 166.

pH

pH, where the p probably stands for potential and the H definitely stands for hydrogen, is a concept developed over 100 years ago by Danish chemist, Søren Peder Lauritz Sørensen, to determine how acidic or basic (alkaline) water-based solutions are. Acids are substances that in water-based solutions can release hydrogen ion H^+, while bases release hydroxide OH^- ions. If a solution contains more H+ ions it will be acidic, and if it contains more OH- ions it will be basic. If it contains equal numbers of H+/OH- it will be neutral.

The pH scale operates between 0 and 14, where 0 is extremely acidic, 14 is extremely alkaline and 7 is neutral. The pH scale is logarithmic and works exponentially, so a solution with pH 3 is 10 times more acidic than one with pH 4, 100 times more acidic than pH 5 and 100,000 times more acidic than pH 8.

Now, fermentation was part of human survival for thousands of years before pH was even imagined and many fermenters never check pH, preferring to use their senses of sight, taste and smell. However, it is sometimes useful to know, and if you are fermenting anything unusual, it could be important to ensure that your ferments do reach the magic figure of pH 4.5. If you intend to produce fermented foods commercially it will be essential for you to do so.

There are two simple ways of determining pH in a home kitchen: with yellow universal indicator paper, or a pH meter. When using paper, simply tear off a piece, dip it into the ferment and compare the resulting colour to the chart provided. Be aware that, when making kimchi, which is bright red, the true reading may be altered slightly.

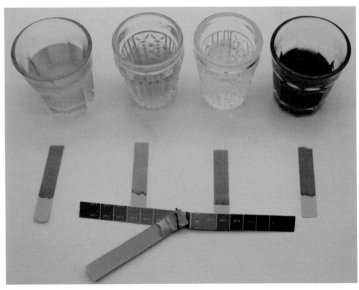

Measuring pH with pH paper (left to right): apple cider vinegar in progress, pH 2.5; continuous brew kombucha, pH 4; tap water, pH 7; newly set up kvass, pH 6.

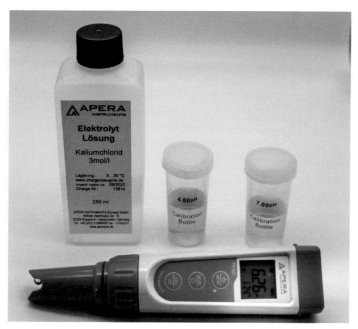

An electric pH meter makes life very easy (with buffers and storage solution).

Anaerobic Environment

It may be necessary to create an anaerobic environment, but not always. The exclusion of air is crucial for vegetable fermentation, but it is less important for milk and water kefir (depending upon the desired end result), although it is recommended. Kombucha, on the other hand, does require oxygen.

The purpose of excluding oxygen is two-fold: first, to provide an environment that will favour the growth of LAB, which will produce carbon dioxide and displace further oxygen in the system, and second, to prevent the growth of almost all moulds.

Bacterial Competition

In their ideal mesophilic, anaerobic environment, LAB will be happily and rapidly increasing in numbers. This has several effects on less favourable organisms that might be present:

- It limits nutrient availability.
- LAB can produce hydrogen peroxide and other antibiotic compounds to inhibit other organisms.
- They can 'crowd out' any unwanted microbes that are not part of the establishing ecosystem/existing SCOBY (symbiotic culture of bacteria and yeasts).

Hygiene

I am always keen to lower barriers to entry for fermentation. Do you need filtered water? Probably not. Do you need organic veg/fruit/sugar? Not so much. Do you need sterile jars? Not really. Do you need specialist equipment? Although it will help, it is not essential. However, one area where corners should not be cut is basic hygiene: specific elements of this are covered in each chapter but there are some rules that generally apply.

Whether fermenting vegetables or straining milk kefir, you should always ensure that your kitchen work surface has been washed down with an antibacterial

Battery-operated pH meters are available for less than £10. They may not be the most durable on the market but are worth the investment. They need to be calibrated before use, following the instructions and using pre-made buffer solutions at known pHs, so that the readings are accurate.

Concentration of Acid

Acidity may also be considered in terms of the concentration of the acid, which is thought to be a better guide than pH to judge the endpoint for kombucha or vinegar. pH measures only the free H+ ions in the brew, but measuring concentration takes into account all of them – and they all contribute to the taste of the finished product! A 5% acetic acid concentration means that 5ml of 100ml are acetic acid.

If you are planning to use home-made vinegar for preserving foods, you will need to ensure that it has a concentration of at least 5%, so that it will still have the power to preserve. Acid concentration can be calculated by using an acid titration test kit, but amateur-level ones are tricky to use.

cleaner and a clean cloth. Hands must be clean and free from possible contamination by raw animal, pet or grubby-vegetable matter. Remove all pets from the work surface (someone once asked me if the strange bacterial colonies growing on their kombucha SCOBY could have been caused by their cat licking it!). Work smartly to minimize the chance of uninvited air-borne microbes joining the party.

Equipment does not need to be sterile (free from all microbial contamination), but it does need to be 'dishwasher clean' – that is to say, thoroughly washed, rinsed and dried at a hot temperature. If you do not have a dishwasher, wash everything in hot soapy water, rinse thoroughly to remove soap residues and dry off either in a low oven or with a freshly washed tea towel. If you have had any contamination problems, pop a Milton tablet in a bowl of water and leave your equipment to soak before washing well. This is suitable for plastic too.

The exception to sterilization is when you are making fruit syrups: these contain no LABs to keep opportunistic moulds at bay, and should be either microwave sterilized (rinsed in warm water, then microwaved for 1–2 minutes on high power until the water has evaporated) or baked in the oven for 15 minutes at 150°C.

Tea towels and dishcloths are often a source of opportunistic pathogens. A daily change is a good idea – put them in with the washing.

Common Sense
Physical Safety
There is always a slight risk of things exploding, especially as glass is commonly used. Fermentation is a live continuous process, sometimes producing (except vinegar) copious quantities of carbon dioxide, which can potentially cause a hazard. Here are some pointers on how to avoid disaster:

- For kombucha and water kefir, always use either clip-top brewer's or screw-top glass bottles that are suitable for carbonated drinks. They can be purchased online. Never use square clip-top bottles as the edges weaken the structure. Wider-necked 'milk' bottles seem to suffer from less pressure build-up.

- Use one plastic 'guide' bottle for secondary fermentation to tell you when your batch is ready (the bottle will go hard, reflecting what is happening in the glass bottles).
- Consider storing your kombucha or water kefir at room temperature in an icebox or cupboard during secondary fermentation, in order to contain any breakages.
- The same goes for vegetable ferments in closed systems, although these tend to crack at the base rather than explode. You can replace the metal catch with a rubber band wound round a few times, which has a bit more give.
- Open bottles of water kefir and kombucha over the sink, making sure they are pointing away from your face.

Using your Senses
The final way to ensure you are fermenting safely is to use your senses – sight, sound, smell, taste, touch, and gut feeling – to guide you. When dealing with natural systems, as you will be here, no troubleshooting guide will be able to predict exactly what might happen.

If your fermentation looks different from what is described or shown, take a moment to work through some options. Were the conditions you fermented under correct in terms of salt content, fermentation vessel, temperature, and oxygen exclusion?

Your sense of smell is crucial too – although you might want to wait a few seconds before sniffing your sauerkraut for the first time, to allow the sulphur to dissipate! If vegetable ferments smell cheesy, something has gone awry and butyric acid has probably been produced. If your milk kefir smells of gone-off milk, then perhaps the base product was on the turn and Paenibacilli in it have outgrown the kefir microbes. If the smell of any of your ferments turns your stomach, do not taste them; there is no need. They should smell vinegary and intensely of vegetable, or yoghurty and wholesome.

If in doubt, you can use a pH meter or indicator paper to establish whether a safe pH of 4.5 or less has been reached before sampling a little.

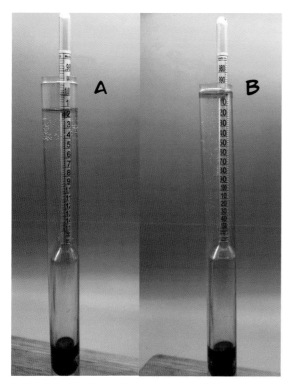

Before fermentation with a 3.5% sugar solution (A), and after (B), where the difference corresponds to a 0.5% concentration of sugar in the finished water kefir.

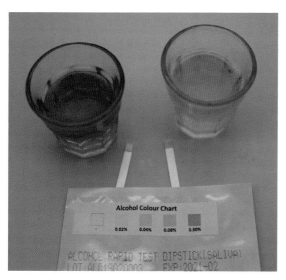

Testing the alcohol content of continuous brew kombucha (none detected) and 5-day-old water kefir made with 3.5% sugar (0.08%). The yellow colour of the lemon ginger and turmeric has slightly affected the reading.

MEASURING SUGAR/ ALCOHOL CONTENT

Using a hydrometer is a very easy way to determine the sugar content of a water kefir or kombucha. This is an inexpensive piece of kit comprising a glass weighted tube, designed to measure the specific gravity or relative density of liquids, based on buoyancy, and a plastic tube. A sugar solution will have a higher density than water. Take a reading with your hydrometer before you begin fermentation, and then take another after fermentation. When taking the second reading, the hydrometer will sink much deeper into the liquid. This indicates that it is now low in density, because the sugar has been utilized by the microbes.

By using the tables that accompany the device, you will be able to tell how much sugar has been used up, and therefore calculate the sugar content of your water kefir. In a pure system, for example, when making wine using just a single known species of yeast, sugar usage will predict how much alcohol has been produced. In kefir and kombucha, however, things are much more complicated. Different organisms are utilizing that sugar, but they are not all converting it to alcohol, so it is not a reliable indication. There are test strips available online that can detect 0.3% alcohol. If there is more than 0.3% alcohol, you will have to dilute the ferment by a known amount and try again.

A refractometer can also be used for working out the level of sugar concentration. Instead of measuring the density of the solution, this will measure its refraction, which changes with the dissolved solids (sugar). It will be more expensive than a hydrometer, but it can be more accurate and easier to read. Sometimes, the sugar content is described in Brix or bx. This simply means 1% sugar. Just as with a hydrometer, the measurement is complicated by other dissolved components, including acetic acid, glucluoronic acid and ethanol.

KEEPING RECORDS

Labelling
Label everything. Even if you think you will remember what you have got, you probably will not. Keep a roll of masking tape handy and a reliable marker pen. Writing

MAKING TIME

One frequently asked question is how is it possible to keep kefirs, kombuchas, sourdough starters and vegetable ferments on the go as part of a busy life. The answer is to make things easier. The thought of spending time using scales and measuring jugs with any degree of precision can be off-putting. Sometimes it is unavoidable, when weighing vegetables and calculating salt, for example, but for maintenance of cultured fermentations, it is less critical.

If you do things American style – measure once into a designated spoon, cup or bowl – you will never need to fiddle about with measuring implements again. For example, a 'Night Nurse' medicine dispenser contains 28g of sugar. This can be tipped directly into a Kilner jar of water, which, with approximately 3cm gap at the top, contains 800ml of water. In just 30 seconds, this will give a 3.5% sugar solution, without the need to weigh or measure.

The same goes for salt. This book does not often reference teaspoons or tablespoons of ingredients (other than spices in recipes), because it all depends on crystal size. For example, Maldon sea salt has very large crystals, but a tablespoon is about 11g, which is a useful guide when weighing out.

on a label is best as the organic acid/alcohol content of most ferments means it will just run off the glass if anything spills.

Fermenter's Notebook

Sometimes, no matter how many rules you follow, something will go wrong. If you take the information and apply it, it should almost always work, but there will be occasions when, no matter what you do, nature will get in the way and something will not go according to plan. The kefir might curdle before it makes kefir, the carrots might grow mould on top, but it is all OK. You will be on a learning curve that never ends – after several years of fermenting, I recently learned that lacto blueberries are delicious after one week, but taste strangely alcoholic after two, and that shredding carrots too finely can lead to a jar of slime.

A fermenter's notebook will become one of your most useful tools. Even though there is a huge temptation to think it can all be done by memory, a notebook can save you a lot of time. You will be less likely to repeat mistakes and you will have a permanent record of your most delicious recipe concoctions.

RESEARCH

Robust human trials in the field of fermented foods research are virtually non-existent, and not all scientific research is created equal. All research costs money and that has to come from somewhere. Often it is from an academic institution or a research council, but sometimes research can be sponsored by a private company, which may of course have an impact on the outcome. For example, if a kefir company does some research on kefir, there could be an element of bias.

Making notes is extremely beneficial. It only takes moments to scribble them down – and you might even end up writing a book yourself!

This is by no means always the case, but it is worth bearing in mind.

There is a lot of 'in vitro' research on the effects of fermented foods, which is carried out in a laboratory outside of the normal biological environment; studying the effects of bacteria or kefir on human cell lines growing in a petri dish would be an example. These experiments show that something can

PICKLE OR FERMENT?

Not all fermented foods retain their probiotic and nutritional qualities until consumption, and not all preserved vegetables in jars are probiotic and/or good for you. What is the difference?

- For retail, any live probiotic food needs to be refrigerated to halt the fermentation process, which could damage the packaging and reduce food stability. They are often labelled as 'live' or 'raw' and, if purchased from a market stall, will require refrigeration at home.
- Sauerkraut or kimchi in the pickle aisle in the supermarket will have undergone a canning process, which will have killed the probiotics. They may retain some nutritional benefits, if fermentation really was used in their production.
- Vegetables pickled in hot vinegar, which may also be sweetened, have not been fermented, are not nutritionally enhanced and have no probiotic benefit. The vinegar acts as a preserving agent; indeed, acetic acid, or vinegar at 5% concentration, is an effective household antibacterial cleaner. In addition, these are usually factory-canned under pressure, to ensure that they are stable.
- Vegetables pickled in raw apple cider vinegar are not fermented. Lactic acid bacteria involved in fermentation are inhibited by high concentrations of acetic acid.
- Although fermentation is used in the production of olives, chocolate, coffee, wine and most beers, by the time they reach the consumer, various cooking processes have eliminated any benefits.
- Tempeh, prepared from fermented soybeans, is cooked before consumption, so does not retain its probiotic properties, although the breakdown of the soybean to remove phytic acid is nutritionally beneficial.
- Miso, yoghurt, kefir, many cheeses, kombucha (unpasteurized) and raw fermented vegetables that you make yourself at home are both probiotic and nutritionally enhanced, as long as they are not heated.

Even though fermentation is used in the production of many supermarket food products, by the time they reach the consumer, they are as dead as a doornail, with zero probiotic benefit.

happen in an isolated environment – for example, 'antioxidant activity' – even though attempts to detect the effects of this in real people are not very successful.

With 'in vivo' research, the system is studied in a living biological entity, animal or human. Many metabolic studies are done on laboratory mice, which may be fed an exact and prescribed diet and may be closely genetically related, which is rather different from being a human.

There are several reasons why there are relatively few human studies on the effects of fermented foods. Humans are very different from laboratory mice. They are not just notoriously unreliable – not always telling the truth about what they have eaten that day – but also genetically and microbiotally hugely variable. Human experiments are also often complicated by the placebo effect, in which taking any sort of medication, even medication that is known to be a placebo, can have a positive effect on well-being.

Human clinical trials are also costly, labour-intensive and generally lengthy, sometimes taking five years from start to finish. Some effects could be long term or preventive in nature and are therefore difficult to identify. In these cases, it might be necessary to accumulate as many as 20 years of data to be able to assess the impact.

Another hurdle is how to determine the size of a study. Researchers can use complex equations to calculate the number of subjects to include. Typically, large sample sizes are required to demonstrate statistical validity but sometimes it is not affordable, practical or possible. Studies on small numbers of subjects (say, less than 100) can be useful indicators for future research, but they need to be interpreted carefully, as they may not yield results that can be extrapolated easily.

The Hierarchy of Research Importance

Type of Study	Characteristics
Opinon	There is a theory; at this stage, it can inform the research but it has not been proven yet.
Case-control studies	Researchers compare people with a known existing health problem, and a similar control group without a health problem to see the effect of an exposure/intervention. It is possible to look backwards at existing data.
Cohort studies	A cohort is a group of linked people, for example, those who have been exposed to a particular treatment/variable. In a cohort study they are compared with another group that were not exposed to the intervention. No attempt is made to 'hide' what treatment is used.
Randomized controlled trials (RCTs)	The gold standard of evidence-based medicine, designed to remove bias. There are usually two groups of subjects: one receiving the treatment and another receiving a placebo/standard treatment. Patients are randomly assigned to a group to eliminate bias. If the study is 'blind', then it becomes even less susceptible to bias, as neither researchers nor patients, and sometimes even data handlers, will know which treatment has been received.
Reviews of RCTs with meta-analysis	Several RCTs in the same subject area are analysed to provide the most compelling evidence of cause and effect in a given subject; data for all reviews is examined (meta-analysis).

CHAPTER 3

YOGHURT

Everyone should make their own yoghurt at least once, even if it seems far easier to just buy it. It almost always works, and it is an exciting thing to wake up to in the morning.

A BRIEF HISTORY

Yoghurt is a type of fermented milk. During the process, milk is soured by the bacterial production of lactic acid, which changes the protein structure, giving a smooth texture. Its name is derived from the Turkish *Yoğurt* and, with a history stretching back over thousands of years, it is one of the oldest and most prevalent fermented foods in the world. Its exact origins are unknown, but the birth of yoghurt was just waiting to happen. Without refrigeration, milk would frequently sour and separate into curds and whey.

Presumably there were occasions when a particular batch of soured milk would taste better than others, and this would then be used to 'seed' another batch. Perhaps something fell into some warmed milk one day, and a delicious thickened yoghurt resulted.

In one of the earliest written records, Roman author Pliny the Elder wrote about certain barbarous nations, who 'knew how to thicken the milk into a substance with an agreeable acidity'. It has been known since as early as 1700 that living microbes are present in raw milk and, by the end of the nineteenth century, LAB had been isolated by Louis Pasteur during his studies on wine spoilage. Their presence in the gut had also been verified In 1905, a type of *Lactobacillus* was isolated from yoghurt by Bulgarian researcher Stamen Grigorov, which became known as *Lactobacillus bulgaricus*.

Yoghurt.

Ilya Metchnikov, father of gut health. ADOBE

At the beginning of the twentieth century, Nobel-prize winning scientist Ilya Metchnikov became particularly interested in the longevity of Bulgarian peasants. He had a theory that old age was an unnatural state, because of chronic intoxication by putrefactive bacteria in the gut. He made the link between the long life of the peasants and the *L. bulgaricus* microbes in the yoghurt they regularly consumed, suggesting that these good bacteria were preventing the putrefactive bacteria from prevailing.

Publishing his work in 1907, he made a great impact for a time, giving public presentations explaining that eating yoghurt could contribute to a long life. He consumed gallons of yoghurt himself, but sadly he did not live to a great age. He suffered a series of heart attacks and died in 1916, at the age of 71. On his deathbed, he is reputed to have suggested to a pathologist friend that he might like to examine his intestines carefully….

The production of yoghurt remained very much a home-based pursuit, until 1919, when a Greek Sephardic Jewish immigrant doctor, Isaac Carasso, based in Barcelona, began to be concerned about the poor digestive health of the local children. In Carasso's view, the problems were due to a lack of hygiene. He knew of Ilya Metchnikov's work and believed that yoghurt might strengthen the children's bacterial flora and improve their resilience. He began production using original Bulgarian cultures, at a time when yoghurt was virtually unheard of in Western Europe. Initially, it was sold through pharmacies as a health tonic. Carasso named his brand 'Danone', or 'Little Daniel', after his son Daniel, who later took over the company, after training in microbiology at the Louis Pasteur institute in Paris.[19]

Today, the Turkish people have the highest annual average per capita consumption of yoghurt in the world, at 35 kilos per person. The UK manages a mere 12 kilos per person.[20] Interestingly, consumption in Bulgaria has decreased over the years, and average life expectancy in that country is now one of the lowest in Europe.

THE HEALTH BENEFITS OF YOGHURT

It is well known that consumption of live yoghurt (as opposed to yoghurt that has been heat-treated) improves lactose digestion and eliminates symptoms of lactose intolerance; the microbes responsible for making yoghurt generally produce high levels of the enzyme lactase.[21] Reduction of gastrointestinal symptoms has also been recorded. Yoghurt bacteria have been recovered from human faeces, showing that survival through the GI tract is possible. Just as with kefir, there might also be an immunological role. In one randomized controlled trial, a year of live yoghurt consumption was found to decrease allergic symptoms.[22] However, there is still some debate over whether all yoghurt starters can be considered to be probiotic, as health-giving properties could be specific to a particular strain. These days it is common for known probiotics to be added to yoghurt cultures.

ALL ABOUT MILK

Humans have been consuming milk for millennia as a wholesome source of proteins, fat and carbohydrates. Cow's milk accounts for over 95% of all milk consumed worldwide, but it is not always all it seems: there are differences in nutritional value, depending on its origin. The most nutritious milk comes from animals that are fed their natural diet, and this does not include the grains used in factory feed. A recent paper by Newcastle University confirmed that organic, grass-fed dairy contained 50% more beneficial omega 3 fatty acids than conventional milk. This is important in the UK as the British diet is deficient in omega 3.[23] It also has more conjugated linoleic acid, vitamin E, iron and carotenoids.

Cows producing organic milk must be fed predominantly on grass and reared outside most of the time. This is also ecologically advantageous, as they can nourish the soil with their own waste products. While it is possible to make yoghurt and kefir from conventionally farmed milk, it will often form weaker curds than milk produced by grass-fed cows, and may lack flavour. If you are going to the trouble of making your own yoghurt, it is worth choosing the best milk you can find.

Goat's Milk

Goat's milk is gaining popularity as there is evidence that it is less likely to induce allergies. It is much whiter than cow's milk, forms softer curds, and has smaller fat globules that are well incorporated, so it does not form cream. It also has higher levels of available iron.[24]

LACTOSE INTOLERANCE

When a human baby is born, it produces the enzyme lactase in the small intestine to break down lactose in its mother's milk. As humans grow up, production of this enzyme stops in some people, leading to problems of lactose intolerance. However, about 90% of the UK population experiences lactase persistence, where mutations in a section of DNA that controls how the lactase enzyme is produced, allows them to keep on drinking milk into adulthood. Although adults rarely drink as much milk as children do, they often enjoy cheese and yoghurt, which contain reduced levels of lactose.

Sheep's Milk

Sheep's milk is almost always used for cheese in the UK and there are only a handful of suppliers. It is interesting that it is not popular for drinking as it has a milder flavour than goat's milk, is rich in protein and does not seem to cause allergies.

Milk Alternatives

There are several reasons for the growing market in non-dairy milk alternatives, including growing self-diagnosis of lactose intolerance, increasing dairy allergies (for which there is some evidence), disenfranchisement with the dairy industry, environmental concerns and veganism.

Cow, sheep and goat. ADOBE

There is a wide variety of 'mylks' (EU law prevents use of the word 'milk' for a product that does not come from a lactating mammal) available in supermarkets today, including soy, almond, hazelnut, oat, coconut, cashew, peanut, tiger nut, walnut, hemp, quinoa and pea. Most are heavily processed and fortified to at least in part replicate the nutritional benefits of milk. There is little research at the moment on the effects of substituting mylks for milk in western societies, which could be a concern, especially for children. The most nutritious substitutes for cow's milk are soya and almond milk.

Raw Milk

Raw milk may be sold in England and Wales, but not in Scotland, at the farm, or at farmers' markets, or from a milk float. Unpasteurized and untreated, it comes straight from cow to bottle. Because of this, it carries a risk of bacterial contamination, and occasional outbreaks have been recorded. Milk is thought to be

Milk alternatives: almond, oat, hazelnut, rice and coconut. ADOBE

Nutrient comparison table for different milks and mylks

Milk	Calories	Fat	Protein	Carbs	Pros	Cons
Cow	66	3.9	3.3	4.5	Traditional, nutritious, versatile	Dairy allergy, farming methods
Goat	61	3.6	2.8	4.3	Less allergenic	Taste
Soya sweetened	25	2.6	3.5	0.4	Protein and essential amino acids	Taste, allergies, environmental impact
Coconut	27	0.9	0.1	2.8	Taste	Low protein, high fat
Oat	45	1.5	1	6.5	Low environmental impact	High sugar, low in other nutrients
Almond	24	1	0.5	3	Taste	Allergies, environmental impact
Cashew	23	1.1	0.5	2	Taste	Allergies, environmental impact

sterile until it leaves the udder cells, but then sources of possible contamination include the teat apex, milking equipment, grass, soil and the environment of the milking shed. Raw milk may be nutritionally superior, retaining the LAB, enzymes and vitamins that are lost through pasteurization. Making kefir is a way of putting that goodness back (and more) into pasteurized milk.

PASTEURIZATION AND HOMOGENIZATION

In order to help keep milk fresh and safe, it is still today subjected to the process of pasteurization, developed by Louis Pasteur in the 1880s. Investigating ways of preventing the spoilage of wine by acetic acid bacteria, Pasteur found that, by heating the wine to a certain temperature for a fixed time, he could destroy the bacteria and spoilage enzymes without affecting the flavour. The process was later applied to milk. At the time, the aim was to destroy the causal agent of tuberculosis, but it was found to kill all manner of other human pathogens too. The incidence of food poisoning from milk these days is usually due to contamination at other points in the food chain post-pasteurization, or when the correct timings for the process are not observed.

Pasteurization does not kill all of the microbes in milk. A species called Paenibacillus not only survives the process, but is also capable of growing at low temperatures, which is why treated milk will eventually turn, even in the fridge.

After pasteurization, milk is often homogenized. This is a mechanical process by which fatty globules of cream are broken up into tiny pieces, too small to coagulate, so they do not float to the top of a cup of tea, for example. This does not apply to skimmed milk, which has had the cream removed already. Many people feel that homogenization improves the consistency of milk and it certainly makes lovely smooth kefir and yoghurt. Some have concerns that the altered globule configuration could have health implications, but these are unsubstantiated.

HOW YOGHURT FORMS

Milk Proteins
Milk contains two types of protein: casein and whey proteins. These exist in an approximate 4:1 ratio, and make up about a third of the milk's content. They contain all nine essential amino acids that are required by humans.

Casein proteins include several different types, each with a different amino acid composition. They are

STRUCTURE OF A CASEIN MICELLE

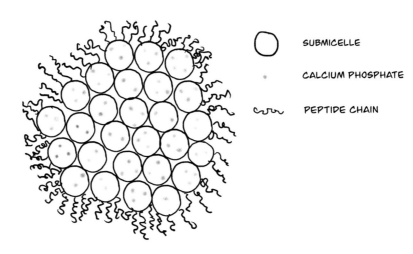

SUBMICELLE

CALCIUM PHOSPHATE

PEPTIDE CHAIN

Casein micelles make up about 80% of milk proteins.

loosely folded, with open structures. They coagulate at pH 4.6 and are suspended in milk in micelles – little globules that water can freely move in and out of. Caseins have a random coil structure and are not susceptible to denaturation (bonds breaking) upon heating. They are stable.[25]

The whey protein elements form a compact spherical shape, because of disulphide bonds that link amino acids together. Upon heating to just below boiling point, these bonds can be broken, leading to loss of compact structure and denaturation. This enables the proteins to hold more water, which improves the texture of yoghurt.

The milk sugar lactose is a disaccharide comprising glucose and galactose. During fermentation by LAB (usually in the low-oxygen environment they prefer), it is cleaved into its two components. Further processing results in the production of lactic acid and acetaldehyde, which flavours the milk, giving the sour, tart taste, and lowers the pH. The acidity affects the milk casein, causing it to coagulate and precipitate. Whey proteins are denatured by temperatures of about 90 degrees, which is helpful when trying to make yoghurt, as their structure then enables them to bind more water. It also increases the cross linking between the whey and casein micelles, increasing gel strength. This forms the yoghurt curd, which can be described as a gel or a soft solid.

Yoghurt Types and Their Characteristics

Type	Thermo/Mesophilic	Texture	Taste	LAB involved
'Normal yoghurt'	Thermophilic	Soft, spoonable	Mild, slightly tangy	*Streptococcus thermophilus*, *Lactobacillus bulgaricus*
Greek yoghurt	Thermophilic	Thick – may have been strained	Mild, creamy	*Streptococcus thermophilus*, *Lactobacillus bulgaricus*
Set yoghurt	Thermophilic	Set – can be cut with a spoon. Not stirred, so curd remains intact	Mild	*Streptococcus thermophilus*, *Lactobacillus delbrueckii* subsp. *bulgaricus*
Viili – functional food (Finland)	Mesophilic	May be thick and viscous, gelatinous (long strain) or moussey (short strain). Can be cut with a spoon	Mild, very yoghurty	*Lactococcus lactis* subsp. *cremoris*, also fungi and yeasts
Filmjölk (Sweden)	Mesophilic	Thick, custardy	Tangy	*Lactococcus lactis* and *Leuconostoc mesenteroides*
Matsoni	Mesophilic	Thick, smooth	Mild, creamy	*Acetobacter orientalis*, *Lactococcus lactis* subsp. *cremoris*, also yeasts
Piimä	Mesophilic	Thin, smooth	Mild, cheesy, buttermilk substitute	*Streptococcus lactis* var. *bollandicus* and *Streptococcus taette*
High-protein yoghurt (strained, made from skimmed milk)	Thermophilic	Thick, chalky	Mild, tangy	*Streptococcus thermophilus*, *Lactobacillus bulgaricus*

Note: the popular Icelandic 'yoghurt' Skyr is not included here, as rennet is used in its production, so it is technically a cheese.

The starting pH of milk is usually 6.7, and after fermentation it lowers to about 4.6. Gelation of the yoghurt begins to occur at about pH 5.2. As the milk acidifies, the casein micelle structure becomes altered and casein chains and clusters can form a network to which the heat-denatured whey proteins can attach themselves.

Microbes for Making Yoghurt

Making yoghurt requires microbes that will consume the lactose and create lactic acid. *Streptococcus thermophilus* and *Lactobacillus delbrueckii* subsp. *bulgaricus* are most commonly used. In commercial situations, known strains are added separately. However, originally yoghurts were formed by mixed symbiotic cultures – rather like kefir grains (*see* Chapter 4), but without the matrix to hold them together. These days, a number of probiotic strains may be added, for extra health benefits. These include *Bifidobacterium bifidum*, *Lactobacillus acidophilus*, *Lactobacillus rhamnosus*, *Lactobacillus casei* and *Latobacilus delbrueckii* subsp. *lactis*.

For a worldwide product such as yoghurt, with thousands of years of history, it is not surprising that there are several different types. The table opposite lists some of the better-known varieties and their characteristics, showing how different combinations of microbe can subtly alter the texture and flavour. Some are mesophilic, meaning that they can be cultured at room temperature, whilst others are thermophilic, requiring gentle heat for optimal bacterial growth and metabolism and curd formation.

Commercial production methods may differ from those used at home. For example, Greek yoghurt can be artificially thickened with added protein instead of by straining. This is not necessarily a bad thing, as it solves the problem of dealing with quantities of acid whey, a waste product from the straining process that is difficult to discard.

INFLUENTIAL FACTORS IN YOGHURT MAKING

Choice of Milk

The final firmness of yoghurt is heavily influenced by the concentration of milk solids, especially protein. Virtually any type of mammalian milk (and some plant milks) can be used, as all those bacteria need is a source of lactose (or other carbohydrates will do). However, the most luxurious result will be achieved with some lovely fat-containing grass-fed milk. In order to make a high-protein, lower-fat, Skyr-like yoghurt, use skimmed milk and then strain it. This will concentrate the proteins.

Homogenized Milk

Homogenized milk tends to give a smoother consistency and a more stable product as it prevents fat separation during fermentation. This can result in a layer of grease on top of the yoghurt, although this can be removed by skimming after heating. Homogenization enhances formation of cross-structures, which can improve texture, although this is not necessarily noticeable to the home yoghurt maker.

UHT Milk

Although the fermentation community tends to be more inclined towards fresh produce (and rightly so), UHT milk can be used, if that is all that is available. As UHT milk is homogenized and has been heat-treated, the proteins are already denatured, and it actually makes decent yoghurt without having to be heated first. Sometimes, home yoghurt makers add dried milk powder, which further increases the protein content and makes the resulting yoghurt firmer.

Raw Milk

Yoghurt can be made from raw milk without heating it. The end product will have a runnier consistency – the proteins will not have been denatured, so coagulation will not be as efficient – but it will retain its raw nutritional properties. Use the freshest raw milk you can lay your hands on – bacterial counts in raw milk can be extremely high, which will provide too much competition for the starter, and could result in some 'off' flavours. If you are using a starter that you have made yourself, or you have purchased an heirloom culture, remember to keep some of this separate, as unknown microbes in the raw milk could permanently alter its balance. Of course, you can heat/denature, which effectively pasteurizes it, for improved texture.

CHOOSING A STARTER CULTURE

LAB need to be present to sour the milk to make yoghurt and there are a few ways to achieve this.

Shop-Bought Yoghurt Starter

Common practice these days is to purchase a favourite live yoghurt and use a spoonful of it to 'seed' your own batch. The probiotic potential may be increased, for a wider range of microbes in your finished product, by combining starters from different commercial yoghurts.

You can usually use a spoonful of your own resulting batch of yogurt three or four successive times before it stops working. The reason it 'wears out' is because commercial strains of LAB are selected to be good at working in very specific factory conditions; they might not replicate with such vigour in a home environment.

Shop-bought yoghurt, with *Bifidobacterium* sp., *Streptococcus thermophilus* and *Lactobacillus bulgaricus*.

Single-Use Sachets of Yoghurt Cultures

Sachets of yoghurt starter culture that contains a particular combination of strains are available to buy. These are usually labelled as 'single-use', but you will probably be able to get successive batches from one sachet.

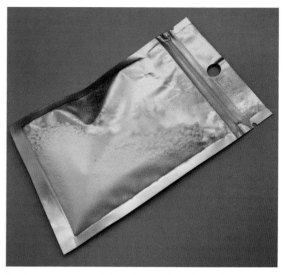

Yoghurt cultures look like skimmed milk powder – they almost are, but they also contain dried microbes that can be easily reconstituted.

Heirloom Cultures

Successful continuous yoghurt production requires an heirloom culture. These are largely uncharacterized communities of microbes that work together, and have evolved together – rather like kefir grains without the grain. Because they occur naturally and have developed a symbiotic rhythm, they can keep going indefinitely, as long as you look after them: they are quite demanding and ideally need to be propagated weekly, to keep the microbes alive. A neat trick is to arrest their growth by popping them in the freezer – put spoonfuls into ice-cube trays.

When making yoghurt, add the culture at about 2.5–5%; too much of a starting inoculum can lead to rapid acid production, which can adversely affect the formation of the curd.

A Starter from a Friend

If you know someone who has an heirloom culture up

and running, why not ask for a spoonful? Just like kefir grains or sourdough starter, a yoghurt starter can easily be donated.

Your Own Starter from Scratch

It is perfectly possible (and really exciting) to make your own yoghurt starter from natural sources, although this is not without risk, as you will not be sure what microbes you are growing. The yoghurt pH of 4.6 and temperature of 46 degrees should, however, be suitable for the growth of thermophilic LAB.

All of the following are said to contain the right sort of LAB to make yoghurt:

- *Cornus mas* (dogwood) stems;
- chilli stems;
- ants' eggs;
- goat droppings.

Making a yoghurt starter with (front to back) chilli stems, lentils (control), dogwood and, at the back, shop yoghurt.

Individual jam jars used to make set yoghurt in an Instantpot. Alternatively, it could have been made en masse for straining.

Dogwood and chilli stems can both be used to make yoghurt starters. The method is simple: place chilli stems and/or sections of dogwood stem into heated and cooled milk then incubate just as you would normal yoghurt. After 4 hours, you may already have achieved a set. In my own experiment, the flavours were interestingly different: the chilli stem starter was much more flavoursome than the dogwood. I tried just a quarter of a teaspoon in the first instance to check that there were no ill effects for 24 hours, before scaling up and offering it to the family.

MAKING THERMOPHILIC YOGHURT

Equipment

Making your own yoghurt is very cost-effective. You can easily make a couple of litres at a time, which will keep successfully in the fridge for at least a couple of weeks, if not more. If you have a yoghurt maker, simply follow the instructions that come with the machine. As with any other branch of fermentation, a lack of gadgetry should not hold you back,

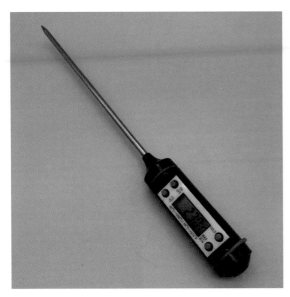

A thermometer really does make life easier.

although life will be easier with a thermometer, which you should be able to pick up for less than a fiver.

When making thermophilic yoghurt (heat-requiring), to keep the milk and microbes warm you could use a large thermos flask. Alternatively, use any lidded container or wide-mouthed bottle wrapped in a towel and kept in an insulated cool box or an airing cupboard, although it might take a few hours longer to set this way. You can also put your oven on its lowest heat setting.

The equipment you have will help you decide what vessels to use for your yoghurt. If you are using a yoghurt maker, it is decided for you; if using an 'instant pot', you can either make it in one large volume, or fill individual jars so it sets in the jar.

'Scalding' the Milk

The scalding is the stage of yoghurt preparation that is most likely to put people off, as it does involve an element of pot-watching. There are four reasons for heating the milk to almost boiling temperature:

1. Even if it has been previously pasteurized (usually at 72°C for 15 seconds), milk will still contain spores and *Paenibacillus* sp. A higher/longer heat treatment will reduce their numbers so they will not interfere with the yoghurt-making process.
2. The high temperature causes denaturation of the whey proteins (90% denaturation gives optimal yoghurt texture) and increases their cross-linking.
3. Holding the milk at just below boiling for 30 minutes causes evaporation, increasing the proportion of milk solids and improving the texture, although only if it is heated in an open pan. Although it is not essential, stirring prevents a skin forming and can contribute to the formation of a silky-smooth yoghurt.
4. Scalding the milk removes dissolved oxygen that can affect the performance of the starter cultures.

Despite all these reasons, if you are going to strain your yoghurt to make it thicker anyway, and are prepared to compromise a little on texture, this step is not essential for pasteurized milk or UHT.

You can choose to scald your milk either fast and short or slow and long; both methods will work. An impatient person might use 95°C for 5 minutes, but many commercial machines do a 30-minute 85-degree heating. Generally, the shorter higher temperature tends to be more successful in terms of a firmer curd. If you heat for longer, or boil the milk, it is not a disaster, but you might be able to taste the difference in the finished product.[26]

Cooling the Milk

Rapid cooling of heated milk to inoculation temperature may help to give a firmer set, although there are divided opinions on this. Perhaps it is to do with reduced dissociation of whey proteins as they cool rapidly. This can be achieved by standing the scalded milk pan in a sink of cold water and whisking.

Incubation Temperature and Time

A high incubation temperature speeds up the process of yoghurt formation but results in a weaker structure and greater whey separation (syneresis), which is what happens when liquid gets excluded from the gel structure. A lower incubation temperature results in slow protein aggregation, with more cross-protein bonds and small pores.

This is better for trapping liquid, but is slower. Some people start off at a higher temperature of about 45°C to allow the yoghurt bacteria to get going, and then allow this to fall to around 37 degrees. Many commercial yoghurt makers will include this stage in their set programmes. Most people settle for around 42 degrees for about 8 hours.

RECIPE: THERMOPHILIC YOGHURT

Ingredients:

Milk, preferably fresh and organic (full fat and high protein for a firmer set)
Starter of choice (3.5–5%)

Method:

1. Ensure that all equipment is 'dishwasher clean', and the work surface prepared.
2. Heat the milk either in a saucepan or 'instant pot', or in a yoghurt maker, holding it at either 95°C for 5 minutes, or 85 degrees for 30 minutes. (UHT milk needs heating only to culturing temperature.)
3. Stir the milk, unless you have a machine that can heat and stir at the same time.
4. Cool the milk to 45 degrees. It can be left to cool naturally, but rapid cooling seems to help form a firmer yoghurt. Stand the saucepan in cold or even iced water in the sink, and whisk to speed things up.
5. Add your starter culture at a ratio of 3–5%; for a litre of milk, that is 30–50g (approx. 3 tablespoons).
6. Place in a suitable vessel and incubate for at least 8 hours. (Home-made starter may be effective in as little as 4 hours.)

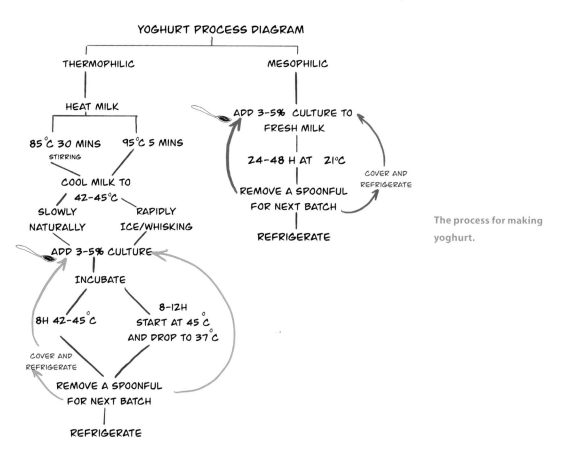

The process for making yoghurt.

7. Do Not Disturb! Do not stir the yoghurt whilst it is fermenting, as this may compromise the formation of the curd. After 7 or 8 hours at 37–45°C, it is likely to be set; check by gently tilting the vessel. The towel-wrapping method might take a little longer, maybe as much as 12 hours.

8. Yoghurt made in little pots can be transferred straight to the fridge. If you have made it in a large bowl, transfer to clean jars or pots.

9. Before you do anything else, take a spoonful and put it in a little pot to keep in the fridge to inoculate your next batch, or freeze for longer storage.

10. Keep the rest of the yoghurt in the fridge and use it for everything!

· ·

Troubleshooting

Yoghurt has not Set

Either you have forgotten to add your culture (it happens), or it has been added at too warm a temperature, killing the microbes. Perhaps the starter culture is exhausted. You can still use the milk – just add some fresh culture. Although it occurs rarely in home fermentation, bacteriophage contamination may be a problem. Bacteriophages are viruses that infect bacteria and cause their lysis (death). They are the most abundant biological entities on earth, thought to outnumber bacteria by at least 10 to 1. They particularly like man-made niches such as fermentation vats, and have been the bane of the large-scale fermentation industry for years.[27]

Too Much Whey

One of the biggest problems with home-made yoghurt is whey separation, or syneresis. This is when whey is expelled from the protein structure, by spontaneous contraction of the gel. There can be many reasons for this: disturbing the system, fermenting for too long, and too high a temperature are the most common.[28]

Yoghurt is Gloopy

This is a desirable quality in certain yoghurts such as Viili, but it may not be what you are looking for. It can be caused by the temperature not being high enough for the fermentation, or by the presence of contaminating yeasts. Always make sure, especially when using commercial cultures, that everything is 'dishwasher clean'.

MAKING MESOPHILIC YOGHURT

It could not be simpler to make mesophilic yoghurt, such as Viili, as no heating is required. If you have a sachet of culture, follow the instructions, which will probably say the following: stir into fresh milk, cover with a piece of kitchen roll held tight with a rubber band and leave at room temperature for 48 hours. If you are given some culture by a friend, simply stir a dessertspoonful into a jar of milk, cover and leave at room temperature for up to 48 hours, or until set.

Viili is a Finnish yoghurt that cultures at room temperature; there are several different types, which vary in their 'gloopiness'. There is even one that grows a thick fungal crust on the top, caused by *Geotrichum candidum* – some people say this is the best bit! The flavour is deliciously mild, if you can get to grips with the texture.

Again, remember to keep a spoonful back for your next batch. Remove it straight away and keep in a covered ramekin in the fridge or freeze it, to avoid the possibility of it being eaten.

STORING YOGHURT

Your finished yoghurt will keep well in the fridge for at least two weeks. After this time, it may become susceptible to contamination from slow-growing pasteurization-resistant microbes, or air contaminants from the fridge. At the first sight of alien growth, discard it. Placing a greaseproof paper disc over the surface, rather like jam makers do with their product, could stave this off a little longer.

Viili has a deliberate gloopiness that makes it like a 'dairy slinky'!

STRAINED YOGHURT

In order to improve consistency, or to make labneh, simply place a coffee filter in a funnel, or some sturdy kitchen roll over a sieve, and pour the yoghurt in. Cover and leave for up to 24 hours, until it reaches a consistency you like. Store in clean pots in the fridge. The whey can be used in smoothies or for cooking.

NON-DAIRY YOGHURT

Making non-dairy yoghurt can be a little tricky, as many milk alternatives just do not have the necessary protein content. However, there are couple of exceptions: soya milk and tinned coconut cream will both work (albeit for different reasons), using an existing yoghurt, a bought culture, or a probiotic capsule as a starter. Capsules seem to be the starter of choice for this type of yoghurt making – probiotic capsules are not always ideal, but they do seem to work extremely well with non-dairy alternatives. You could add cornflour or agar agar for thickening, but you may prefer to keep it simple.

Soya Milk Yoghurt
Soya beans have a high protein content and are well suited to making yoghurt, although most people prefer to sweeten it a little to improve the flavour. You can use shop-bought soya milk, avoiding those with unappealing additives – look for those that are just soybeans and water – or home-made soya milk.

SOYA MILK YOGHURT

Ingredients:

1 litre of soya milk
5% starter yoghurt (50g) or 4 probiotic capsules

Method:

1. Warm the soya milk to 42°C.
2. Add the probiotic capsule or starter.
3. Pour into your receptacle of choice.
4. Maintain heat of at least 37°C for at least 8 hours.
5. Check for flavour. If it is too mild, 'cook' for another 4 hours.
6. Decant if required, and refrigerate. Strain to thicken if required.

Coconut yoghurt has quite a moussey consistency – it is impressive, given how simple it is!

Coconut Milk Yoghurt

Coconut milk works in quite a different way from soya milk, as it is low in protein but high in fat. It seems that carbon dioxide from fermentation actually gets trapped within the matrix, creating a mousse-like texture. Tinned coconut milk can contain stabilizers and thickeners, so look for a make that is unadulterated – Aroy-D (70% coconut) or Biona (50% coconut), for example. Blocks of coconut cream are not recommended, as it ends up separating with lots of bits in.

Method:

1. If you want to make thick yoghurt, refrigerate the cans of coconut milk overnight upside down. When you open the cans the next day, invert them and the water fraction will be sitting on top.
2. Set the liquid aside for use in cooking.
3. Mix in the contents of the probiotic capsules or starter yoghurt.
4. Stir well to incorporate.
5. Incubate covered for 8 hours at about 37°C, using your chosen method.
6. Taste, place in containers and refrigerate.

The finished yoghurt can be used in any context where you would use a shop-bought yoghurt: mix it with kefir (*see* Chapter 4) and strain it to make a delicious labneh-style cheese (*see* page 73), have with Billionaire's Granola (*see* page 71), or make tzatziki.

COCONUT MILK YOGHURT

Ingredients:

2 × tins of coconut milk
4 × probiotic capsules or 50g of shop-bought live coconut yoghurt

MILK KEFIR

KEFIR vs YOGHURT

Kefir, like yoghurt, is a type of fermented milk, but it has many qualities that put it in a class of its own: it is a rich source of probiotic microbes[29], has many proven health benefits[30], is extremely easy to make with reusable kefir grains and can be used with a whole range of animal milks and nut-derived milk substitutes. It is probably the simplest and cheapest way to achieve a positive influence on your health. Whilst commercial kefir does taste rather like drinking yoghurt, home-made kefir has a unique character – tart, tangy and often fizzy. Kefir is much less labour-intensive to make than yoghurt, as there is no temperature management involved, but achieving a good flavour and texture is definitely more challenging. On the health front, however, kefir wins hands down, with its far richer microbial community of up to 25 different species in comparison to yoghurt's two, three or four. It is like yoghurt on steroids! Of course, there may be occasions where the mild tanginess of yoghurt will be preferable from a culinary point of view.

THE ORIGINS OF MILK KEFIR

Kefir may have arrived only recently on the shelves of UK supermarkets, but its origins lie in the distant past and are shrouded in myth and mystery. It seems to have originated at least 2,000 years ago in the Caucasus Mountains, between Georgia and Armenia. According to legend, the first kefir grains were a gift to the Caucasian people from the prophet Mohammed. He showed them how to make a magical elixir that would bring health and longevity, but only if the means and

methods of its preparation were kept secret. As a result, kefir grains became closely guarded tribal treasures. For hundreds of years, kefir was barely known outside this region, although it did receive a mention in the thirteenth century by Marco Polo in the chronicles of his Eastern travels.

Gradually, rumours of a miracle tonic with healing powers began to spread and, by the end of the nineteenth century, the Russian *Universal Encyclopaedia* included a hefty section on kefir. The 'All Russian Physicians' Society' were eager to get their hands on this super food for their patients and to set up kefir production on an industrial scale. They approached

A jug of finished kefir, strained and ready to go.

the most prominent dairy owners in the Northern Caucasus, the brothers Blandov, for their help. The native Caucasians were still intent on sticking to Mohammed's instructions, and were reluctant to share either kefir grains or know-how, so the brothers had to resort to subterfuge: they needed a secret agent. Step forward Irina Sakharova, a brilliant and beautiful young employee at the dairy. At just 20, she was already a graduate in dairy farming, with a gold medal to her name for her butter.

Irina was sent off with a small party to charm some kefir grains from Prince Bek-Murza, a local nobleman who was also a large-scale milk producer for the brothers' dairy. After entertaining her at court for several days, the Prince was rather taken with the young woman. Every day he sent her red roses and invited her to walk in the 'alley of love'. Irina did not return the prince's affections, but it seems that he was besotted enough to bestow 4 kilograms of kefir grains upon her, allowing the Blandov brothers to start

A typical supermarket shelf today may have a number of different manufacturers' kefirs, in many different flavours. A few years ago, there were none!

This tiny region of Eastern Europe is where the first kefir grains originated at least 2000 years ago. ADOBE

production. From 1908 kefir was made available to the Russian public – in some cases provided free of charge – although large-scale production did not begin until the 1930s.

Mohammed-based myths aside, it is generally accepted that kefir came about through an accidental interaction between two different microbial worlds. Fresh milk, a rich source of nutrients and microbes, was stored in goatskin bags, which were covered with their own microbial flora. Shepherds used to take goatskins on to the hills with them and top them up with milk during the day. Presumably, on occasion, the milk turned into delicious fizzy kefir, and at some point the connection was made between the flavour and the presence of the grains. It became common practice to store milk at home in a bag hanging over the door. Whenever anyone passed the bag, they would knock it to help mix the contents. Nowadays, the milk is more likely to be stored in a ceramic pot, although the old set-up is still used by Bedouin tribes to make yoghurt. Without a fridge, there are only two ways to enjoy milk: either fresh or fermented, on the basis that, once it has been acidified, it deteriorates much more slowly.

The kefir grains used today are distant relatives of those same ancient cultures. So far, the creation of kefir grains through any means other than spontaneous natural generation has been achieved only once or twice in laboratories, using mixed cultures of bacteria that are involved in the process.[31]

KEFIR FERMENTATION

Kefir forms as a result of lactic acid bacteria using lactose as a source of energy and creating lactic

Shepherds and goats of the Caucasus, the place where kefir began.

acid in the process. As the concentration of lactic acid increases, the pH of the milk falls. This causes the proteins in the milk to unfold (denature), and allows them to interact with each other, coagulating together to form curds. When enough lactic acid is produced to make this happen, at approximately pH 4.5, the acid helps to act as a preservative, preventing contamination by undesirable microbes. The degree of coagulation depends on the milk substrate used and also the fat content. Goat's milk, for example, forms much smaller curds and the resulting kefir is thinner than that produced from cow's milk. Plant-based milks do not contain casein or whey proteins, so do not often coagulate in this way, although separation into a watery fraction and some type of curd can occur. Yeasts and other organisms are able to convert glucose in the milk substrate (some of the lactose is broken down to

KEFIR ETYMOLOGY

Kefir (Кефир) has certainly been known by this name in Russia since the 1860s, when it was first described in scientific papers. Links to Turkish words for lather or pleasure, *keyif*, have been suggested, or to the Greek work *kefi* meaning 'mojo' or 'spirit'. Today, 'kefir' is the word used in most of the English-speaking world, although pronunciation varies greatly from 'ke-fear' to 'kee-fur' to 'keffa' to 'ke-fur'. In other countries, it is known as Tibetan milk mushroom, *yogurt pajaritos* ('birdie yoghurt') in Chile and *bulgaros de leche* elsewhere in Latin America.

glucose and galactose by other bacteria) into carbon dioxide and alcohol, which gives kefir its fizziness. Some plant-based milks contain sugar, which means the kefir can be extremely fizzy.

KEFIR GRAINS

Kefir cannot be made without kefir grains. Actually they are not 'grains' at all, but clusters of many different species of bacteria and yeast, living together in perfect harmony, bound in a polysaccharide matrix. Their creamy colour makes them look rather like little cauliflower florets. Kefir grains are an example of a SCOBY, a 'symbiotic culture of bacteria and yeasts'. Invented by a kombucha enthusiast called Len Porizo in the 1980s to describe the kombucha 'mother', the acronym has stuck, and is now used to describe other visible biofilms such as kefir grains. This huge and varied population of microbes are able to support and enhance each others' growth, while working together to exclude contaminants.

Although all kefir grains now in existence may have similar origins, there is a great variety in the microbial communities they might contain. More than 300 different strains have been identified across tested grains, but they usually contain between 15 and 40 different types. Some are almost always present, such as *Lactobacillus kefiranofaciens*, which produces kefiran, the polysaccharide matrix that forms the grains.[32] Other most commonly found bacteria are from the *Lactobacillus*, *Lactococcus*, *Streptococcus* and *Acetobacter* species; and yeasts from *Candida*, *Sacchromyces* and *Kluyveromyces* species. Over time, exposure to various milks, from a range of animals, storage in various vessels, airborne contamination and environmental conditions will have resulted in microbes both joining and being eliminated from the original SCOBY.

Species found on the surface of kefir grains differ from those found in the interior and, to complicate things further, the microbial composition of the kefir grains may bear little relation to the content of the finished kefir. For example, a recent study found that although *Streptococcus* sp. were barely present in a tested set of kefir grains, the finished kefir contained approximately 60% *Streptococcus* sp.[33], whereas other kefirs have been found to contain as much as 80% *Lactobacillus kefiri*.[32] There is also a vast range for

A close-up of kefir grains to show their cauliflower-like appearance.

Kefiran forms the strands of gloop that bind the grains together. It has its own benefits.

the final numbers of microbes that can be present following fermentation, from approximately 10^4 to 10^9 bacteria and 10^5 to 10^8 yeasts per gram of kefir.[34]

THE NUTRITIONAL CONTENT OF KEFIR

Cow's milk kefir is packed full of nutrients. Some of these are pre-existing in the milk, but the number and diversity of microbes helps enhance them by partially breaking down proteins into bioactive peptides, fats into free fatty acids, converting lactose into lactic acid and producing B and K vitamins. The exact composition of the kefir product will vary depending upon the kefir grains and their concentration, the type of milk used, and the length of time and conditions for fermentation. However, the following guidelines give a reasonably good idea of what to expect in cow's milk kefir.

HEALTH BENEFITS OF KEFIR

By the end of the nineteenth century, the link had already been made between a healthy constitution and fermented milk. Nowadays, kefir has been extensively studied and, although it is impossible to know exactly what microbes are in it (except for those who have access to a microbial genetics laboratory), there will be several probiotic species of bacteria and yeast. Whilst these microbes do not usually colonize the gut as such, they can live there temporarily – sometimes for up to a month – interacting with the existing commensal gut microbes and receptors on the gut wall and helping in myriad ways.

Research has identified a huge array of benefits, which really mirror what an optimally working gut should be achieving, highlighting once again the role of probiotics as stimulators of the existing commensal gut microbes. In addition, kefiran, the thickening polysaccharide produced by the grains, has also been shown to have its own positive health effects. To date there have been few reliable large-scale studies in humans, and cynics will sometimes mention the placebo effect, which can affect such studies. Does it really matter? If it is a placebo effect, then how amazing to be able to achieve such benefit from so little effort.

Regular drinkers of kefir usually have their own anecdotal evidence for how it has made them 'feel better', although of course how that is defined is entirely subjective. For example, they might describe a reduction in the occurrence and/or duration of coughs, colds, fevers, tonsillitis, an improvement in regularity, texture and smell of bowel movements, reduction in the use of steroid inhalers for asthma or chronic rhinitis, better skin, reduced desire to eat sweet things and an improvement in gum health and energy levels. Some

Guideline content for cow's milk kefir

Component	Approximate content
Water	80–90%
Protein	3%
Fat	0.5–3%
Carbohydrate	6%
Lactic acid	1%
Alcohol	<0.5%
Vitamins	A, B1, B2, B5, A and K (and traces of B6, B9 and B12). Concentrations of some of these may increase or decrease with fermentation
Minerals	Potassium, magnesium, calcium, phosphorus (traces of zinc, copper, manganese, iron, cobalt)
Amino acids	Concentrations often increase with fermentation, including tryptophan, threonine, serine, alanine, lysine
Bioactive peptides	Yes
Acetoin, diacetyl, acetaldehyde, other aromatic compounds[30, 32]	

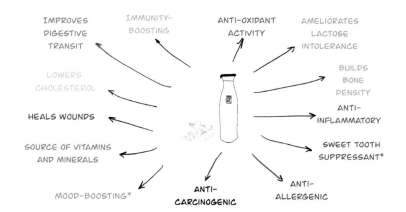

HEALTH BENEFITS OF KEFIR (ANECDOTAL* AND EVIDENCE-BASED)

IMPROVES DIGESTIVE TRANSIT

IMMUNITY-BOOSTING

ANTI-OXIDANT ACTIVITY

AMELIORATES LACTOSE INTOLERANCE

LOWERS CHOLESTEROL

BUILDS BONE DENSITY

HEALS WOUNDS

ANTI-INFLAMMATORY

SOURCE OF VITAMINS AND MINERALS

SWEET TOOTH SUPPRESSANT*

MOOD-BOOSTING*

ANTI-CARCINOGENIC

ANTI-ALLERGENIC

The health benefits of kefir, both anecdotal and evidence-based.

users have reported feeling the benefits as quickly as 48 hours after starting regular consumption, although two to three weeks is more usual.

HOW TO MAKE KEFIR

Kefir is simple to make, as the kefir grain microbes work at room temperature and no heat is required. The basic method is the same, whether using dairy milk or a substitute. In a nutshell, bacteria and yeasts in the kefir grains ferment milk to make kefir at room temperature. When enough acid is produced to make the milk curdle, usually at about pH 4.6, it is done. The grains are strained out and put in fresh milk to make another batch, and the kefir product can be eaten or drunk, or put in the fridge for later.

Just as its composition can be an unknown quantity, almost every aspect of the production of kefir is also variable: the quantity of grains used, the type of milk, the fermenting vessel, when you stop fermenting, what you flavour it with and how you eat it. To make kefir that tastes delicious and is mild enough for all to enjoy, follow the basic method below.

Finding your Kefir Grains

First, you will need some kefir grains. If you know someone who makes their own kefir, ask them for some – you will only need half a teaspoon to get started. Alternatively, they can be purchased online. Fresh

grains are preferable; dried ones are available, but they require prior reconstitution, following the given instructions.

When you get your grains, take a moment to contemplate that these fascinating structures, containing billions of microscopic creatures, are direct descendants of those original kefir grains from thousands of years ago. If you gently prod them with a teaspoon, you will find that they are extremely gelatinous and cannot be easily damaged or destroyed.

If you are using some kefir grains for the first time, it is best to follow the acclimatization instructions below, to ensure that the grains are working before you waste a whole pint of milk. Be sure to follow the basic hygiene principles.

The Fermenting Set-Up

The set-up you use will have a significant effect upon your kefir – indeed, it is one of the easiest ways to influence the flavour. The two set-ups below will result in subtly different kefirs. You might prefer one over the other (the flavour from the anaerobic/closed method is a good starting point for most people), but there are no rights or wrongs. Remember, kefir was originally made in a goatskin bag!

An anaerobic system with a small head of oxygen in the jar provides a microaerophilic environment that favours growth of LAB. While it supports the growth of carbon dioxide- and alcohol-producing yeasts, they grow less efficiently without oxygen, as do oxygen-requiring *Acetobacter* sp. This means that lactic acid will be a more dominant source of flavour in this type of kefir than yeasty or vinegary flavours. Another advantage of this anaerobic set-up is that the low oxygen conditions make it very difficult for any contaminating moulds to grow, although this is quite unlikely in the 24-hour fermentation time.

The aerobic/open system has a cloth cap to keep out contaminants and to allow easy movement of gases in and out. The lactobacilli will be content with the low levels of oxygen at the bottom of the jar, which they like. The yeasts will have greater access to oxygen and will create energy through a much more efficient pathway, enhancing their growth. This will taste yeasty but will contain relatively little alcohol. It may be slightly fizzy, but some of the carbon dioxide produced will escape. If *Acetobacter* sp. are present, which require oxygen to convert alcohol to acetic acid, your kefir might gain some vinegary flavours.

Vessels for Fermenting

For a closed system, you need to use a vessel that will keep oxygen and airborne contaminants out but will allow a little expansion for carbon dioxide production. Good quality clip-top jars with rubber gaskets are perfect for this. Kilner or IKEA jars, for example, have dishwasher-safe metalwork and are extremely sturdy. Similar-looking jars that have been sold with sweets inside are not designed for kitchen use and may not be robust enough. It is not essential to use glass (ceramic containers can be suitable), but glass is non-porous, non-reactive and allows you to see what is going on.

If you do not have a clip-top jar, or are making a smaller quantity of kefir, use an ordinary jam jar. The lid should be left a turn undone, to prevent too great a build-up of pressure. Always make sure that you clean the lid (especially metal lids, which have a lip) as well as the jar. If you do not have a suitable jar, you can just use a bowl with a beeswax or silicone cover, or a plate over the top.

To make an aerobic system, you need a jar of larger capacity than the amount of kefir you want to make. You could use a litre clip-top jar and just fold the lid

Open/aerobic system on the left; closed/anaerobic system on the right.

back, or unclip it all together. You'll also need a rubber band and some sturdy kitchen roll or a piece of linen.

Technically, there is nothing wrong with using plastic containers, although they can make the milk smell slightly odd. If that does not bother you, go ahead; you could even simply put the grains straight into a plastic pint milk bottle (as long as you do not mix up milk and kefir).

CHOOSING YOUR MILK

Animal Milks

Use fresh milk that is not near to being on the turn – pasteurized cow's milk contains *Paenibacilli*, non-harmful psychrotrophic bacteria that survive pasteurization and eventually cause milk spoilage. If you use milk when it is about to go off, they can compete with the kefir grain microbes and the milk will turn before it has a chance to make kefir.

Organic milk is a good option as the cow's natural diet contributes to a product with a superior nutritional composition. The higher the fat and protein content, the more luxurious-tasting and thicker the kefir. In recent years there has been a tendency to opt for 'low fat' products in the belief that these are healthier, but in this context, using 'whole' milk is fine. At least some of the fats will be broken down into free fatty acid components that could be useful for your own commensal gut bacteria. Any fresh animal milk works, from skimmed cow's to full fat Jersey, goat, sheep or even camel if you can find it.

You can use either homogenized or unhomogenized milk. There is some debate about homogenized milk having a reduced nutrient content, but it certainly makes smoother kefir. Given the ability of kefir microbes to break down fats, this may not be as important a consideration. Goat's and sheep's milk have a different structure and are naturally more homogenized.

Raw (unpasteurized) milk can be used, but sometimes people find that it is hard to make kefir from it. This is because there are so many other bacteria, including LAB, already in the raw milk, competing with the kefir bacteria for food. However, turning it into kefir could be a safer way of consuming raw milk: there are so many 'good' microbes in the kefir grains that they can usually inhibit the growth of small numbers of pathogenic (harmful) bacteria that could be present in the unpasteurized milk. On the other hand, studies have also shown that the very nastiest pathogens can survive and even proliferate in kefir cultures. If you are keeping raw milk at room temperature for 24 hours to make kefir, you would have to accept the risk that, if there are pathogens in the starting milk, there could be more of them in the finished kefir. This kefir should not be fed to children, the elderly or those who are immunocompromised. If using raw milk, divide your grains and freeze half, just in case an issue arises.

UHT milk gets a rather bad press, as it is felt to be comparatively poor in terms of nutrients. However, it may be the only milk available, and kefir made from UHT milk is better than no kefir at all. The proteins are denatured by the treatment and it does not seem to make a particularly unctuous kefir, but there will still be some nutritive value from the action of all those microbes.

Fresh milk can also be baked, in order to produce a Russian type of kefir called ryazhenka, which is delicious. Simply bake the milk for 6 hours first in a very low oven.

Plant-Based Milks

Milk kefir grains can be used to make kefir from soya, oat, rice or any nut milk, but it is true to say that some are an acquired taste! The key to success is to use a nutrient-rich substrate. Many plant-based milks have as few as 12 calories per 100 millilitres, which is not enough to support a greedy population of kefir grains. Ideally, you are looking for a product that has a good distribution of protein, fat and carbohydrate, providing a variety of nutrients to match the variety of nutritional requirements of the kefir grains. Home-made nut milks can be a fantastic choice, as they are additive free. Alternatively, you can mix some different types together.

Soya milk has been well studied in the scientific literature and has a reasonable protein content: soya kefir contains several bioactive peptides that are proposed to be beneficial.[35] It also contains all the essential amino acids needed by the human body. A home-made plant-based milk would be an ideal substrate. Additive-free tinned coconut milk (Aroy-D or Biona) can result in a thick, almost yoghurty kefir.

Soya milk kefir thickens nicely.

ACCLIMATIZING NEWLY ACQUIRED KEFIR GRAINS

The kefir grains may already be in some milk, or they may have arrived wet in a packet. If they are in milk, remove them using a sieve or strainer. They do not need to be rinsed.

● ●

ACCLIMATIZATION OF KEFIR GRAINS

Ingredients and equipment:

A small pot or jar and cover
10 × volume of grains of milk (or to cover)
Sieve

Method:

1. Put grains in a small container with some whole organic milk, or soya milk.
2. Cover the container with a lid or saucer and leave on the worktop for 12–18 hours.
3. Check after this time to see whether the milk has set, or whether curds have begun to form around the grains. For plant-based milks, bubbles should be forming on the top of the liquid.
4. If there is no activity, check back every 6–8 hours. When grains are acclimatizing after a period of transport or dormancy, it can take up to 60 hours for them to become active, especially if they have been frozen.
5. When the milk has set, that is proof that the grains are in good working order. Either pick them out if they are in a discrete lump, or separate using a sieve and proceed to scaling up below. They do not need to be rinsed. Discard the small amount of kefir that has been made – it is not harmful, but it might taste odd.
6. If you have more than the required amount of grains, drain them and freeze the extras in a small pot or bag. This has been shown to be the most reliable way of storing kefir grains.

7. If after 60 hours there is no action, you will need to find some more grains.

● ●

MAKING A 500ML BATCH OF KEFIR

Day 1
Ingredients and equipment:

Half a teaspoon of kefir grains (approx. 2–3g)
500ml Kilner jar with gasket ('dishwasher clean')
Spoon
1 pint of very fresh milk, or plant-based milk

Method:
1. Place the kefir grains in the Kilner jar.
2. Add milk to just below the metal band, leaving about 2cm head room.
3. Close the lid.
4. Leave the jar on the worktop for approx. 18–24 hours to ferment.

Day 2
Ingredients and equipment:

Spoon
Sieve or strainer
Storage container that the sieve fits over (a large jar with a lid, or a bowl)
Another 500ml Kilner jar (optional)

You have kefir when the milk has set to a yoghurty consistency. It may also have separated, with pockets of whey forming; this is quite normal. If you do not have time to strain it right away, put it in the fridge for up to three days (this stops it from continuing to ferment, ensuring that the flavour does not get too strong). Of the plant-based milks, only soya or coconut will thicken.

1. Assemble the strainer over the kefir storage container/jar.

MILK KEFIR PROCESS DIAGRAM

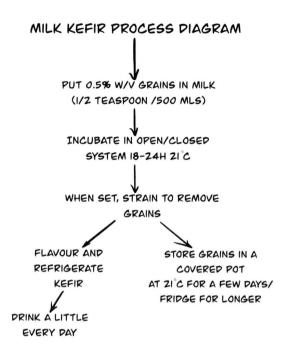

PUT 0.5% W/V GRAINS IN MILK
(1/2 TEASPOON /500 MLS)

↓

INCUBATE IN OPEN/CLOSED
SYSTEM 18–24H 21°C

↓

WHEN SET, STRAIN TO REMOVE
GRAINS

FLAVOUR AND
REFRIGERATE
KEFIR

STORE GRAINS IN A
COVERED POT
AT 21°C FOR A FEW DAYS/
FRIDGE FOR LONGER

DRINK A LITTLE
EVERY DAY

The process of making kefir.

Straining set-up, using a straining funnel and a bottle.
E. MORELAND

The art of kefir straining. E. MORELAND

The finished product can be flavoured with one drop of lemon oil per 500ml. E. MORELAND

2. Pour the fermented mixture through the strainer into the container to separate out the grains, gently agitating, or stirring with a spoon, until only the grains are left. Gentle stirring will not harm them, as they are quite robust. Kefir that has been refrigerated will thicken and will be harder to strain.

3. Do not wash the grains. Put them back into the clip-top jar (after washing it in hot water, or using a clean one if you have it), and start again. The grains can be stored if you do not want to make more kefir immediately (*see* below).

4. The strained kefir is now ready to eat, drink or refrigerate, or to use for a second ferment. It can be stored in a jar, wide-mouthed bottle or jug, depending on the consistency.

• •

FINE-TUNING THE PROCESS

Stirring or Mixing Kefir while it Ferments

When kefir was first made, it was kept in a goatskin bag, which was knocked from time to time to mix the milk. However, in a 500ml Kilner jar in most instances it is not necessary to disturb the kefir at all. As the bacteria and yeasts proliferate through their milk source, they will cause microscopic movements within it, and the bacteria will be thus distributed throughout. The exceptions are when unhomogenized milk with a thick collar of cream is used, or when the milk is fermenting in a tall deep vessel. In these cases, you can either agitate the jar by twisting from side to side, or open the lid and stir with a long spoon during the first 12 hours of fermentation. Disturbing after this time can sometimes lead to the formation of small curds, which can make the kefir grainy (although it will still taste fine).

Metal Implements

Most domestic-grade stainless steel is not made for fermenting, as the acid tends to corrode it. However, short-term contact with a metal spoon and sieve for mere moments will not harm the kefir grains. It is important to stir very gently, though, as some shearing of the grains against the sieve can occur. Some prefer to use a plastic sieve for this reason.

Straining the Kefir

One of the most difficult things about making kefir is the process of getting it out of the fermenting vessel into the storage jar! Many people start with a plastic sieve over a bowl and then transfer it using a funnel into a jar. However, it is much more efficient to use a funnel strainer – either a plastic one that can go in the dishwasher (Oxo Good Grips), or a metal one (for example, from Kilner). If you think a daily dose of kefir is going to work for you and your family, it is definitely worth investing in one of these. The kefir can then be strained directly into its storage bottle.

Some people try to solve the logistical problem by keeping their kefir grains in a little muslin bag attached

Grains may be strained using a plastic sieve and a jug, a metal straining funnel or a strainer.

to an external string that can be pulled out of the fermentation vessel instead of straining. Whilst on many levels this seems practical, it can be messy and rather unhygienic. The milk curds can build up on the bag and become quite sour and it all ends up looking a bit grubby. It is useful to be able to look at the kefir grains to see how they are doing, and to know that the only things in your kefir jar are the milk and grains.

TASTE, STORAGE AND SECOND FERMENTATION

Taste

With such a variety of microbes in kefir grains, and a range of substrates to choose from, it is no surprise that there is a huge variety in the taste of the finished product. Kefir has a definite tang to it, like yoghurt, but this can range from mild to acrid. It may be smooth or slightly grainy, depending on the milk used. It may be thick or thin, depending upon the fat and protein content of the milk. It can be fizzy due to the production of carbon dioxide by yeasts and some bacteria, and its properties may also change with the

Adding lemon oil; a grating of lime zest is also delicious.

seasons, especially when using milk from grass-fed cows.

One of the most popular ways to enhance kefir is to add some to flavour – citrus flavours and spices go surprisingly well, as do some savoury combinations too. To flavour a batch of kefir you can carry out a 'second fermentation' (*see* below) with a slice of lemon or lime peel (avoid the flesh as it can make the kefir curdle, although this is reversible). Even refrigerated, within about half an hour the milk will have taken on a slightly citrus flavour. The lemony acidity seems to legitimize the sourness, and kefir becomes much more acceptable even to those who have claimed not to like it. If you make kefir on a regular basis, you might like to invest in some lemon oil, which is quite costly but lasts for ages – only one drop will flavour 500ml. Plant-based milks are often already quite sweet and nutty in flavour, so do not really need too much enhancement.

Storing and/or Second Fermenting Kefir

Once you have fermented your milk source, reduced the pH and produced lactic acid, with all its protective properties, your kefir will not 'go off' as such, unless you contaminate it. Even with the grains removed, kefir contains billions of microbes and it will continue to ferment, further developing flavour. At low temperatures, the microbes are much less active and fermentation will proceed at a much slower rate.

For a mild-tasting kefir, refrigerate it straight away. There is evidence that the free fatty acid content of kefir increases for the first few days of refrigeration, which could be an added benefit. If you keep it towards the back of the fridge, where the temperature is more consistent, the kefir should remain pleasantly usable for up to a fortnight.

For a stronger natural flavour, leave the kefir strained at room temperature for up to 48 hours, to 'second ferment'. Ensure that the lid of the storage container is loose, as yeasts will continue to produce carbon dioxide and ethanol. This will result in a fizzier, stronger-tasting kefir with a higher alcohol content. (You would have to try quite hard to make kefir appreciably alcoholic, though. Highest recorded levels are about 2%, and this requires an additional 4 or so days under anaerobic

Milk kefir can be mixed with rhubarb and lime, damson compote, billionaire's granola, honey, date syrup, strawberry syrup, cumin and salt, or raspberry sauce.

conditions.) Refrigerate the kefir when you have reached the point at which you like the taste.

Cow's milk kefir may be kept in the fridge with little deterioration to its probiotic activity for up to a fortnight. After this point, some studies have shown that the number of lactobacilli present then start to decrease. Goat's milk kefir is much more stable and is less likely to separate into curds and whey. It can even be successfully frozen in plastic bottles – as long as there is a little room for expansion.

Plant-based milks have a much shorter shelf life. Sucrose is added, which is easily broken down to glucose and fructose, if the presence of glucose can lead to quite vigorous yeast/bacterial growth even at low temperatures. The longest-lasting is soya milk, which retains its flavour/consistency for up to 10 days.

IS IT READY?

The endpoint of kefir fermentation differs according to the milk used. With full fat cow's milk, it can be very obvious – during the process, grains will float to the top and, when the kefir is done, they will be sitting on top of a firmly set curd that will pull away from the side of

The kefir is ready when it has set. The grains almost always float to the top, but not always. They may nestle just below the surface.

Tilt the jar to see whether the kefir has set. Here it has formed a solid mass.

The amount of grains needed to make delicious kefir in 500ml of milk.

the jar if you tilt it slightly. Open the jar and smell the contents. You will soon get used to kefir's distinctive set of odours, and this will help you to decide if it is done. If you have used an anaerobic set-up, when you release the catch on the jar you will hear a hiss of gases. If it still smells like milk, and the milk is runny, it is not ready. If the weather is warm, or you have left your kefir for longer than necessary, pockets of whey may have started to form. These will mix back in without any problem after straining.

With a skimmed-milk source, it is harder to tell when the kefir is ready, as skimmed milk gives a much softer set. Smell it and poke with a spoon if you are not sure how much it has thickened.

Goat's milk presents quite differently. Because of its composition, it does not set so firmly. Instead, the milk tends to thicken and may have quite large lumps – almost like goat's cheese – floating in it. It does not usually separate after a short fermentation, but, if this does occur, again it is not a concern. It becomes more homogeneous after straining and smells just like goat's cheese.

Apart from soya milk, which does set remarkably well, plant-based milks will usually have separated into clear and opaque liquid fractions after 24 hours, with the grains in little pieces sitting at the bottom. Coconut cream will thicken quite well too. There is likely to be a mass of bubbles on top of the kefir, which rarely thickens, and a release of carbon dioxide when the jar is opened. The smell will have altered and will have some slightly vinegary tones.

VARIABLES AND ADJUSTMENTS

Scaling Production Up or Down

How much and how regularly you make your kefir will depend on your own circumstances. If you are a family of four all drinking 125ml a day, you will need to make 500ml a day. Many people like this daily routine, but others prefer to make a larger quantity less frequently, and decant it into smaller bottles for consumption over a few days. Those who are new to kefir will need to acclimatize with a spoonful or two a day at first and build up, so there will be no need to make a new batch straight away. Sometimes, people attack the process with great gusto, then find that they are over-run with kefir sitting in jars in the fridge. You will need to adjust your kefir-making regime to suit you. Either make it less frequently, storing the grains in a little covered pot of milk in between, or transfer to a smaller pot to make less kefir. *See* below for what to do with excess kefir.

Ratio of Kefir Grains to Milk

My personal preference is for a much smaller ratio of grains to milk than is recommended by many other fermenters – just 2–3g per 500ml of milk, or half a teaspoon. This can easily be scaled up; if you are using a litre of milk, use double the amount of grains. Due to the exponential way that bacteria grow, this is not critical – after all, you always start off with millions and end up with billions! However, too many grains can affect the composition of the kefir. It can become rather yeasty and fizzy and taste extremely sour or vinegary. This is because of the complex nature of kefir grains, and the way in which species on the surface can differ from species in the interior of the grain. This is also the reason why results can vary depending on whether you use one large lump of kefir grains or several small pieces.

Timing and Temperature

Getting times and temperatures right can be tricky. In the warmer months, the kefir might well be set in 18 hours, which may not be convenient. If you can find somewhere in the house that is slightly cooler, you should be able to establish a 24-hour routine. Another solution is to refrigerate the kefir when you judge it is almost done and letting it finish off at a slower rate in the fridge. In the winter time, the converse can be true – if you have a relatively cold house, fermentation could take 36 hours. To speed things up a little, try warming the milk to room temperature (approximately 21°C) before adding the grains.

PROPAGATION OF GRAINS

Dividing the Growing Mass of Grains

After a few rounds of kefir making, the mass of your

kefir grains will have grown. This means that your kefir production is going well. When your grains have about doubled in size, take out half of them and give them to

Plant-based milk kefir grains often stop growing and start to break up into smaller pieces.

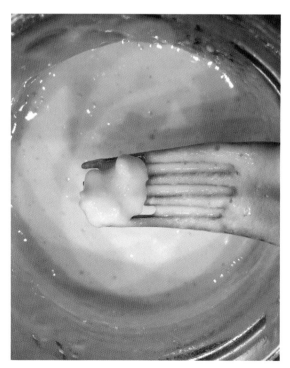

Non-dairy grains are happiest kept in soya milk.

a friend. Or the dog. Or freeze them, just in case your original ones give up the ghost at some later stage. If the grains are in one big lump, you can cut them in half with a knife. This will not harm them.

Propagating Plant-Based Milk Kefir Grains

It is perfectly possible to both grow and maintain milk kefir grains in other substrates for many months, although they seem to be less inclined to increase in size or quantity. Neither do they form clumps or thick strands of kefiran polysaccharide. This is because galactose in milk is a major substrate for kefiran synthesis, which holds the grains together. Adding yeast extract or ground chickpeas (which contain galactose) to non-dairy milks does not encourage propagation. However, kefir grains may be successfully propagated in soya milk; this process also produces kefiran. Use a good-quality soya milk or mixed milk for maintenance purposes and, if the kefir starts to lack vigour, transfer to some whole cow's milk to refresh for a few days.

Passing Grain on to Friends and Family

To make your grains grow as quickly as possible, put them in a Kilner jar with just 100ml milk and leave them out of the fridge in this same milk for three to four days.

They will not smell very nice and the kefir will not taste good, but the grains will grow very happily! Then just change the milk and repeat or share.

Storing Kefir Grains

In between making batches of kefir, keep your grains in approximately 20 times their volume of milk in a covered container. They must be protected from drying out. They can be kept at room temperature like this for about a week without changing the milk, unless the room is extremely warm. They can also be kept like this in the fridge for up to three weeks, but after refrigeration they will take some extra hours before they are ready to make another batch of kefir. Rinse them in fresh milk before using if they smell as though they need it. For long storage, drain the grains and store dry in a small covered pot in the freezer. When you wish to use them again, bring to room temperature and for frozen grains reacclimatize according to the instructions.

TROUBLESHOOTING

The Kefir Has Separated or is Grainy

Upon storage, or over-fermentation, kefir can separate

During straining, kefir may appear grainy. This may persist after straining too.

To lose a grainy texture, use a balloon whisk to re-incorporate the curds.

into curds in whey. There is no need to worry about this. Just whisk it up with a fork or small balloon whisk and it will re-incorporate. If it does not smell or taste unpleasant, it is fine.

The Milk Has Separated

Where there is a thick band of cream – more than 0.5cm – on the top of the milk, the grains may get stuck in it and only the cream fraction will turn to kefir. If you are using this kind of milk, you will need to stir or shake it a few times whilst it is fermenting. Sometimes, the separate milk fraction does not ferment at all. If this has happened, extract the grains from the cream and try again, removing the cream first.

Contamination Problems

Contamination is not going to be a huge issue, especially if you use an almost-full clip-top jar with a gasket, or a jar with a clean lid. This provides a good low-oxygen environment and it is difficult both for surface moulds to grow and for contaminants to enter the jar. There are so many millions of bacteria in the kefir and grains that it is difficult for pathogens and moulds to take hold. Bacteria and yeasts produce antibacterial substances that inhibit the growth of other species. Also, kefir is acidic, which inhibits the growth of many pathogens. If you are using pasteurized milk, it has already been treated to kill pathogenic bacteria. Contamination would be more likely to occur post-fermentation – through putting a used spoon into your kefir jar, for example – and even this would be a rare occurrence, as the same protection from billions of protective bacteria will apply.

If there is a dry-looking white film growing on the top of your kefir, this could be kahm yeast, which can occasionally grow on the surface. If this occurs, strain the grains, place them in a smaller than usual jar (so you do not waste lots of milk), fill it very full to eliminate as much air as possible, and ferment as usual. This may do the trick. Try once more to see if the kahm yeast is still present, or start again from your frozen spares. If it is clearly

Spare kefir grains in their 'hotel', waiting for the addition of some milk.

growing fuzzy mould, it is time to throw the kefir out.

The Milk Has Curdled

Curdling of the milk is much more likely to happen in the summer. You will realize that something is wrong as your kefir will not have its characteristic smell. It will be almost odourless, and the curds will be tiny. This is because the milk has gone off, due to the action of milk spoilage organisms, before the kefir grains have got going. You will have to discard the kefir and start again, using fresh milk and finding a cooler place for the fermentation.

RECIPES AND WHAT TO DO WITH LEFTOVERS

So, how should you include kefir in your diet? The easiest way is to have it as a 125ml shot every morning (when you are used to it), in a glass, knocked back in one or two gulps, just as it is. However, the human palate is more accustomed to processed foods with a carefully designed mouth-feel, which home-made kefir lacks. There are various ways to make kefir more palatable. One of the easiest ways is to add a swirl of date syrup, maple syrup or a fruit syrup.

Milk Kefir Smoothie

Add about 100/125ml of kefir to your usual smoothie. Do not worry about killing the probiotics with a blender: there will be some microbial sacrifice to the blade, but not enough to make any big impact on the numbers. Fruit kefir smoothies are best made fresh as the continued bacterial

CONSUMING KEFIR: WHO, HOW MUCH AND WHEN?

There is a type of kefir for almost everyone, with some caveats, as it is impossible to identify the exact species in every batch of kefir grains. Reports of serious illness following kefir consumption are rare, but if you are immunocompromised, have had recent gastric surgery, or have an underlying serious health condition, please check with a medical practitioner beforehand.

Milk kefir is suitable for lactose-intolerant people, for multiple reasons. First, during fermentation about 60% of the lactose is broken down into glucose and galactose. Second, some LAB die during transit through the gut, releasing the enzymes that can still digest lactose. Third, the kefir microbes that do survive the passage through the upper intestines are able to help the existing gut bacteria to eliminate undigested lactose.

If you have IBS or IBD, your reaction to kefir could be unpredictable, so it needs to be introduced into your diet in extremely small quantities – as little as half a teaspoon a day. Kefir is suitable for pregnant women and nursing mothers, as long as the grains have not been exposed to raw milk.

When you are a newcomer to kefir, you must start slowly. Occasionally, people are over-enthusiastic, and suffer from diarrhoea as a result of the massive sudden influx of new microbial species. Start with just a teaspoon or two the first day, and build up slowly, through 5, 10, 20, 50 and 75ml to a maximum of 150ml. This is a perfect portion to have with muesli or as the basis of a daily smoothie.

Stomach acid levels are lower in the morning and this is often suggested as the best time to have kefir, to increase the chances of the microbes surviving the GI tract (although dairy products are quite good at protecting them). There have been positive reports on levels of bone mineral density in post-menopausal women who took kefir at night.[36]

A favourite receptacle, like this jug and beaker in Bristol Blue glass, can make a daily kefir shot taste even better.

action tends to change the flavour, and not always for the best.

Quick Banana or Mango Milk Kefir Ice Cream

Blitz pieces of frozen banana or mango with some kefir to make an ice cream that completely hides the flavour of the kefir. Also works with frozen mango. It freezes solid if it is re-frozen, so it is best eaten immediately.

Proper Kefir Ice Cream

This works well and is usually very popular – a cross between an ice cream and frozen yoghurt. Use it with any of the leftover fruits you might have from making kombucha or water kefir, or with fruit syrups. The dried skimmed milk is not essential, but it does increase the protein content, to improve the final texture.

• •

KEFIR ICE CREAM

Kefir mango lassi.

Ingredients:

4 egg yolks
100g caster sugar
500ml milk
50g skimmed milk powder (optional)
Vanilla pod
125g strained kefir (can be strong-flavoured)

Method:

1. Whisk the egg yolks and caster sugar together in a bowl until pale.
2. Bring the milk, milk powder if using, and vanilla pod just to the boil.
3. Pour over the eggs and sugar, whisking all the while.
4. Return to the pan and cook over a low/medium heat, stirring until the mixture coats the back of a wooden spoon. Do not let it boil, otherwise it will become grainy.
5. Leave the custard to cool.
6. Add in the kefir, and any other flavourings, and mix well.
7. Put in an ice-cream maker and freeze.

• •

Kefir Mango Lassi

Making a lassi is probably the best way to encourage a reluctant kefir drinker. Use some tinned mango pulp (available in most supermarkets; Sainsbury's does an unsweetened one) at about 15% volume, and mix into some kefir. This lasts for about a week in the fridge with cow's milk, but with plant-based kefirs it can be thoroughly explosive.

Billionaire's Granola

Perfect for a 'kefir breakfast', this gut-healthy granola with 12 different plant-based ingredients is great in terms of diversity. The orange peel makes it taste really special. The term 'cup' in the recipe represents ratios; you can use whatever cup size you like. A half cup measure (120ml) makes a litre jar of granola.

BILLIONAIRE'S GRANOLA

Ingredients:

3 × cups whole rolled oats

1 × cup of mixed nuts (for example, $\frac{1}{3}$ almonds, $\frac{1}{3}$ pistachios, $\frac{1}{3}$ pecans)

1 × cup of mixed seeds (for example, $\frac{1}{3}$ sesame, $\frac{1}{3}$ pumpkin, $\frac{1}{3}$ sunflower)

Teaspoon of cinnamon

A couple of drops of vanilla essence (optional)

$\frac{1}{2}$ cup rapeseed or extra virgin olive oil (you cannot taste it, but go easy if you are not sure about the olive oil)

$\frac{1}{2}$ cup maple syrup or honey

1 × cup of mixed dried fruit (for example, $\frac{1}{3}$ raisins, $\frac{1}{3}$ cranberries, $\frac{1}{3}$ candied orange peel)

Method:

1. Heat the oven to 150°C fan.
2. In a bowl mix the oats, nuts and seeds, cinnamon and vanilla essence.
3. Add the oil and maple syrup and stir well.
4. Place on a baking tray and bake for 15 mins.
5. Stir and bake for another 5 mins, until golden and crispy. Do not worry if it is slightly wet-looking at this stage; it does dry.
6. Stir in the dried fruit and, when cooled, put in a jar.

Kefirdelphia

If you are over-run with kefir, strain it through a coffee filter overnight in the fridge to make what is basically a cream cheese. This works well for dairy. If you are plant-based, use a good-quality tinned coconut cream, which strains brilliantly. Sometimes it can taste a little

Straining kefir to make Kefirdelphia cheese, using a funnel lined with a coffee filter.

E. MORELAND

After 24 hours, the whey and curd have separated. This may take a day longer for goat's milk kefir. E. MORELAND

Tear away the paper filter to release the cheese.

E. MORELAND

strong, in which case filter with 50% of your home-made yoghurt to make a delicious, creamy and probiotic labneh. Flavour with dukka, ras al hanout or garlic and herbs.

Do not waste the whey. It can be used in smoothies. It is full of probiotics and you will never taste the difference.

Labneh Balls

Oil your hands and roll teaspoons of the cheese into little balls. Store them in a jar of extra virgin olive oil in the fridge to go with salads or pitta bread.

Labneh balls in extra virgin olive oil. ADOBE

Chickpea and mixed torshi salad, with kefir dressing drizzled over.

Kefir dressing.

KEFIR DRESSING

Ingredients:

200ml kefir
50ml extra virgin olive oil
Squeeze of lime juice
1 crushed garlic clove
Handful of chopped coriander, parsley, mint or dill, or any combination of these
Pinch of salt and black pepper

Method:

Whizz ingredients together using a stick blender. Serve over salads. The dressing can also be used with hot food, as long as you put it on just before eating it, so that some of the probiotic microbes are preserved. It is especially good with roasted vegetables, curries and chilli.

Kefir Icing

Mix 50g yoghurt kefirdelphia (*see* above) and 50g butter with 250g icing sugar to make probiotic icing. This will need to be applied just before eating, as the high sugar content might not be ideal for the survival of probiotic microbes.

For a plant-based alternative, use strained coconut cream kefir.

OTHER USES FOR KEFIR

It is recommended never to put kefir on an open wound, as it is impossible to be certain of the microbes it contains. However, it is commonly used in the Middle East to make a face cream; strain it, add a little essence of rose to cover up the smell, and keep refrigerated.

Kefir can be used just like yoghurt to clear up mild thrush infections and athlete's foot, on unbroken skin. Clearly, this would have to be at your own risk.

Kefir icing (arranged by Sarah @rightgoodkitchen).

CHAPTER 5

WATER KEFIR

Water kefir is a fascinating phenomenon – a drink that sparkles like lemonade but also comes with proven health benefits. Sustainable and requiring only the simplest of ingredients and equipment, it is also incredibly versatile; it can be made to taste tart or mild, it can be almost completely non-alcoholic or approaching 3%, it can be fizzy or still. Once fermented, it can be flavoured in a multitude of ways, using flowers, herbs, fruit, or even coffee. Unlike its milky sibling, it also opens up the world of probiotic drinks to those who are dairy-intolerant/allergic, or who follow a plant-based diet. Water kefir grains contain fewer species than milk kefir, and the end product will not have the same huge range of nutrients, but it is definitely worth having in your repertoire.

WATER KEFIR GRAINS (WKG)

Water kefir grains are another type of SCOBY (symbiotic culture of bacteria and yeasts), but they use sucrose as their energy source and are bound together by a dextran polysaccharide matrix. They look quite different from their milky counterparts, ranging in size from 1 to 30mm in diameter, with a glassy appearance, reminiscent of the silica gel that is used in plant pots for retaining water. They feel crumbly, and are much easier to destroy than milk kefir grains. They can be crushed to smithereens between your fingers, or when being pushed through a sieve, so do be gentle with them.

There is a great variety in both the appearance and behaviour of the grains; they will all make water kefir, but they may have slightly different nutritional requirements.

Water kefir grains are known by many other names worldwide, including *tibicos* in South America, Japanese water crystals, beer seeds, California beers and ginger beer plant (GBP).

Both of these different types of grain make water kefir. The flavour is different but the fizz is still the same. They probably have different origins. E. MORELAND

Opuntia **cactus (prickly pear).** ADOBE

THE ORIGINS OF WATER KEFIR

The origins of water kefir are nebulous: it is likely that it originated in more than one world location, and there is some confusion over whether it is the same thing as the ginger beer plant (GBP) that was common in Western Europe during the early part of the twentieth century. GBP always contains both *Saccharomyces florentinus* and *Lactobacillus hilgardii*, but it is impossible to tell just by looking, so it remains an unknown.

The first mention of GBP in the scientific literature was in 1887, when Prof. Harry Marshall Ward studied the microbes involved.[37] In a paper to the Royal Society, he cited a wide range of sources as diverse as Italy, North America and Edinburgh. At about the same time, Dutch microbiologist Martinus Beijerinck attributed the origins of GBP to soldiers bringing it with them upon their return from the Crimean War. The first mention of *tibicos* comes in an 1899 paper by L. Lutz, who describes *tibi* as (translated from the French) 'native of Mexico, where it grows on pads of *Opuntia* [cactus], which in the presence of water containing dissolved sugar determines an active fermentation of the medium by producing a sparkling liquid with tart flavour, slightly butyrous, used as a drink by factory workers'.[38]

Tibicos (WKG) have been used in Mexico for many years, perhaps even for centuries.[39] Interestingly, there seems to be no evidence in the research of such grains being found on cactus pads since that first report in 1899.

THE SCIENCE OF WATER KEFIR

While there is plenty of sugar available, several species of LAB can synthesize the dextran matrix from sucrose, producing an enzyme called dextransucrase. This dextran is an ideal surface upon which other organisms can aggregate. The microbes in the grains also propagate into the sugary water, turning it cloudy. There may be as many as 100,000,000 microbes per millilitre.

Lactic acid bacteria (LAB) use the carbohydrates (provided by sugary liquids) and minerals to produce lactic acid, ethanol, a range of flavour molecules and organic acids, and carbon dioxide, which gives the carbonation. The LAB work optimally in a lower-oxygen environment, whereas acetic acid bacteria (AAB) require oxygen to metabolise. Yeasts can survive and produce CO_2 under both sets of conditions.

Yeasts in the WKG produce an enzyme called invertase, which breaks sucrose down into its constituent glucose and fructose sugars. These can then be utilized by the lactobacilli, resulting in lactic acid formation. The alcohol produced by the yeasts from their own metabolism is the energy source needed by *Acetobacter*, from which they make acetic acid (vinegar), which keeps levels of alcohol in the water kefir low. There will be many more reactions going on, but they are difficult to study in isolation. When the bacteria in the grains are separated, the relationships no longer exist. Also, some LAB can produce substances in addition to lactic acid that can inhibit the growth of yeasts and some pathogens, complicating the story further.[40]

The presence of *Saccharomyces* yeasts seems to be an important factor in kefir grain performance, as it is able to synthesize co-factors for other members of the SCOBY. In its absence, other sources of co-factors might be required. These can be provided by figs or unrefined sugars, for example.[41]

The pH of water kefir when it is ready for drinking is usually slightly acidic, approximately 4–4.5. Like most other ferments, it is relatively hard to contaminate, as few pathogens are able to thrive in these circumstances.

COMPOSITION OF WATER KEFIR

Nutritional Composition

Before fermentation, water kefir contains about 3.5% sucrose, and minerals either from the tap water, or any additional fruit that has been added, such as traces of potassium, calcium, phosphorus, manganese, iron, sodium, magnesium, zinc and copper. It lacks the bioactive peptides and partially digested fats found in milk kefir, and contains fewer vitamins, but its microbial content alone makes it a worthy addition to the diet.

Water kefir does initially contain sugar, although much of this is metabolised; after a few days, very little will remain. When the fermentation process is near completion, after about 48 hours, it is likely that the water kefir will contain probiotic microbes, trace amounts of sugar, B vitamins, lactic acid, ethanol, glycerol, acetic acid, mannitol, and various volatile aromatic compounds which contribute to the final flavour, with complicated names such as ethyl acetate, isoamyl acetate and ethyl hexanoate.

Microbial Composition of Water Kefir[44]

Group	Common species
Lactic acid bacteria, responsible for production of lactic acid	*Leuconostoc mesenteroides, L. citreum, L. brevis, L. buchneri, L. casei* subsp. *casei, L. casei* subsp. *rhamnosus, L. diolivorans, L. fermentum, L. harbinensis, L. hilgardii, L. hordeii, L. kefiranofaciens, L. kefiri, L. lactis, L. mali, L. nagelli, L. paracasei, L. parafarraginis, L. perolens, L. plantarum, L. satsumensis*
Acetic acid bacteria, responsible for the production of acetic acid *Zymomonas* sp., the only bacterium known to be able to produce alcohol (this is usually done by yeasts)	*A. fabarum* and *A. orientalis, A. lovaniensis Zymomonas* sp.
Yeasts responsible for the production of alcohol and carbon dioxide	*Dekkera* sp., *Hanseniaspora*, sp. *Saccharomyces* sp., *Zygosaccharomyces* sp., *Torulaspora* sp., *Kluyveromyces* sp., *Khazakstania* sp., *Hanseniaspora* sp., *Pichia* sp., *Lachancea* sp.
Bifidobacteria sp. production of B and K vitamins	*Bifidobacteria* sp.

Microbial Composition

There is huge variety in the composition of water kefir grains, which reflects their world-wide occurrence. They may contain between four and ten different species of organism and then several different strains of each.[42, 43, 44, 45] This may alter during the lifetime of the grains due to aerial contamination, especially if ferments are kept near each other, as there could be some transfer of ferment-friendly microbes. If the grains are under-fed, loss of species could occur. Depending on the grains, there may be more yeasts present than bacteria or vice versa.

Even though you will never need to remember any of these names, the table shows the huge variety of life inside those grains, not only busily metabolising nutrients to make bioactive molecules, but also exerting probiotic effects on their journey through your digestive system.

In contrast to milk kefir, much the same population of microbes exists both on the grains and in the liquid. Curiously, even though all the microbes are present in the kefir, it is not possible to spontaneously make WKG from kefir solution.

HEALTH BENEFITS OF WATER KEFIR

Most of the health benefits of water kefir probably come from the probiotic microbes that it contains. There have been no studies in humans as yet, but 'in vitro', water kefir has shown antibacterial activity against a range of pathogenic bacteria. In gel form it seems to enhance wound healing[18], and has been found to lower blood sugar and total cholesterol in diabetic rats.[46] Another study showed that water kefir has significant antioxidant potency, so could be a good source of natural antioxidants.[47] On this basis it seems possible that regular consumption of water kefir could reduce the likelihood of developing diseases associated with reactive oxygen species, such as atherosclerosis, cancer, emphysema and arthritis, although this is conjecture at the moment.

Many of the other benefits remain as hearsay for now but anecdotally may include the following:

- Rapid relief of cold symptoms, sore throats, swollen tonsils.
- A feeling of temporary euphoria a few minutes after drinking.
- Diuretic effects, which could be due to the presence of mannitol in some water kefirs.

MAKING WATER KEFIR: GETTING STARTED

Finding Your Grains

When looking for water kefir grains, the advice is more or less the same as that in the milk chapter: find a friend if you can! Water kefir needs a heftier initial inoculum than milk kefir, so you will need approximately 50g per litre. This should not be too much of a problem as, when water kefir is growing happily, the volume of grains can easily double within a couple of rounds of fermentation.

If you are buying online, there are several reputable companies. Buying dehydrated grains is not recommended, and it really is not necessary – the wet grains are perfectly able to withstand posting, and rehydrating is just another stage to worry about. If you do have dehydrated grains, follow the instructions to the letter.

With the diversity in their microbial composition, different grains might have different nutritional requirements. If you have been given your kefir grains by a friend, or have grains from a source that comes with instructions, do heed the advice you are given. Although the advice here aims to cover all bases, it is difficult to predict which conditions will work best for your particular grains. A little experimentation may be required.

Choosing a Vessel

LAB work optimally in a low-oxygen environment, whereas AAB require oxygen to metabolise. Yeasts can survive and produce oxygen under both sets of conditions. By changing the amount of air in the system, you can change quite drastically the final flavour of your water kefir. Just as with milk kefir, you can choose either a 'closed' or an 'open' system for water kefir, depending upon the flavour profile you are after.

Closed System

This method makes water kefir that is light on vinegar tones, not too sweet, minimally alcoholic and a perfect base for adding flavour.

LAB are facultative anaerobes and thrive in a low-oxygen environment. In a closed system, with a little headroom, you will ensure that they grow more voraciously than the AAB, which require oxygen. Potentially, yeasts could produce a lot of alcohol that would then not be metabolised by the AAB, but this is limited by the amount of sugar you add and the fact that the LAB will be using some of this to make dextran.

In a closed system, carbon dioxide is generated, which cannot escape. The amount is limited by the sugar added, so, as long as you do not overdo it, you are unlikely to get a dangerous pressure build-up. The rubber or silicone gasket of the clip-top jar should allow enough expansion to prevent an explosion. However, if you are concerned, you can replace the metal catch with a rubber band, which would allow a little more movement.

The advantage of fermenting anaerobically is that the resulting water kefir is fizzy and ready to drink straight away.

Open System

In an open system, the LAB can produce lactic acid, although not as voraciously, the yeasts can produce alcohol and the AAB are much more active converting that into acetic acid. This means that the water kefir will have a much more vinegary taste, which some people love. It will also not be as fizzy, as the carbon dioxide will be able to escape, but you can add carbonation during second-stage fermentation. For this method you can use any large jar with a paper towel or cotton cover over the top, to keep out flies and airborne contaminants.

Other suitable vessels include:

- Recycled plastic bottles – these can withstand a good deal of expansion, although it depends upon your attitude towards the potential leaching of chemicals from plastic.
- Large drinks dispensers with taps – these look like they are going to be ideal for scaling up, but there are a couple of caveats. First, you must ensure that the internal tap exit pipe has a mesh over it, to prevent the grains getting stuck – otherwise, it will be a source of great frustration! Also, when you turn the tap on, remember to open the lid or nothing will come out, as a vacuum will have been created.
- Ceramic crocks can be used, but it is easier and more exciting to see what is going on with a clear vessel.
- Food-grade stainless steel may be suitable for large-scale fermenting.

Basic Instructions

Ingredients:

Approx. 5% w/v water kefir grains: 50g or 2–3 tablespoons per litre

3.5% w/v white sugar (35g per litre)

Tap water (can be filtered. Can also be slightly warm <30°C)

1 unsulphured dried fig or 5g coconut sugar (may be optional)

If you are fortunate and have hard water and perfect grains, you may not need to add figs or brown sugar. To scale up to fit your chosen vessel, see the ratio table below.

Equipment:

Fermentation vessel of choice

Spoon

Sieve and funnel

Plastic bottles or screw-top jars for storage

Method:

1. Ensure your equipment, hands and work surface are clean.
2. Add sugar(s) and water directly to the jar to save time, stirring well until the sugar is dissolved. Ensure there is a good 7–8cm of headroom.
3. Add your kefir grains.
4. Shut the lid or arrange the cap, depending on whether you are using a closed or open system.
5. Leave to ferment on the worktop for 48 hours, away from bright sunlight. After 24 hours, if you move the jar or bottle slightly you should see bubbles of carbon dioxide forming and rising to the surface and the liquid becoming cloudy. This is a sign that fermentation is well under way. (This stage may take a little longer after transit.) Your grains will mostly be settled at the bottom of the jar, occasionally floating up.
6. Carefully open the lid and taste a little, using a spoon. If it is to your liking, with a good amount of fizz (closed system) and just a hint of sweetness, it is ready for straining. If not, leave for another 24 hours and then try again.

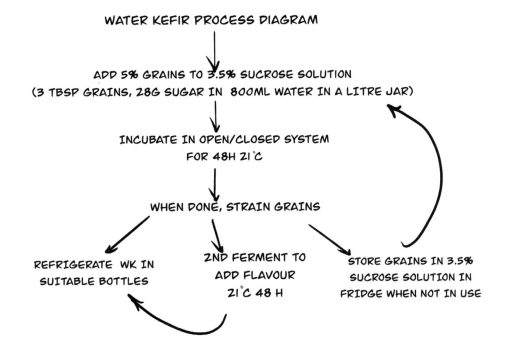

WATER KEFIR PROCESS DIAGRAM

ADD 5% GRAINS TO 3.5% SUCROSE SOLUTION
(3 TBSP GRAINS, 28G SUGAR IN 800ML WATER IN A LITRE JAR)

INCUBATE IN OPEN/CLOSED SYSTEM FOR 48H 21°C

WHEN DONE, STRAIN GRAINS

REFRIGERATE WK IN SUITABLE BOTTLES

2ND FERMENT TO ADD FLAVOUR 21°C 48 H

STORE GRAINS IN 3.5% SUCROSE SOLUTION IN FRIDGE WHEN NOT IN USE

The process of making water kefir.

Setting up the water kefir: measuring in the sugar using a cup measure. E. MORELAND

Adding in the water by eye, and allowing the sugar to dissolve. E. MORELAND

7. When it is ready, strain out the grains using a sieve or straining funnel, either directly into suitable bottles or into a jug. It is now ready to use, or can undergo secondary fermentation – *see* below.

8. Set up your next batch: while the grains are in the sieve, rinse out the vessel with hot water, and repeat the preparation protocol above.

READY FOR STRAINING AND STORAGE?

Water kefir is a slightly cloudy, fizzy liquid that should not be at all thick or viscous. The taste is hard to describe: a bit soda-watery with a hint of bicarb, balanced by a touch of sweetness and a touch of whey (although there is absolutely no animal product in it).

Ratios for Scaling Up

Jar size	Water	Sugar	Coconut sugar (optional)	Grains (approx.)
1ltr	800ml	28g	4g	40g
1.9ltr	1.5ltr	52.5g	7.5g	75g
5ltr	4ltr	112g	20g	200g
Ratio		3.5%	0.5%	5%

Spooning in the water kefir grains. E. MORELAND

Straining out the kefir grains. E. MORELAND

Fermentation time can be affected by a number of factors: the ratios of sugar to water in the solution, the ratio of grains to sugar water in the vessel, and the temperature. Add to that your personal preference for flavour and fizziness and you have a highly variable situation. You are the only person who can decide when your kefir is ready, as it depends very much on your taste. After about five days, the microbes will have consumed all of the sugar. At that point, you can end up with some rather strange flavours, due to over-production of aromatics and microbial cell death releasing substances into the mixture.

Stages of water kefir development: the left-hand jar is the most mature and is slightly cloudy; the one on the right is 24 hours old and tiny bubbles are beginning to form.

Once it has been strained, your water kefir is ready to drink just as it is, or to be a mixer for fruit juice or cordial. If you have made it in a closed system, it will already be fizzy and can be bottled and refrigerated for storage. It will keep for two to three weeks in the fridge. The cold will slow down but not stop the activity of the microbes, which will continue to slowly utilize the sugar, improving carbonation and reducing sweetness.

When choosing suitable storage vessels for water kefir, avoid those lovely little square flip-top 250ml bottles. Sadly, they are not up to the task.

SECONDARY FERMENTATION (2°F)

This simply means adding some flavour to your strained water kefir and leaving it to ferment again

Different flower petals – roses, geraniums, white and pink elderflowers (the pink are the best, if you can find them!).

Water kefir with raspberry and rose.

for a day or two at room temperature. Never add anything other than sugar or the odd fig directly to your kefir grains, as particles of fruit will become mixed up in them and this can create a bit of a mess. At this stage you can let your imagination run away with you – any fruit, herb, spice, flower petal, even vegetable combination is possible.

2°F has four effects:

1. To infuse flavour into the water kefir.
2. To add even more complex potential bioactive compounds into the mix.
3. To improve carbonation.
4. To utilize any additional sugar from syrups or fruit ensuring that even flavoured water kefir is a low-sugar beverage.

2°F with Fresh Fruits

You can use whatever fruit you have to hand, but there are a few tried and tested combinations that work well: lemon, ginger and turmeric; rhubarb and hibiscus; lime and mint; strawberry, basil and black pepper; raspberry and rose; apple juice and cinnamon; orange and elderflower; and pineapple, cinnamon, clove and chilli with brown sugar, known as tepache.

Method:
1. Cut up bits of fruit to increase the surface area.
2. Add to strained water kefir in a Kilner jar with gasket (to increase carbonation if desired), or cover with paper or a cloth.
3. Leave for 48 hours for the flavour to infuse.
4. Strain to remove any discoloured fruit (add this to a smoothie), and bottle or serve.

2°F with Herbal Infusions

You can use virtually any kind of herbal teabag to infuse flavour into your water kefir. Use 1 teabag per litre and leave for 24 hours. For something a bit different, try adding about 10% dissolved coffee and a touch of muscovado sugar.

2°F with Cordial

If you regularly make water kefir, it can be more

Freezing cordials for storage: ice cubes and flavour in a 2 in 1 solution!

economical and practical to have a syrup or cordial that you can easily add. I will usually have a bottle of lemon, ginger and turmeric cordial in the fridge, but use leftover strawberries, raspberries, citrus peels as they become available. Below are some cordial recipes that can easily be adapted to other fruits. These can be refrigerated for up to a month in glass jars or bottles that have been sterilized for 15 minutes at 150°C, or they can be frozen as ice cubes for longer storage.

FRUIT OR VEGETABLE FERMENTS

The incredible versatility of WKG means that they can be used to ferment almost any other substrate that contains a source of sugar, including fruit and vegetable juices. This is a wonderful way of probiotically enhancing any type of bought fruit or vegetable juice, as well as releasing a whole range of other bioactive compounds.

When using your WKG with anything other than

Recipes for Cordials

Cordial	Ingredients	Method
Lemon, ginger and turmeric	80g fresh ginger, grated; 50g lemon juice; 450g water; 30g fresh turmeric, grated; 600g white sugar	Add all ingredients to a pan and simmer gently for about 15 mins. Strain to remove the bits, which will be a delicious addition to kefir or yoghurt, or mixed into granola.
Rhubarb and hibiscus	500g young juicy rhubarb stems; 200g caster sugar; 2 tbsp dried hibiscus flowers	Put all ingredients in an oven-proof dish, cover and bake at 150°C in a preheated oven for 20 mins. This should release a lovely clear juice; boiling would break up the fibres and make it cloudy. Strain the juice through a sieve and have the fruit for pudding!
Frozen berry cordial	1 bag frozen fruit; sugar to taste (about 100g)	Add ingredients to pan and heat slowly to thaw fruit and release the juice. Simmer for 10 mins on a low heat. Strain, applying gentle pressure only to keep the juice clear. Use the leftover strawberries to make fruit leather: pulverise and spread on baking parchment and dehydrate on the oven's lowest setting.
Elderflower cordial	30 elderflower heads; 1.5 litres of water; 1kg sugar; juice and cut-up remains of 2 lemons and 1 large orange; 1 tsp citric acid (optional – will help it keep for longer)	Put the elderflower heads in a large bowl with the citrus juice and leftover fruit. In a pan, heat the sugar and water to boiling point, ensuring that the sugar has dissolved. Pour over the flowers and citrus. Cover and leave for 24 hours. Strain and bottle.

sugar and water, use only some of them, as they may react to the new substrate. For example, grains used in spirulina and apple juice seem to stay green for weeks, becoming more opaque in appearance and are definitely less feisty in their production of carbon dioxide.

Use the ratio of about 3 tablespoons of grains per litre. You will only need to ferment juices for 24 hours before straining, bottling and refrigerating – after then, some pretty strange flavours may start to emerge. Due to the very high concentration of sugars in fruit juices, longer fermentation times can lead to the production of alcohol, especially in a closed system; clearly, you need to be aware of this if you are planning to give it to children or you need to drive after consuming it.

You do not even have to use your grains for this process. Because the content of the grains and of the water kefir is very similar, you can achieve the same result by 'backslopping'. This rather unappealing term refers to the act of adding something already fermented to something that is not – 25% water kefir will be enough to get things going. This works well with coconut water, for example, and seems to reduce the development of strange flavours; 24 hours may well be long enough, but it can be left for up to 48 hours, according to your palate.

You can ferment any fruit juice with your kefir grains to give it a probiotic boost.

Coconut kefir water made by 'backslopping' for 24 hours with 25% water kefir.

Fruit ferments should be ready when some bubbles start to form. The opaque appearance might not change at all, unless they contain polyphenols that change colour with acidity. In term of taste, they will have a slightly more acidic or vinegary tang.

FACTORS THAT CAN AFFECT FERMENTATION

Ratio of Kefir Grains to Liquid

If you make milk kefir according to the advice given here, you will be accustomed to using just a tiny amount of grain for a large quantity of milk. Things do not work in the same way for water kefir; if you do not have enough grains, the process is much slower, which is interesting, because the exponential growth pattern of bacteria and yeasts should overcome this. An inoculum of 15g/ltr of grains seems to take almost four days to reach the same pH and level of carbonation,

as opposed to 48 hours for 50g/ltr. It also seems to develop some strange flavours along the way.

The reasons seem to relate to the symbiotic nature of the organisms; perhaps they require high concentrations of nutrients, which are not achievable with a small number of grains in a large volume. At the other end of the scale, having too many grains is not really an issue – it seems to be self-limiting and will usually sit at a maximum third of the volume of liquid. There is little change to the flavour whether the minimum 50g/ltr or 300g/ltr is present, but if you have too many grains you will not have room for much water!

Water

The content of tap water varies enormously throughout the UK. About 60% of it is termed hard or very hard, meaning it has at least 60 mg/ltr of calcium carbonate and often contains other minerals. If you have hard or very hard water, you may find that your kefir grains

WATER HARDNESS IN THE UK

SOFT ● VERY HARD ○ HARD

Do not use distilled water for making water kefir. Distilled water can actually kill some kinds of LAB because of osmosis, as it will flow into the bacterial cells to equalize the osmotic pressure and could burst them.

Sugar

The type of sugar you use will strongly influence the flavour of your kefir. Some prefer the darker caramel tones of brown sugars, others the lighter end of the spectrum, to let the colour of added fruits and cordials shine through.

Organic sugar is less processed and still contains some molasses, which gives it a pale golden colour. It is a good way of consistently providing your kefir with trace minerals without adding any additional flavour. In general, the darker the sugar, the higher the molasses content and the less you need to add for a mineral boost. In fact, if you use too much, you can interfere with the dextran-making machinery of the SCOBY and the grains may break up and turn to mush. When changing to a darker sugar, always use some spare grains. If you are using filtered or soft water you might find you need to include some browner sugar in your brew.

Using Alternative Sweeteners

There is an urban myth that honey is not suitable as a sugar source. However, as long as it is pasteurized, it is fine. Honey's contents are variable and, as it contains only about 80% sugars, you need to add slightly more to get the same concentration, but also to let the flavour come through. A 5% solution generally works well, but sometimes you need as much as 10% to get the flavour. Of course, this will depend on the particular honey. It is not advisable to use honey consistently as

need no other support to grow. In Bristol, for example, they are happy doubling with nothing other than tap water and organic sugar. Soft water can have very different effects and you might need to supplement.

In theory, water should be filtered to remove traces of chlorine or chloramine, which is added to ensure that tap water is safe from pathogens. In practice, however, it seems to make little difference to the growth and proliferation of either water kefir grains or the resulting kefir. If you do filter the water, you will be removing trace minerals that do benefit the microbes, so you may need to introduce either a fig or some coconut sugar.

If you know that your water contains chlorine, it will evaporate if you either heat the water and let it cool, or leave it in a shallow vessel with a large surface area for an hour or so. Chloramine, which is sometimes used these days, is less easily removed. The effects of chlorine or chloramine on fermented foods and, indeed, on the gut microbiota have not yet been well studied.

the kefir grain dextran matrix is made from sucrose, which is not present in large quantities in honey (it is fructose and glucose mainly).

While raw honey is a lovely thing, it is not recommended for use in this context, as it contains yeasts that could interfere with the action of the water kefir grains, or even permanently change their nature. If you want to experiment, do remember to keep some grains back.

Two other readily available sweeteners are agave – a plant-based syrup with a similar sugar composition to honey, which is suitable – and stevia, which is not, as it is devoid of both sugar and calories, and therefore cannot provide an energy source for the microbes.

Sugar Concentration

The 3.5% sugar suggested here is lower than in many other recipes. The reason for this is because it produces water kefir quickly, with little residual sugar and alcohol. The more sugar there is in the mix, the longer it will take for the microbes to metabolise it. In a closed system, more alcohol will potentially be able to be produced from the sugar by the yeast. In an open system, more of this will be able to be converted to vinegar so you can end up with stronger flavours. If you want a stronger-tasting kefir, add 5% sugar at the start. If you use 10% sugar, in a closed system, you can create an alcoholic version.

Temperature

The grains will grow best in the range 21–30°C. If the kitchen is feeling a little chilly and they seem sluggish, put them nearer the radiator – but not on it. If you leave your grains in the fridge in fresh sugar water for three weeks, you may be lucky and find that slowly but surely they have made water kefir, even at this low temperature.

WKG MAINTENANCE AND STORAGE

Adding Fruits to WKG

Traditionally, figs have been added to water kefir to introduce micronutrients. Other common choices are raisins and apricots. The fruit should be unsulphured; sulphur is sometimes used as a preservative, and can slow down bacterial activity. Figs have been shown to produce the most grain growth, and in a litre jar you only need to use about half a fig. This might be completely unnecessary for regular maintenance of your water kefir grains. Co-factors that are needed by the microbial community in your grains are also produced by the yeast *Saccharomyces cerevsiae*, so if this is present in your grains, you will not need to add fruit. It might also be unnecessary if you have hard water. Try first without adding fruit and then add some fruit if it seems sluggish. You can also add a pinch of coconut sugar instead.

Grain Storage
Setting up a 'Hotel'

When your first set of grains have doubled in volume, remove half of them and transfer to a jar of fresh sugar water, three times their volume, with a couple of inches of air, in the fridge. If you use a slightly higher sugar concentration of 5% (5g sugar in 100ml), you can forget about them for longer. Put the lid on, but not too tightly. They will be fine for several weeks. Unfortunately, freezing can destroy *L. hilgardii*, one of the WKG microbes that could be responsible for making the dextran that keeps the grains together, so refrigeration is best.

Going Away

To take a holiday, either put your grains in the 'hotel', or put them in the fridge in their usual vessel in fresh sugar water. They will keep quite happily there for up to three weeks and if you are lucky, will have slowly made water kefir while you are away.

What to Do with Any Excess

Especially in the summer, you will find that the grains increase at an alarming rate! Remove them when you notice that they are taking over, and either share them, experiment with them or compost them. Mix them into smoothies – they can be blended in so you would never know. Pets also seem to love them.

TROUBLESHOOTING

To troubleshoot, first you need to answer this question: when you pour your water kefir into a glass, is it thick or thin?

Thick and Gloopy

Your kefir grains are still working. They have started to make too much of the dextran that binds them. In fact, LAB are used in the commercial production of dextran, which is a thickener used in food manufacturing. They normally go into dextran-producing mode when they are over-fed or too warm. Drinking water kefir that is too thick will not do you any harm, but it is usually not very fizzy and tastes rather sweet. To resolve this problem, start again using only 3% sugar water, and make sure your kefir grains are somewhere a bit cooler. You can also add a few strips of lemon peel to reduce the pH and turn off the dextran-making mechanism, or a pinch of potassium chloride (lo salt), also works.

Still Thin and Clear

If the liquid has not become at all cloudy after 72 hours, it is not looking good, but there is one more thing you can try: Put the grains in a very small quantity of 3.5% sugar water, cover and leave at room temperature (two times volume of grains max). The kefir microbes make bioactive compounds that support each others' growth and putting them in a small volume increases the concentrations of these products. Add a piece of dried fig or 0.5% coconut sugar to the sugar solution. WKG love these and they may be just what they need.

If still nothing happens, they may well be dead.

Mushy Grains

Over-fed and under-fed grains can both go to mush. Interestingly, they will still make decent water kefir, although it will be cloudier than usual. There are ways to rescue them, but it does demand patience and can take months, as it will require a change to their usual regime.

1. Strain the grains using a sieve with a big mesh to select some of the larger grains and get rid of the mush.
2. Reduce the size of your jar if necessary.
3. Grow anaerobically (in a closed system), to encourage LAB.
4. Use 3.5% sugar solution.
5. If you usually add extra coconut sugar or fig, do not do so in this case.
6. If you do not usually add these, do so in this case.
7. Repeat this opposite cycle every three days.

Gradually, very gradually, you should see some improvement in grain health and volume.

Mushy vs normal water kefir grains: they can be rescued, but it takes time and patience.

Contamination Problems

Contamination is rare with water kefir, especially if it is being cultured in a low-oxygen environment, where it will be hard for mould to grow. In the unlikely event that there is something fuzzy growing on the surface, you should throw it away and start again from your hotel.

CONSUMING WATER KEFIR: WHO AND HOW MUCH?

In addition to considerations mentioned in the Introduction, as there are no animal products involved, water kefir is suitable for vegans and vegetarians. It will contain traces of sugar, but these can be quantified. It is safe for children and preferable to fizzy drinks or those containing aspartame, but there may be a very low level of alcohol present. It will contain histamine and is not suitable for those with a histamine allergy.

How much you should have is about finding your personal tolerance. When you drink it at first, try just a little, about 20ml or so. If you have IBS/IBD, try 5ml and build up from there. There is no 'top end' as such, but do bear in mind the residual sugar content.

CHAPTER 6

KOMBUCHA

'Tea, best drink of the day' was the slogan for the British Tea Association during the 1970s. Today, its fermented cousin kombucha is taking centre stage, as more and more people recognize its potential health benefits. Naturally carbonated and slightly alcoholic, it usually tastes nothing like the tea that it is made from – it can resemble anything from a vinegary cider to fizzy pop. Like water kefir, it is delicious just as it is, but it can also be flavoured in infinite ways.

Kombucha is now available bottled and even on draught in pubs, restaurants and health food shops, often for a fantastic price. It is popular partly because of its low alcohol content: under-25s in the UK today apparently drink less alcohol than any other generation in recent years. Be aware, however, that not all kombuchas are 'live'; some are filtered to remove bacteria and yeast to make them shelf-stable, and some are even pasteurized. Kombucha is as cheap as chips and incredibly satisfying to make at home. Be warned, though: the SCOBY is a startlingly unappealing-looking thing, and visitors may well raise an eyebrow when they see it brewing on your kitchen worktop!

THE ORIGINS OF THE KOMBUCHA CULTURE

The origins of the kombucha culture are as obscure as those of the other SCOBYs, lost in the mists of time. However, it certainly makes sense to imagine Manchuria, now in China, as its birthplace, since tea-drinking began there about 5,000 years ago.

One credible theory, proposed in 1913 by Dr Anna Bachinskaya, one of the first kombucha researchers, suggests that insects (for example, fruit flies, who carry species of *Acetobacter* and *Lactobacilli* as part of their natural microflora) were attracted to some sweetened tea that had been left and forgotten. Combining with yeasts that had begun to colonize from the air, the first SCOBY mat began to form. In Eastern cultures, where unusual foodstuffs were regularly consumed – think of the 'thousand-year eggs', which are 'fermented until the yolk goes black and the white goes green' – it is easy to imagine the SCOBY being viewed with interest rather than with horror, which may have been the case elsewhere!

Tea picking in China began 5,000 years ago.

Drosophila (fruit flies), much enlarged for detail and (inset) as they appear to the human eye.

By 220 BCE, during the Tsin Dynasty, kombucha was apparently prized for its energizing properties. Its use probably spread via the Silk Road to Korea, where, according to legend, in 415 CE a Korean physician named Dr Kombu was summoned to heal the sickly Japanese Emperor Ingyo. Dr Kombu must have had a remarkable reputation – it is a long way from Korea to Japan! – and his name is often cited as the root of the term 'kombucha'. However, there is no written evidence that what we now call kombucha was involved. The story is further confused by the existence of kombucha, a Japanese tea made from kelp that has been enjoyed for centuries, but is not related to the SCOBY-requiring drink.

Gradually, kombucha travelled along various trade routes until by the early twentieth century it was commonplace in Eastern Europe and Germany, passed on from family to family, and used for its health benefits in a similar way to kefir grains. Its popularity continued until the Second World War, when rationing of tea and

'Thousand-year eggs', intact and sliced.

Tastes like cider, but is made from tea!

sugar brought its use to an abrupt halt. Despite a slight surge in popularity in France and Italy in the 1950s, it is from the United States that today's enthusiasm has issued; that market is now valued at around $700 million, and is growing.

COMPOSITION, DYNAMICS AND NUTRITIONAL CONTENT

Microbial Composition

Due to the world-wide distribution of kombucha SCOBYs, their microbial content has been found to differ quite substantially, but they all seem to contain predominantly two types of organism: yeasts and AABs. AABs are vinegar microbes and can withstand very acidic conditions. There tends to be one predominant type of yeast, which might be *Candida* sp. (not the thrush-causing *Candida albicans*), or *Saccharomyces* sp., but studies have found up to 24 other kinds present in smaller quantities.[49] Similarly, almost all the bacteria present in the SCOBY are *Acetobacter* sp. or *Komagataeibacter* sp. (named after Dr K. Komagata, who recently reclassified these bacteria).

The microbial content of the SCOBY and the brew it generates are dissimilar, often with completely different species dominating in each environment. Yeasts often outnumber the bacteria in the brew. In fact, the *Lactobacillus* sp. that are so prevalent in kefir may be completely absent in some kombuchas[49], but constitute about a third of others.[50] However, although various kombuchas can have very different microbial contents, broadly speaking, they make a similar-tasting brew.

The Dynamics of Kombucha

The kombucha SCOBY is a fascinating beast. It grows quite differently from kefir grains, gradually forming a mat across the liquid-air interface, which can seal off the tea underneath. This provides two completely different environments for the microbes during the process: first, an aerobic one with the brew exposed to oxygen, and second, as the SCOBY forms a seal, the system becomes anaerobic.

In a new batch of kombucha, there is a high concentration of sucrose and plenty of oxygen.

Yeasts hydrolyse sucrose into its glucose and fructose components and may use the efficient respiration process to get their energy, or they may still produce alcohol from fermentation, while sugar is in abundance.

In this oxygen-rich environment, *Komagataeibacter* sp. use sugars for energy and in the process become prolific producers of cellulose. Tiny fibrils form that are attached to each cell, knitting together to form a biofilm to which the other symbiotic microbes can cling, resulting in a thick jelly-like membrane, or zooglea (the SCOBY). The zooglea remains well hydrated, ensuring survival of the microbes. Air also becomes trapped between the layers of cellulose, helping it to float on the surface of the tea, rather like a jellyfish. Caffeine, theophylline and theobromine, all components of tea, have been found to stimulate the production of cellulose up to a point, but very high levels can inhibit it. Gradually, it grows to the sides of the vessel, excluding oxygen from the tea below and the microbes will switch to fermentation mode: yeasts will produce alcohols and carbon dioxide; other microbes, various organic acids. With a well-fitting SCOBY, carbonation will occur as the carbon dioxide struggles to escape. AAB remaining near the top of the brew can convert the alcohol to acetic, gluconic and glucuronic acids.

Acetic acid can even stimulate the yeasts to produce more alcohol for AAB consumption, so it is a perfect loop. Antimicrobial/antiviral compounds in the brew help to keep contaminants at bay. Meanwhile, death and lysis of a proportion of the yeast cells provide vitamins and other nutrients that stimulate bacterial growth.

Nutritional Content of Kombucha

Given that its ingredients are so simple, the complexity of a kombucha brew is staggering. While it is hard to say whether all of the following will be present in your particular kombucha, as the content depends up the SCOBY and the substrate, it does show the potential range.[51]

- Amino acids – up to 14.
- Organic acids – predominantly acetic, gluconic, glucuronic, with lactic, citric, butyric, malic, pyruvic sometimes detected.
- Vitamins – B1, B2, B3, B6, B12, C.
- Tea polyphenols – catechins, theaflavins, thearubigins, flavonols.
- Essential elements – Cu, Fe, Mn, Ni, Zn.
- Flavour compounds – alcohols, aldehydes, ketones, esters.
- Biogenic amines.
- Hydrolytic enzymes.
- D-saccharic acid.
- Antimicrobial substances.
- Probiotic species of bacteria and yeasts: *Komagataeibacter xylinus*, *Lactobacillus* sp., *Saccharomyces* sp.

The kombucha SCOBY itself is composed of cellulose, hemi-cellulose and protein and is, in fact, edible!

HEALTH CLAIMS FOR KOMBUCHA

'Kombucha is not a panacea – it doesn't cure anything', according to one of the USA's premier kombucha makers, Hannah Crum. However, it seems to be a supporter of good health for 'everything'. Potential benefits may be due to the presence of polyphenols, organic acids, vitamins, amino acids, antimicrobials and a variety of micronutrients. However, with no robust human trials yet, hard evidence is hard to come by. Highlights of recent research include the following:

- Positively influencing circulating levels of HDL and LDL.[52]
- Antioxidant activity from green and black tea.[53]
- Cytotoxic effects against human cancer cell lines.[54]
- A role for kombucha in controlling diabetes: a study in rats showed that drinking kombucha slowed down the digestion of carbohydrates, which reduced blood sugar levels.[55]

Glucuronic Acid

This is normally produced in the liver and is involved in detoxification processes in the body (removal of drugs and certain hormones), and is a component of hyaluronic acid, an important component of synovial fluid. It is also a potent cellular protectant. It is not known whether glucuronic acid that is ingested as opposed to synthesized internally has the same effects[56], which could be altered after ingestion.

Polyphenols

These compounds are a hot topic these days, since it has been discovered that not only are they excellent protectors for cells again oxidative stress, which can cause cancers and heart disease, but they are also food for the gut microbiota.

Probiotics

One of the cellulose-producing organisms, *Komagataeibacter xylinus*, has been very recently designated as a probiotic, due to its incredibly efficient metabolism of glucose.[57] In some kombucha, probiotic *Lactobacillus* sp. and also probiotic yeasts such as *S. cerevisiae* or *S. boulardii* will enhance these effects still further.

Anecdotal Evidence

Kombucha's long history, however, tells a bigger story about its possible benefits. Anecdotal observations from regular drinkers include the following favourable effects: improving hair, skin and nails; reducing stress and anxiety; helping with insomnia; relieving headaches; preventing bladder infections; reducing kidney calcification; helping with digestion; alleviating arthritis; facilitating excretion of toxins; influencing the gastrointestinal flora; promoting a healthy gut lining; reduction of hot flushes and other menopausal issues; detoxification; improvement of eyesight; cellular regeneration; relieving allergies; and weight loss.

Looking at this list, it is a wonder anyone drinks anything else!

MAKING KOMBUCHA: GETTING STARTED

Because of the complexity of kombucha biochemisty, making your own can be slightly unpredictable at first. Fizziness and flavour may alter from one batch to the next, even if you have done everything in your power to control it. The best approach is to embrace the variation rather than to seek perfect reproduction every time.

Finding a SCOBY

A good-quality SCOBY can guarantee success for your first batch. If you do not already know someone who is brewing successfully, who has a spare to give you, buy a fresh one from a reputable source (*see* Recommended Suppliers). There is no need to buy a dehydrated SCOBY, or attempt to grow one from shop-bought raw kombucha. Some of the organisms in the SCOBY do not tolerate refrigeration, so if someone offers you one from their fridge, you can politely decline.

Whilst your SCOBY might develop any number of interesting characteristics under your care, a purchased SCOBY that has been grown in green or black tea will be pale in colour, smooth, glossy and firm. One from a friend might be bumpy with less shiny patches, or thicker in one part than another. Ideally, it should be about 1–1.5cm thick, and it is quite normal for it to have some brown stringy yeast strands attached to the underside. Dark, floppy SCOBYs might well be on their last legs, and should be avoided.

Starter Tea

Any reliable SCOBY supplier will also provide at least

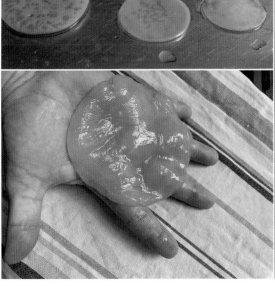

All these SCOBYs are healthy and will make delicious kombucha. The patchier ones have been growing at a lower temperature. They could do with a bit more heat, but will still function.
E. MORELAND

200ml of starter tea, which is used to lower the pH of your base liquid, protecting the brew from mould, and contains many microbes from the previous batch that can set to work immediately, without having to grow from the SCOBY. Starter tea should always be taken from the top of the batch, because at the

A wooden barrel – one for the serious kombucha enthusiast. ADOBE

bottom there are many yeast cells that could affect the balance of the brew. Ideally, it should have a pH of 2.5–3.5. The usual recommended amount is 10%; more than this could affect the flavour of the new batch.

If for some reason you do not have any starter tea (if you have spilled it or thrown it away before reading the instructions, for example), buy a bottle of live kombucha and add this.

Some recipes will say that distilled vinegar is an appropriate substitute. There are a couple of issues here: well-aged starter tea might contain a range of organic acids at a concentration of about 3–4%, including acetic acid at around 1%. White distilled vinegar contains just acetic acid at a concentration of 5%, so your brew could end up being overly acidic because of the concentration of acetic acid. If it does, you might need to save this first batch as kombucha vinegar, reserving some starter tea for your next batch. Then it will be fine.

The second issue is that distilled white vinegar does not contain any kombucha microbes. Vinegar really should be used only if you absolutely cannot get any starter tea. If you do have to use vinegar, do not use raw or home-made as it could harbour vinegar eels that could have a field day in your brew.

Choosing a Method

There are two methods for making kombucha: single batch or continuous brewing (CB). Most people start off with a batch system and, if they decide they like it, upgrade to continuous culture, which allows you to draw off a proportion of the brew every day, without any bottling

These gorgeous jars look as though they would be perfect for kombucha, but they are old, so they could contain lead. Such jars are best avoided.

Continuous Brewing vs Batch Fermentation

A continuous brewing system for kombucha on tap.

E. MORELAND

A batch brewing system. When it's gone it's gone.

Continuous Brewing

Batch Fermentation

Pros

Kombucha available every day so consumption can be regular, which is important if you are to enjoy the preventive benefits
Works best for plain kombucha
Works well for smaller amounts, drawing off max. 15% daily
More organic acid-rich than a batch-brewed product
Possibly contains more variety of end products
Can still be bottled and second fermented
Can achieve a very good balance between sweetness and sourness – regular addition of fresh tea can add agitation and aeration to the brew
From a 5ltr vessel you can draw off 750ml every day, or 1.5ltr every other day. Good for impatient people

More manageable (smaller) quantities
Great for flavouring at primary fermentation stage
Can be bottled for storage so you do not have to worry about maintenance
No special equipment needed (other than a large jar)
Ideal for occasional use
Generates pretty SCOBYs
Good for experiments!

Cons

Need special equipment – large glass vessel with spigot
Less suitable for experimental batches
Only a limited amount may be removed at one time, or you might as well batch brew
Not practical if you only want to drink kombucha occasionally. You will end up making lots of vinegar
Maintenance required.
SCOBYs can look a bit ropy

When it has gone, you will have to start again
Easy to forget about as you leave it for five to seven days before tasting
Less rich in bioactive compounds

are planning to make more than 8 litres, as they are heavy and is pretty disastrous if you drop one.

The artisan option is a wooden barrel, to which you can add additional layers of flavour, as in wine- or beer-making. Ceramic pots are also an option, but do ensure that they are suitable for high-acid beverages – sometimes, they contain lead. Again, potential breakage when cleaning out can be an issue, and they are not cheap.

To set up a CB system, you will need a large vessel with a spigot. Check that the tap and its parts are made from good-quality stainless steel or food-safe plastic that can withstand the acidic brew, as this is not always the case. Most people opt for a 5-litre glass vessel. If you decide to go bigger, a food-grade (304) stainless-steel vessel is recommended. A much more economical choice is BPA-free plastic, which is lighter and at least partially see through.

MAKING KOMBUCHA: THE PROCESS

The process of producing kombucha basically involves making a base of sweetened tea, adding a SCOBY and leaving it to ferment a while. Of course, there are a number of variable factors that will affect the outcome; these are discussed later. This recipe uses black tea, which is thought to have been the original substrate. If the instructions seem irritatingly imprecise, that is

required. This is perfect for impatient people who do not want to wait up to a couple of weeks for a batch to be ready. Compare the pros and cons, to see which will work best for you.

Suitable Brewing Vessels

Glass containers are a good option as they are safe for use with acidic foods and they allow you to see what is going on. They become impractical, however, if you

Formulas for Kombucha

Vessel (ltr)	Water (ml)	Tea (g)/Bags	Starter tea (ml)	Sugar (g)	SCOBY (g)
1.8	1.5	7.5–15g/2–3	150	82.5	75
2.5	2.1	10–20g/2–4	210	115	105
5	4.2	20–40g/4–8	420	230	210
8	7	35–70g/7–14	700	385	350
	Formula (% based on water content)	0.5–1%	10%	5.5%	5%

because a decent brew can result from within quite a wide range of parameters.

Using the formula can give quite precise numbers, but you can round up or down to make life easier. Do not worry too much about the SCOBY size – as long as there is some in there, it will be fine.

KOMBUCHA BASIC RECIPE

Ingredients:

Black tea, either loose or in bags (quantity depends entirely on quality)
Water (tap or filtered)
White sugar (preferably organic)
Starter tea
SCOBY (healthy)

Equipment ('dishwasher clean'):

Fermentation vessel
Jug
Strainer
Spoon
Scales
Paper towel
Rubber band
Bottles for storing/second fermenting the finished brew
pH strips or meter

Method:

1. Follow all the usual hygiene steps. It is fine to handle the SCOBY as long as your hands are clean.
2. In a jug, combine the tea and about a quarter of the total water, just off the boil (black tea brews most successfully at 95°C). Stir gently and brew for 3–5 minutes for teabags, and about 10 minutes for larger tea leaves, because of the difference in the surface area; bag tea tends to be much finer.
3. Taste the tea base before you start. Adjust so that it is not fiercely tanninish, nor as weak as dishwater.
4. Add the sugar and stir until dissolved.

5. Strain the sweet tea into your fermentation vessel.
6. Add the remaining water.
7. Check the temperature is lukewarm; if it is too hot, you will kill the microbes.
8. (**Optional**) Check the pH with test strips or a meter and add starter tea to get to an ideal starting pH of 4.5. Do not forget to stir.
9. Or add your starter tea and stir in.
10. Add the SCOBY. It may sink or float – either is fine.
11. Cover with the paper towel and secure with the rubber band.
12. Leave on the worktop out of bright sunlight for 5–7 days. Do not put the vessel near plants or other ferments because of the possibility of airborne contaminants. Do not disturb it, as this can affect the development of a new SCOBY. This will not be harmful but it could destroy your chances of getting carbonation from a SCOBY-sealed vessel.

For Batch Fermentation:

1. After day 5 if it is warm, day 7 if it is not, taste either using a straw inserted gently down the side where the SCOBY meets the vessel, or by pushing the SCOBY aside and using a tasting cup.
2. You may be happy with it already. If, however, you want more acidity or less sweetness, leave it for longer, up to 14 days. When done, remove the SCOBY(s) to a bowl with about 200ml of starter tea from the top. This can be used to start your next batch.
3. The kombucha is now ready for drinking straight away, or bottling and 'second fermenting' to add more flavour and fizz (*see* page 64).
4. If you have grown a new SCOBY, you can add this to the original when making your next batch, or put it in your SCOBY hotel (*see* page 107).

For Continuous Brewing:

1. Up to the point of fermentation (5–7 days, depending on the warmth of the environment), the instructions are exactly the same for batch fermentation and continuous brewing. Thereafter, this is what to do for CB.

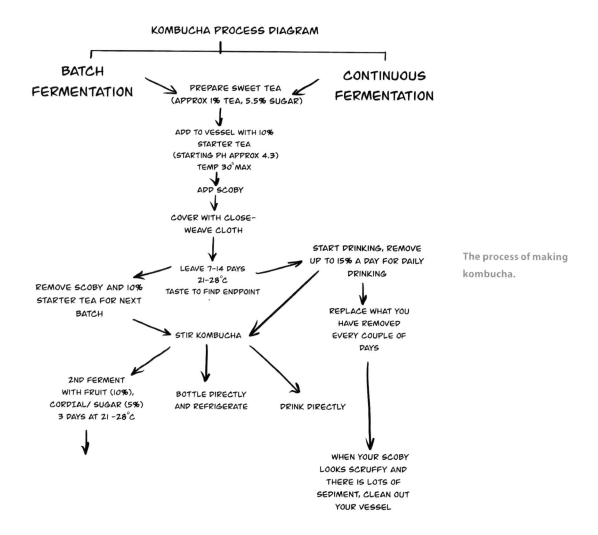

KOMBUCHA PROCESS DIAGRAM

BATCH FERMENTATION

CONTINUOUS FERMENTATION

PREPARE SWEET TEA (APPROX 1% TEA, 5.5% SUGAR)

ADD TO VESSEL WITH 10% STARTER TEA (STARTING PH APPROX 4.3) TEMP 30° MAX

ADD SCOBY

COVER WITH CLOSE-WEAVE CLOTH

LEAVE 7-14 DAYS 21-28°C TASTE TO FIND ENDPOINT

REMOVE SCOBY AND 10% STARTER TEA FOR NEXT BATCH

START DRINKING, REMOVE UP TO 15% A DAY FOR DAILY DRINKING

REPLACE WHAT YOU HAVE REMOVED EVERY COUPLE OF DAYS

STIR KOMBUCHA

2ND FERMENT WITH FRUIT (10%), CORDIAL/ SUGAR (5%) 3 DAYS AT 21 -28°C

BOTTLE DIRECTLY AND REFRIGERATE

DRINK DIRECTLY

WHEN YOUR SCOBY LOOKS SCRUFFY AND THERE IS LOTS OF SEDIMENT, CLEAN OUT YOUR VESSEL

The process of making kombucha.

2. After 5–7 days, open the spigot and pour some into a glass for tasting. The kombucha may well emerge ready carbonated, and will be absolutely delicious served as it is over ice.

3. If it is already to your liking, great. If you are using a very large vessel, or the weather is chilly, it might take a few more days to get there. Keep testing every couple of days.

4. When it has reached the point that is right for you, you can start to draw off up to 15% of the kombucha a day, or 25% every other day, replacing it with the same volume of 5.5% sweetened tea. The well-formed SCOBY on top of a CB will not be bothered by having fresh cooled tea poured over it.

5. If you decide you want to bottle it, you can do so, but you will need to replace the volume that you have removed and wait a few days for the brew to reach its perfect point again.

6. For maintenance, get into the habit of making a jug of sweet tea along with your morning cuppa. Keep a cup measure handy so you never need to weigh the sugar out. The tea can be left covered at room temperature for the day, or refrigerated if you do not need it. You will not need to add any starter tea, as the continuous brew will be awash with protective organic acids already.

7. Remember: if you take tea out, put some more tea in. You do not have to do this every time you draw,

but, if you leave it too long, there will be a lot of sugar in the replacement tea that will need to be metabolised before it tastes right again. You will hardly notice smaller amounts.

● ●

IS IT READY?

Acidity Levels

Because of the number of variables – the health of the SCOBY, temperature, humidity, tea, system dynamics – it is difficult to give more than a guideline as to when the kombucha is ready for consumption. The finished product can be anywhere between pH 2.5 and 3.5, but pH is not really the best way to judge, as it does not take into account all of the acid groups that you can taste. Unless you are planning to sell it, in which case measurements are essential, you will be better off using your senses of taste and smell and a little common sense.

At its endpoint, your brew should have a lovely amber hue, may be slightly cloudy, and taste more like cider than tea. You are looking for a hint of sweetness (not as sweet as a canned fizzy drink), and a fruitiness that has an acidity, but is not enough to make you wince, or burn your throat when you swallow.

Your kombucha is unlikely to reach too high a level of acidification in 10 days, but the general rule is, if it tastes like vinegar, it is vinegar, and has gone too far for regular drinking. It is probably not good for your teeth, could give you guts ache and, if you have an underlying serious health condition, could make you ill. If you are an advocate of apple cider vinegar, you will be aware that it is normally taken diluted in water. If your brew has gone too far, it does not have to go to waste, as there are plenty of ways of using kombucha vinegar.

If you are planning to bottle and second ferment your brew, you can stop when it tastes a bit on the sweet side, as it will be undergoing further fermentation.

Visible Changes

The first change will occur when you add your starter tea; it will become a much paler colour with the addition of just 10% of acidic starter tea, as it lowers the pH of the brew and is like a pH indicator. Your kombucha may well continue to lighten over time, because some of the polyphenols in it might undergo microbial transformation.[53]

After a day or two, you will notice a thin film of newly developing SCOBY, with some bubbles of carbon dioxide trapped underneath it, showing that fermentation has begun. The brew will

ACIDS IN KOMBUCHA

Your starter tea should taste quite vinegary, and should have a pH of 2.5 to 3.5. If you do not have a pH meter, just dip your finger in to taste. The pH dynamics of continuous culture can be altered to some extent to suit how you like it. If you regularly remove large quantities and replace, it will have a higher pH.

The concentration of acid is a better indication of when your kombucha is ready than pH. For example, most commercial vinegar has a concentration of 5% – 5g of acetic acid per 100ml. In a 10- to 14-day brew of kombucha, you might expect to have a concentration of about 3.5% total acids, but the pH might be anywhere between 2.5 and 3.5. This is because kombucha contains up to eight different acids, all of which can undergo different interactions in the complex brew – there may be hydrogen ions tied up with other things that pH cannot detect.

Long-brewed batches of kombucha can develop very high concentrations of organic acids, including acetic, gluconic and glucuronic. Be aware that kombucha that has been left for a month can become extremely acidic – too acidic to be drinkable – even if the pH has not changed much.[58]

Tea as a pH indicator. You can clearly see the colour difference upon addition of just 10% volume of acidic starter tea to the jar on the right.

The top layer of new SCOBY is growing right up the sides of the jar, forming a seal. Strings of brown yeast will often hang down from the underside.

begin to look cloudy, as yeast and bacterial cells proliferate.

After about five days, either a new SCOBY will be visible across the top of the brew, or the old one will have signs of new growth attached to it – probably growing slightly up the sides of the jar – and more bubbles will be present.

After about seven days, brown strings of yeast may also have begun to form; although not very attractive, they are a sure sign of fermentation. Sediment may have started to form on the bottom; this will contain end products of metabolism from the microbes, and also a few dead cells. It is not harmful.

VARIABLES AFFECTING THE END PRODUCT

Temperature

The optimal temperature for the perfect batch of kombucha is 26–27°C. In Britain, for example, for about 46 weeks of the year that is pretty hard to achieve without assistance. That does not mean the kombucha will not develop, but it may take a little longer. In the

winter, when the heating is on, it might brew more rapidly, but there may still be some seasonal changes. These could be due to cold draughts blowing through nooks and crannies, or other changes that are less noticeable, such as air pressure, for example. Also, at higher temperatures there is less dissolved oxygen available in the system, which could affect the balance between the microbes. If you want to keep it warm, you will need to work out a way of heating it from the sides. Bottom heat, via a heat mat for example, can result in the formation of kahm yeast on top.

Sugar and Other Sweeteners

Kombucha is usually made from white sugar, but it does not have to be; other types can be substituted and these will give a range of different and more caramel-y flavours.

Brown sugar kombucha tastes significantly less

sweet. Researchers have found that, with molasses, much more lactic acid is produced than acetic acid, which can give the brew a less vinegary taste, although it does taste quite strange!

If you are experimenting with different sugars, use a spare SCOBY from your hotel in case you do not achieve the desired results. The suggested 5.5% sugar content is on the lower side – some research papers and recipes suggest using up to 10% – but you may find that this makes a brew that is too sweet by the time it reaches a pleasant acidity. It is your kombucha and only by experimenting will you be able to decide how it suits you best.

You can use pasteurized honey with kombucha. Substitute it at a slightly higher concentration, because honey is only about 80% sugar, although it has more fructose in it than glucose, which makes it taste sweeter. Try using about 7.5%. If you are using honey, you will want to taste it – if you are lucky, you may be able to detect some of the floral or citrus notes. Green or white tea are the best bases for a honey ferment as they are mild enough not to mask its flavour.

Using unpasteurized honey with green tea forms the basis for a variation of kombucha called jun, which you can set up with an existing kombucha SCOBY (even though some people believe that it is a different type of SCOBY). Yeasts present in wild honey can potentially interfere with the dynamics of your SCOBY, so, if you decide to experiment with it, use a spare.

There will be an amount of residual sugar left in your kombucha by the time you come to bottle it. Within the first three days of fermentation, yeasts will have cleaved the sucrose into glucose and fructose, which will be utilized more slowly over the coming days. As the amount of oxygen and sugar in the brew drops, yeasts and LAB will begin to get their energy from anaerobic pathways, which are much less efficient than their aerobic counterparts. Without access to oxygen there simply is not enough energy in the system to utilise all the sugar. This can be measured using a hydrometer (see page 32). In tests on my own batch, after 10 days, there was a sugar concentration of 2.75g per 100ml. This compares with 11g typically in a can of regular Coke.

In an experiment when enough molasses was added to provide 7% sucrose (it is about 70% sucrose), the dynamics of the brew changed and by the end of the experiment 97% of the sugar was used up. This was thought to be due to the presence of microbially useful compounds including biotin and amino-nitrogen in the molasses.[59]

Batch Size

The size of the batch will make a difference to the timeframe. The five to 14 days required for 2 litres of kombucha can extend to over a month for a 5-gallon batch. The dynamics of a large system can be quite different, especially if it is not stirred, with a marked separation of microbes. The yeast cells precipitate out into strands or at the bottom, and obligate aerobic AAB to concentrate at the surface, so they will not meet! In industrial processes, tanks are stirred to avoid such problems.

The Tea

Any combination of the *Camellia sinensis* var *sinensis* teas – white, green, oolong, black, Pu-erh – will make delicious kombucha. Some say that organic tea leads to enhanced SCOBY growth. You can also use speciality teas, such as Darjeeling or Assam, but occasionally people have reported slower SCOBY growth with teas containing oils, such as Earl Grey or Lady Grey. This is likely to be SCOBY-specific, so, just to be on the safe side, use a spare when choosing these teas.

Loose Tea or Teabags?

There is no denying the convenience of teabags to make kombucha, but you do get a better-looking brew when you use 'proper' tea. Standard teabag tea is much finer than leaves and can make your kombucha slightly murky if you over-steep it, unless they are very 'posh' teabags that contain larger bits. Do not squeeze teabags out, as this can make the brew a touch bitter.

Caffeine

Kombucha contains about one-quarter of the caffeine of a cup of tea for the same quantity. Although caffeine is supposedly pivotal for the proliferation of the SCOBY, there are several reports of people successfully using decaffeinated tea. However, it might be a good idea to

THE WORLD OF TEA

The most widely consumed beverage in the world (water aside), tea is believed to have originated as a medicinal drink 5,000 years ago in Manchuria. By the late eighteenth century, it had been well and truly discovered in England, and became affordable for all after the government removed tea taxes to thwart the lucrative smuggling trade. Black tea rapidly became more popular among the English than other varieties, and they soon adopted the custom of adding milk and sugar, which was newly available. The importance of tea in world history cannot be underestimated, from the protests of the Boston Tea Party in 1773, which escalated into the American Revolution, to

Leaves of Camellia sinensis from the tea plantation at Bristol Botanical Gardens. E. MORELAND

the Opium Wars fought between Britain and China in the 1800s, which could also have been called the 'Tea Wars'. Britain was instrumental in spreading the tea trade to India and, today, China and India are the world's first and largest producers, in a world tea market worth about 50 billion US dollars.

The five different types of tea – black, green, white, oolong and Pu-erh all come from the same leafy perennial plant, *Camellia sinensis*. They differ according to the way they are processed, which involves up to five steps; plucking, withering, rolling, oxidizing and drying. White tea is the least processed: the name comes from new or very recent growth at the tip of the stems, which is often covered with a white down. Essentially, these very young tips are simply picked and withered dry, or heated extremely gently. The resulting tea is very pale.

Green tea is produced by heating the tea using steam or pan frying, to inactivate the enzymes that would cause oxidation and subsequent colour loss of the leaves. Leaves are rolled and shaped, and dried.

Oolong tea is fully oxidized, so allowed to go brown. All five processing steps are used, but very slowly over several days, allowing rich and varied flavours to develop. Black tea is also fully oxidized, but more completely and the process is usually carried out over just one day. Black tea contains the most caffeine and purines.

Pu-erh tea is like green tea, but before it is dried it undergoes a fermentation step. This can take months or even years, allowing rich dark flavours to develop.

Within each of the different types of tea, there are a range of specialities, such as Darjeeling, Assam, Ceylon, Lapsang Suchong, Earl Grey, Lady Grey. These teas may be made from different cultivars of the *Camellia sinensis* plant. They may also be grown in different regions, which alters their properties (rather like grapes in vineyards of the world), or contain additional flavourings.

Tea is rich in flavonoids: tea polyphenols, catechins. It also contains caffeine, which is important in brewing kombucha. Caffeine has different roles in different places: it is present in the plants as a pesticide, and in humans it acts as a stimulant. In your kombucha brew, it is an important nutrient for the organisms that grow the kombucha SCOBY.

keep your SCOBY hotel full of caffeinated kombucha, so you have a back-up if it does not work out.

Steeping Time and Temperature

The aim is to make a base with the goodness of the tea leaf extracted into the water and the best flavour. Green teas tend to require a lower steeping temperature (around 80°C) than black teas (95 degrees). If you are using a blend of teas, steep at the lowest temperature – there will be less chance of the more delicate tea flavour being overpowered. Tea leaves will need longer to steep than a teabag; follow the instructions on the box.

LOOKING AFTER THE SCOBY

Making a SCOBY Hotel

The importance of maintaining a SCOBY 'hotel' cannot be underestimated! It will mean ultimate security for you and your kombucha-ing, and provide SCOBYs for all your friends too. It is very simple to set up. After your first brew, remove a single layer or a chunk from

the SCOBY, and place in some finished kombucha in a large jar with a lid on. Have enough kombucha so that it could provide emergency starter tea if required. Now you will have some back-ups if you are feeling experimental, or you experience a growth of mould (rare), or (worse, but even more rare) an appearance of vinegar eels. When you have made one hotel, make another so that you have a back-up for your back-up! Leave at room temperature, where it will persist indefinitely, gradually growing a new SCOBY on the top. Do not refrigerate, as this will compromise some of the AAB, whose populations might never recover.

SCOBY Health and Culture Maintenance

After some cycles of fermentation, whether batch or continuous, your SCOBY might be looking rather scruffy and thick, and you might notice that your kombucha is getting tart rather quickly. If this is the case, it is time for some maintenance. If it is more than half an inch thick, you can remove it from the vessel to a chopping board and give it a trim. Underneath where the oldest SCOBY is, gently pull and remove some

You will not regret setting up a SCOBY 'hotel', which will provide the ultimate security. E. MORELAND

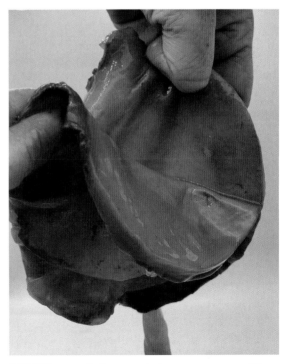

A SCOBY can easily be separated, to remove some of the layers when it becomes thick and scruffy. E. MORELAND

STIRRING THE BREW

It might be tempting to stir your kombucha as it begins to ferment. It may seem like a good way to keep the organisms in symbiotic contact with each other as they grow throughout the brew, and it is true that the presence of oxygen can help with the conversion of both glucose into carbon dioxide and alcohol into acetic acid. However, you should resist the temptation! If you stir, you will disturb the formation of the new SCOBY and it will probably sink to the bottom. It will not affect the ability of your tea to make kombucha, but it will upset the natural ecosystem that arises when it is allowed to grow to the edges of the jar and seal it.

layers. These can either be placed in your compost bin or hotel, or given away. Or eaten!

In your CB, when you find a layer of scum sticking to the sides of the jar as you drain it, and a thick layer of sediment at the bottom, it is time for a clean. Remove most of the liquid through the spigot, pouring gently to leave some of the sediment behind to be rinsed away. Thoroughly wash the jar

Adding hibiscus flowers for colour and flavour. The microbes also enjoy the polyphenols in the flower pigments.

and the spigot, letting hot soapy water run through the tap, followed by clear hot water to rinse. A wipe of the inside with distilled vinegar will not do any harm. Reassemble the system and you will be good to go.

What to Do With Extra SCOBYs

- Give them to everyone you know! Spread the word and your new-found expertise. (Do not forget the starter tea.)
- Use them to make vinegar (*see* page 113).
- Find some chickens and goats – apparently they love them!
- Put them in the compost.
- Blend them up into a thick paste, store in a jar in the fridge, and use as a vegan thickener in cooking. SCOBYs are full of fibre, so both probiotic and prebiotic. A spoonful can be easily added to many recipes.

AFTER FIRST FERMENTATION

You may prefer your kombucha just as it is, but, just like water kefir, it can also be used as a base for an almost endless range of additions – fruit, flowers, spices, and so on – for both flavour and nutritional benefit. There are three ways of doing this: at primary fermentation stage (1°F, not suitable for continuous method), when bottling, which is called 'secondary fermentation' (2°F), or just by using it as a mixer. This last option is the simplest: try mixing with any fruit juice. Tomato juice and a dash of fermented chilli sauce makes a surprisingly good pairing.

Flavouring at Primary Fermentation (1°F) Stage

This works well for batch brewing and is a good way of adding immediate depth and flavour, with no bottling or 2°F required. You can also develop even more beneficial metabolites from the added flavourings, as the microbes will be able to utilize them too – hibiscus flowers, for example, are a rich source of anthocyanins, beloved of probiotic microbes. Some flavourings – cinnamon sticks, ginger, dried rose petals, vanilla – can be popped straight into your vessel, or you can use a herbal teabag or infusion.

Others, such as hibiscus, yerba Mate, rooibos and nettles, can be steeped when preparing your kombucha base. Reduce the normal tea by 50%, and use green or white tea so that the added flavours will come through more distinctly.

You can go one step further, and at 1°F stage substitute 50% of the tea with fresh fruit juice – you will still need some tea to provide caffeine and flavonoids for the SCOBY. Researchers have recently found that using pomegranate juice in lieu of most of the tea increases the amount of antitoxicant glucuronic acid in the brew several times over.[60] You will still need to add the starter tea; while the pH does not usually need to be lowered for safety reasons with fruit juice, which is generally acidic, the microbes in the starter will help to get the fermentation going and antimicrobial compounds offer further protection to the brew.

Bottling and Secondary Fermentation

These processes go hand in hand. If you want to flavour your kombucha and add carbonation, you will need to perform a 2°F in a sealed bottle. Even if you want to add carbonation without any flavour, the process is the same. This is also the method of building up a store of kombucha to keep you going while you are waiting for your next batch.

After primary fermentation, some of the yeasts in your brew will have entered a dormant phase, and may precipitate as strings or rest on the bottom of the jar in the sediment. This happens when their nutrient source begins to run down, or when levels of organic acids begin to inhibit their growth. When they are moved to a new environment and given a fresh source of energy, they will awaken. This is where a sugar primer, or the addition of some fruit or fruit syrup, is needed.

Aeration caused by the bottling process will introduce some oxygen into the mix, enlivening both yeasts and the *Acetobacter*. When the oxygen is depleted, the yeasts will start to make alcohol and carbon dioxide but how much is limited by the amount of sugar added. The carbon dioxide is trapped inside, and will escape as bubbles upon opening.

BOTTLING

Equipment:

Suitable bottles (use a guide bottle)
Long-handled spoon/stirrer
Funnel
Bowl and cover
Ladle
Flavourings/sugar or fruit purée or fruit cordial/extra sugar
A plastic bottle as a guide (optional)

Method (CB):

1. Insert the spoon or stirrer down gently beside the SCOBY and agitate the brew.
2. Draw off directly from the tap, using a funnel if you are putting it straight into bottles.

Method (Batch Brewing):

1. Remove the SCOBY with clean hands or a fork and place it in a bowl.
2. Use the ladle to remove starter tea from the top, for your next batch.
3. Cover and set aside.
4. Stir the kombucha to distribute the yeasts in the sediment at the bottom of the jar throughout your brew.

AFTER BOTTLING

After bottling, you can either leave the kombucha as it is, and store it straight away; you can add carbonation without flavour; or you can add carbonation and flavour.

Storing As Is

You do not have to add either flavour or fizz to your brew, if you prefer it as it is. Simply pop the bottles straight into the fridge.

Adding Carbonation Without Flavour

You can add carbonation to the brew, without adding flavour (bottle conditioning). Stir up the sediment to ensure that yeasts are included, and bottle the brew

Second/intermediate fermenting may be done either in an open system or by putting the fruits directly into the bottle. Left to right: raspberry and rose flavouring a hibiscus and green tea kombucha; orange and pomegranate with 'builder's' tea; and ginger, also with 'builder's' tea.

VENTING AND OPENING BOTTLES

Try to resist checking the bottles before three days, as, once the lid is opened, the carbon dioxide will escape, and all the microbes' hard work will be wasted. The lone plastic bottle approach is definitely recommended as a safe way to monitor this. Otherwise, be sure to do the following:

- Place your 2°F bottles in a place where they will do no damage if they do explode, for example, in a cool box.
- Open bottles with great caution, especially if they have a flip top. Point the bottle away from your face and open it over the sink, just in case.

while it is still on the sweet side – with the aeration of bottling this should provide the right conditions for the yeasts to start producing carbon dioxide. If you have missed this point, add some sugar as an energy source (35g/ltr or 10g in 300ml). Fill the bottles to 2cm from the top and leave at a warm room temperature for three or four days. Feel the plastic guide, if using, or try a bottle. If you are happy with the carbonation and flavour, refrigerate.

Adding Carbonation and Flavour

These flavour suggestions may get you started: raspberry and rose, orange and ginger, pomegranate molasses, watermelon, peach and orange blossom, peach and gooseberry, blackberry, apple and cinnamon, cherry, coffee. If using fresh fruit, cut it up into very small pieces, or mash it, so you can get the bits out of the bottles again as they will swell up. Remember that not all fruit is sweet, so you need to taste before you add. If berries are sour, add 3.5% sugar (35g/ltr). Put the mashed fruit directly into the bottom of the bottles you are using.

Cordial is a simple way to add flavour on a regular

basis. Make a flavoured syrup (using one of the template recipes on page [00]), and add about 5% of the volume to a bottle.

If you want to add herbs, spices or infusions, remember that these do not contain much sugar generally, so you may want to compensate by adding 3.5% sugar (35g/ltr). You can use literally any herbal tea, or separate components of them, to add flavour, at the ratio of a teabag per litre bottle.

To make flavoured brews look professional in the bottle, with no bits in, another option is to add in an intermediate fermentation stage. Fortunately, this is not as cumbersome as it sounds. After you have removed your SCOBY and next starter tea from your vessel, add your flavourings – for example, crushed raspberries and strawberries – directly to the brewing vessel. Cover with a paper towel secured with a rubber band and leave to infuse for one to two days. Taste to check that the flavour has permeated the brew, then strain through a fine sieve and bottle as above, leaving at room temperature for a further three to four days to add carbonation.

TROUBLESHOOTING

Problems with Carbonation

Too Much

Kombucha can produce an extremely feisty reaction, especially if it has been flavoured with mango, pineapple or watermelon. If carbonation builds extremely quickly, put your bottles straight into the fridge to help them calm down.

Too Little

Too little carbonation is the more common problem. It can be such a disappointment to open a bottle expecting a pop and to experience nothing! Usually, it is more of a gentle fizz than the explosive bubbles of champagne, especially with plain kombucha. A number of factors can affect the amount of carbonation you will get, including the exact balance of microbes in your SCOBY and brew, the type of tea used, the temperature and the amount of dissolved oxygen. Also, it might take a couple of batches with a new SCOBY to get it right. Try not to let disappointment put you off – it is a

challenge that occupies the thoughts of many a home kombucha maker.

The following tips may help with carbonation:

- Stir the brew before bottling to give yeasts throughout, and to aerate it.
- Add some sugar to wake them up.
- Fill the bottles almost full.
- Purées of pineapple, mango or watermelon are all excellent enhancers of carbonation.
- Leave the bottles somewhere warm (up to about 30°C).
- Do not open the bottles to check – use a plastic guide bottle.
- Smaller bottles are often more successful than larger ones.
- Bottle a sweeter, younger kombucha for better carbonation.

If after three or four days nothing seems to be happening, and you would really like some carbonation, you can cheat by adding a pinch of brewer's yeast to your bottles.

My SCOBY Looks Ugly

SCOBYs, especially in continuous culture, may not look like beautiful smooth golden discs, but that does not mean that there is anything wrong with them. Black or dark brown patches on or seemingly within your SCOBY are usually colonies of yeasts, as are the brown strings that often form on the underside, and are not usually cause for concern.

Moulds have a fuzzy appearance and, whether they are white, green or black, a mouldy SCOBY should always be discarded. Some moulds produce mycotoxins that could have pervaded the brew. Also, as kombucha is usually able to stave off mould formation, if it does occur, it is an indication of a problem. Discard everything, thoroughly clean your vessel, using distilled white vinegar to finish off with, and start with a new SCOBY from your hotel.

It Smells…Wrong

If the smell is not of the vinegar/cider variety, and resembles that of sileage, vomit or nail polish, it could be a sign of contamination. Discard the entire brew and SCOBY and retrieve one from your hotel with some starter tea to start again. Make sure that you have properly decontaminated all your equipment, including the spigot, if you are continuous brewing. Milton sterilizing fluid is good for this.

Fruit Flies

Fruit flies really love kombucha – indeed, they were probably involved in its development in the dim and distant past. They will take advantage of any

opportunity to get into your brew, so it is important to use a tight-weave cloth, or robust kitchen paper cap. In the height of the summer, you can make a fruit fly trap, just like a wasp trap, by inverting the top half of a cut bottle over the bottom half and filling with kombucha. If they do find their way into your brew, get them out of there quickly before they lay eggs.

Not Quite Vinegar…

If you have just missed the point of kombucha perfection, and do not want more vinegar, you can

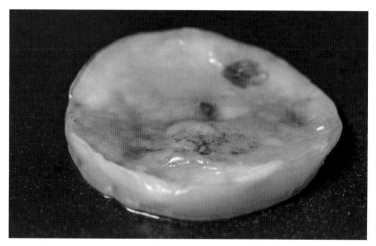

rescue your brew by adding a splash of it to water kefir, to create a fizzy, tart and delicious drink. You could also dilute it with fruit juice.

A mouldy SCOBY is a rare occurrence, but it can happen if a brew is not appropriately acidic. The system should be discarded and a new one begun from your SCOBY hotel. E. MORELAND

TAKING A BREAK

If you are batch fermenting, just put the SCOBY in your hotel, making sure there is enough old tea in there to keep it covered.

If you have a CB system and want to go on holiday for a fortnight, you can leave the kombucha in its continuous brew vessel. Draw off to tap level (this can be bottled) and either just leave it like that until you get back, or replace with fresh sweet tea before you go. You might well have a perfect batch upon your return.

HEALTH AND SAFETY

Important Health Caveats

Kombucha is a potent broth of bioactive compounds. There are no guidelines on its consumption in the UK at the moment, but the CDC in the USA recommends no more than 125ml three times a day. That is just over a small bottle, which is not much.

The guidelines arose because, in the US in 1995, two people became ill, one fatally, after drinking kombucha

The cap must be suitable to prevent fruit flies getting in. The one in the middle has too big a weave; finer cotton (left) is perfect (perhaps made from repurposed old shirts), or use a piece of kitchen towel (right).

brewed independently from the same SCOBY. It seems that both had underlying health conditions, leaving them vulnerable to acidosis (where the body loses the ability to regulate the pH of the blood). No similar incidents have been recorded since and the conclusion was that kombucha per se does not lead to acidosis. However, anyone with a pre-existing condition that makes them potentially susceptible to it should not consume kombucha.

In the USA, kombucha is also contraindicated for pregnant women.

Lead poisoning has occurred from fermentation in an unsuitable ceramic pot, and there has been an incident of cutaneous anthrax as a result of applying a SCOBY directly to an open wound. Also, a mouldy batch containing toxins was responsible for an outbreak of illness in Georgia.

Those who are diabetic must take care. Studies on rats have shown that kombucha can regulate sugar levels, but you are not a rat. If you are immune-compromised, then the same rules apply to kombucha as with other fermented foods: exercise moderation, and check with a health professional if you are unsure.

Quantities

How much you drink is of course up to you, but the maxim 'water kefir for quaffing, kombucha for drinking' is a good one to follow, especially if the kombucha is home-brewed. If you want a longer drink, mix with water kefir to maintain the carbonation.

When deciding whether to give kombucha to children, remember that it is not sugar-free, although it contains much less than a Coke, for example. It also contains alcohol, which may well be at less than the 1% found in over-ripe fruit, but the level is not easy to determine. Another reason to hold back is that acidic foods can attack tooth enamel and children's milk teeth are very susceptible to damage. To be on the safe side,

if you are going to give kombucha to children, it should be diluted with water or water kefir.

General Considerations

Never do any of the following:

- Apply your SCOBY directly to an open wound.
- Drink your kombucha in huge quantities, especially if it tastes like vinegar.
- Brew your kombucha in vessels that are not classified as being food-safe.
- Attempt to reuse a mouldy SCOBY.
- Keep your SCOBY hotel or any SCOBY in the fridge. They do not like it.

MAKING KOMBUCHA VINEGARS

Cooking Vinegar

When life gets in the way, an untended brew can easily turn to vinegar, as the AAB continue to work in their aerobic environment. If this happens to yours, it might well contain about 3% acetic and other organic acids after about a month. (Remember that the pH will not tell you how much acetic acid you have, just that it is acidic.)

Sometimes, though, there is just something lacking and it does not taste quite like a vinegar with the oomph to cook with. You may think, 'I'll just boil off some of the water to concentrate it!', but, as the boiling point of acetic acid is only slightly higher than that of water, it will also be evaporated, leaving you exactly where you started.

There is a better way of enriching it so it can match up to any kitchen-grade vinegar:

1. Add 10g/ltr of sugar to your kombucha vinegar to refuel the yeasts and the AAB.
2. Leave for two weeks, with a SCOBY in, and taste.
3. Repeat until you achieve a vinegar that pleases you.
4. Bottle and store at room temperature, infusing with herbs or spices if you like.

Note: unless you carry out a titration to assess the percentage acidity, you have to assume that your kombucha vinegar is not concentrated enough to use in making pickles for long-term storage, as 5% acetic acid is required for this purpose. You can however, use it to make quick pickles for refrigerating and eating within a few days, and they will be delicious.

• •

APPLE CIDER VINEGAR

Apple cider vinegar is extremely popular and easy to make.

Ingredients:

Apple cores and skins 750g
Sugar water solution (10%)

Equipment:

2ltr capacity Kilner jar
Paper towel
Submerging device
Rubber band

Method:
1. Put your apple cores and peels in a jar and top up with approx. 1 litre of 10% sugar water, leaving a couple of inches of headroom.
2. Use a plastic lid or a piece of baking paper scrunched up to keep the apples submerged.
3. Cover with a paper towel or close-weave muslin square and secure with a rubber band.
4. Leave at room temperature for up to two weeks, stirring vigorously daily to prevent mould settling, and to oxygenate.
5. After a couple of weeks, the liquid will be cloudy, slightly alcoholic and vinegary.
6. Strain out the apple skins and peels. Do not forget to keep the liquid!
7. Put the liquid back into the jar. If you have some ACV with a vinegar mother, add a couple of tablespoons of this to speed up the process.
8. Put the paper towel back on and leave for about another month or so at room temperature. If you are lucky, after a few days a pale skin of vinegar mother will begin to form across the top of the jar, from AAB present in the air.
9. Bottle when it tastes vinegary enough – this could take some weeks.

Alternative method:
Place a kombucha SCOBY on top of your hard cider (after putting the liquid back in the jar), and leave for one month. Taste and replace the SCOBY for longer if necessary.

Shrubs or Drinking Vinegars
These drinking vinegars are essentially vinegar sweetened with fruit syrup and left to steep, to be used diluted with a mixer. Usually, distilled 5% white vinegar is used, but we are going to substitute kombucha vinegar. As we aren't sure of the acid concentration, we're going to double it and keep it refrigerated. You can use any fruit: gooseberries, strawberries apples. For soft fruits, berries, etc. there is no need to make a hot syrup: for apples and pears and old rhubarb you will need to stew it to make a compote and then strain out the fruit.

The formation of a vinegar mother appears as a pale cloud on the top of the vinegar (not to be confused with kahm yeast). It will sink if disturbed but another will form. E. MORELAND

FRUIT-FLAVOURED DRINKING VINEGAR

Ingredients:

1 cup of chopped-up fruit
1 cup of sugar
2 cups of vinegar

Method:

1. Mix the berries with the sugar and leave in the fridge for 48 hours, stirring regularly, until plenty of juice has come out of the fruit. Alternatively, make a compote with hard fruits by boiling them with sugar and a little water until they have softened.
2. Mix the juice with the vinegar, then bottle and refrigerate. This will keep for several months in the fridge. It is ready to drink straight away, but the flavour will improve with age.

Continuous brew, delicious just as it is. E. MORELAND

Kombucha Vinegar Cleaner

Vinegar is a potent antimicrobial, degreaser and glass polisher! Simply add a few drops of essential oil to some kombucha vinegar in a spray bottle. It might not pass muster with the Environmental Health department, but it can be used domestically.

CHAPTER 7

WILD FERMENTATION

The process of wild fermentation, or lacto-fermentation, relies on the invisible world of microbes that are naturally present on fruit and vegetables. Lacto-fermented vegetables are tart, tangy and sour. They are less sweet than their pickled counterparts, but this is a small price to pay for the enormous nutritional benefit they offer, and it is not too hard to get used to.

MECHANISMS OF VEGETABLE FERMENTATION

The exact process of lacto-fermentation is likely to be similar with most vegetables, but to date there is not much research on individual systems. The best characterized are sauerkraut and kimchi, which are sufficiently important in certain territories to have spawned industries that are willing to fund studies.

Fundamentally, vegetable fermentation occurs when LAB use carbohydrates for energy, in the process producing lactic acid, acetic acid, alcohol and carbon dioxide. This lowers the pH of the vegetables, to the point at which other bacteria cannot survive, thus preserving the food from further deterioration. Salt is added to the ferment to prevent the growth of unwanted bacteria, yeasts and fungi, especially in the early stages. LAB are salt-tolerant, so they are able to start growing quickly and triumph over these other microbes. Lacto-fermentation is an anaerobic process – it occurs in the absence of oxygen, which is achieved

by excluding air from the fermentation vessel. This also prevents oxygen-loving yeasts and mould from taking hold.

NATURALLY OCCURRING MICROORGANISMS

The soil in which vegetables are grown contains about 10^{10} bacteria and up to 50,000 species per gram, depending upon geographical region and terroir, before you include any equally numerous fungi, algae and protozoa. Nowadays, new advances in molecular genetics have made it easier to study these soil organisms and their role is gradually being explained, although science is so far only in the foothills of an enormous mountain. It is clear that the soil microbiota is crucial in the establishment and productivity of crops, and is the main driver of nutrient cycles, enabling nitrogen and mineral uptake by plants. The soil microbiota will also influence the microbiota of the vegetables you are fermenting; without the microbes, the fermentation cannot get started.

Microbial communities on fresh produce are affected by several factors, including natural habitat, environmental factors, produce type and cultivar, storage conditions and farming methods; plants that are grown near to the ground are more likely to have soil-type microbes than bananas, say, and cold-stored fruit and veg will probably have higher populations of cold-tolerant microbes. Many vegetables are grown hydroponically these days and may never see a grain of soil in their lifetime, however they are still able to develop microflora, albeit different from the one nature intended. Microbes exist in all parts of plants – stems,

OPPOSITE: **Wild fermentation just needs naturally occurring microbes to get started.** M. GILMARTIN

pips, cores and flesh – not just on the outside skin. Disparate parts of the same fruit or vegetable may even contain different types of microbe.

CHOOSING THE RIGHT VEGETABLES

Organic vs Conventionally Farmed

Recent studies have shown that there are differences in the microbes on organic and conventionally farmed beetroot, apples and tomatoes. Interestingly, fewer obvious differences exist with cabbages, which seem to be variety-specific. It is not yet clear what this means in terms of the body's gut microbiota, but it is another indication that any divergence from a more natural path will have an impact on the hidden microbiological world. The precise consequences are not yet known, but at least some of the microbes in your gut will come directly from the raw fruit and vegetables you eat.[61-64]

Organic beetroots and cabbages contain significantly more vitamin C than their industrially farmed counterparts, and some studies have found significant nutritional differences between these classes of vegetables[65, 66,] but others, not so much[67]. Organic vegetables will have been subjected to fewer pesticides, which is desirable in terms of soil and human health, but they are also more expensive than conventional produce, which is not something everyone can absorb. The general message is that the choice is yours; fermentation will work whether your vegetables have been produced organically or conventionally, even if people tell you otherwise.

Quality of Vegetables

Fermenting vegetables requires time and patience, so it would be a shame to ruin any ferment through poor vegetable choice. If you use the best-quality, tastiest and freshest vegetables you can get your hands on, you are much less likely to be disappointed. As vegetables age, flavours can change and a certain bitterness can develop, especially in courgettes, cucumbers and aubergines. Older cabbages also have a slightly funny taste, so the fresher the better. It is worth bearing in mind that some supermarket vegetables look fresh but might be several weeks old. Older produce is more likely to have a collection of moulds beginning to develop. Even though it is very unlikely that any mould will grow on your ferments, there is no need to challenge the system unduly.

Ideally, you should buy your vegetables from a local greengrocer who specializes in produce from small-scale farmers, where quality is of prime importance and the vegetables have not travelled too far, and have not been hanging around in a depot for weeks.

Washing Your Vegetables

As already discussed in the Introduction, fermented foods, especially those made on a small scale at home, are incredibly unlikely to make you ill. The salt you add, the acid produced by the LAB, the anaerobic environment, the competition for resources with more numerous species, bacteriocins produced by the LABs: all of these factors make it very difficult for pathogens to take hold. That said, there's no need to take chances. If you have just dug your vegetables up from the allotment, do give them a good wash, just to make sure you have removed any clumps of dirt that could harbour potentially pathogenic microbes from animal faeces in the soil.

Tasting the Vegetables

It is crucial to taste the raw vegetables before embarking on any fermentation. Anyone who has made a bitter kimchi, revolting pickled gherkins and slimy carrots, will know that it takes a while to learn from such mistakes.

If your cucumbers or lettuce are bitter before you ferment them, they will certainly be bitter afterwards – and fermented. Carrots need special attention. Some supermarket carrots are grown to be so sweet as to be almost fruit-like. The middle core is ill defined and they are full of sugar. Carrots like this will tend to stimulate the formation of dextran in your ferment, which can give a slimy texture. It is not harmful, but it is really unpleasant, so it is advisable to buy greengrocers' carrots or organic ones. Additionally, given a choice of a bitter organic courgette and a delicious fresh-tasting conventionally farmed one, most people would choose the latter.

Frozen Vegetables

Many species of LAB will be quite happy in the freezer, so you can usually use frozen vegetables – with emphasis on the 'usually'. To alleviate any problems, always include at least one source of fresh vegetables in the mix. For example, if you are using a bag of frozen sweetcorn, include some fresh garlic, herbs and a couple of slices of celery, to help to get things going. Alternatively, you could add some kefir whey or sauerkraut juice.

As long as your vegetables have not been irradiated (which is most unusual in the UK), there are likely to be enough microbes to start fermentation. Bacteria and yeasts grow exponentially, with one becoming 2, becoming 4, 8,16, 32, 64, and so on, so low bacterial populations in the right conditions can recover within just a few hours.

Find a decent greengrocer who really knows his stuff. M. GILMARTIN

LACTO-FERMENTATION: GETTING STARTED

Preventing Potential Problems

Lacto-fermentation can be as simple or as hi-tech as you like, but the principle remains the same: when fermenting vegetables, it is important to provide an anaerobic environment for your microbes, as these conditions allow LAB to thrive, and produce lactic acid and carbon dioxide. You must also consider how that gas is going to escape. An anaerobic environment will prevent two potential problems: contamination and oxidization.

Contamination is possible because the starting vegetables are not just covered with bacteria, they may also harbour mould spores and yeasts. Mould spores travel through the air all the time – witness an unattended fruit bowl to see the potential for decomposition – and most moulds thrive in an oxygen-rich environment. Keeping air out of the vessel will minimize the risk of mould growth.

Oxidation is another potential problem with a poorly

Yes, the process needs the microbes, but not this many! Give vegetables a thorough wash. ADOBE

sealed fermentation vessel, or a vessel that has been repeatedly opened to release pressure or to taste the contents. The contents in the top two or three centimetres will have a duller, less appealing colour than the rest of the jar. When the microbes are exposed to oxygen, some of them are able to use this to generate energy, but they do not make lactic acid this way. Instead, many different pathways are activated, forming products that do not enhance either the flavour or the appearance of fermented foods.

The vessel you choose for your ferment depends to some extent upon the type of ferment you are making. If you open the jar, you will disrupt the environment that you have tried so hard to create, so it is important to consider this. The longer the fermentation time, the greater the chance of contamination and/or oxidation occurring, especially if you keep opening the jar. Sometimes, fermentation can proceed more rapidly in a Kilner jar if it is not vented. This is because the carbon dioxide is not able to escape, and can become dissolved in the fermenting mixture, as carbonic acid, thus lowering the pH even further. This can influence the growth of certain types of LAB. It is not usually a problem – it actually seems to help kimchi!

Suitable Vessels
Fermentation Crock
If you decide to go 'old school' and use a ceramic crock, you must find one that is designed specifically for the purpose, as some ceramics can contain lead. They use a water seal to prevent mould contamination.

The porosity is said to improve the quality of the fermentation.

Pros: usually capacious; unlikely to explode; attractive addition to kitchen, exciting when it is time to open up!
Cons: hard to see what is going on inside; expensive; channel must be kept full of water to maintain seal.

Wooden Barrel
This traditional vessel is not commonly used in the UK, but may impart an additional layer of flavour, rather like ageing wine.

Pros: flavour enhancement; natural material; porous; good for large quantities.
Cons: hard to clean; expensive; not see-through.

Kilner or Other Clip-Top Jar
Kilner jars and other clip-top vessels are very popular for fermenting, especially in the UK, despite their limitations. Make sure they are designed for culinary purposes and not 'gift-type' jars, which may not

Different vessel options: jam jar and lid, plastic kimchi box, ziplock bag, mason jar with two-part lid, clip-top jar, lidless jar and bag of brine, wooden barrel, ceramic crock and Sterilock jars.

be sturdy enough. Replacing the clip with a rubber band wound around a few times, giving slightly more expansion than a metal clip, can avoid the need to vent. They are best for short ferments, and not ideal for long ferments.

Pros: cheap; available; transparent; ideal for small quantities; easy to clean; does not retain odours; replaceable gaskets.
Cons: breakable – glass is a liability and must be checked for weaknesses; could crack under pressure, although gaskets usually prevent this.

Plastic Box
Vented food-safe plastic boxes are now available for fermenting.

Pros: safe; easy to clean; come in all sorts of shapes and sizes.
Cons: do not allow view of what is going on inside; cannot use full capacity as lots of room is needed for generation of carbon dioxide; the smell of the plastic is rather unappealing, although it does not transfer to the food.

Mason Jar with Screw-On Two-Part Lid
These are a popular choice for fermenting in the USA, although the quality of the metal lid is not always the best.

Pros: cheap; easy to find; easy to wash.
Cons: rust can form on the lid, which could taint the ferment; the lids are not really suitable for venting – they are really for canning.

Vented Fermentation Jar
Can be used with a standard mason jar, with a valve mechanism that will let carbon dioxide out of the jar without letting oxygen back in. Easy-to-use valves with membranes are available these days, although you can also use a traditional glass tube set-up if you prefer, or if you already have one.

Pros: removes the need to vent; can be extremely reliable (depending on manufacturer); membrane

versions easy to clean; one-time purchase; look efficient.
Cons: high cost; can get blocked with mashed-up ferments.

Large Glass Jar with Lid
For no-frills fermenting, and short ferments only.

Pros: inexpensive; economical; reusable; recyclable.
Cons: no mechanism for release of carbon dioxide, so must be vented, with risk of oxidation/contamination; may not have shoulders for easy submersion of brine; lids can rust and harbour contaminants.

Large Glass Jar with Plastic Bag-of-Brine Stopper
This is great for no-frills fermenting. Filling the bag with brine means that, if there is a leak, the salt concentration in the ferment will not be diluted.

Pros: inexpensive and easily available; safe; see-through, no venting required; suitable for long or short ferments; reusable.
Cons: bag can burst; uses plastic.

Ziplock or Vacuum Seal Bags
The bags need to be sturdy with a good seal, and made of a high-quality material. Ziplock bags can be reused until the seal fails.

Pros: inexpensive and easily available; safe; see-through; suitable for long or short ferments.
Cons: may need venting; plastic can make 'sweaty' flavours long-term.

Submerging the Vegetables
When fermenting vegetables (with the exception of short, paste-based kimchi and piccalilli ferments), it is important to ensure that they are completely out of contact with the air and in contact with the salt-containing brine – at all times. If portions of your vegetables stick up above the level of the brine, they will be more susceptible to the effects of oxidation and discolouration, and could provide a tasty source of carbohydrate for mould growth, if any oxygen

is present. There are various ways of achieving this submerging, dependent to some extent upon the type of vessel you are using.

Re-Purposed Food-Safe Plastic Disc
This works well for a mason jar, or any vessel with shoulders. You can easily recycle any piece of food-safe plastic for the task. Cut a circle from a lid or tub that is about 1cm larger than the mouth of the jar. Ease it into the jar and position it so that it sits on top of the vegetables, held in place by the shoulders. In some countries, it is possible to buy special inserts called 'pickle pushers', but these do not seem to be readily available in the UK yet.

Glass Weight
Be sure to use a weight that is designed for the purpose, as some decorative glass contains lead. They are quite expensive but very effective – perhaps something for your Christmas list.

Vegetable Pieces
If you are fermenting a cabbage, you can use the end to keep the rest of it under the brine. You could also use carrot sticks that are longer than the jar opening, or anything else that springs to mind. Ensure that this is also included in your brining.

Small Glass Jar or Shot Glass
These can work well in a jar that does not have shoulders and for tightly packed vegetables. Place the glass on top of the vegetables to bridge the gap to the lid. When the lid is shut, the jar or glass will press down on the vegetables underneath and keeps them below the brine.

Plastic Bag Filled with Brine
Fill a bag with 2% brine and secure it with a rubber band. The water needs to be brined in case the bag bursts. If it just had plain water in it, it could reduce the salt concentration in the vessel to potentially unsafe levels. If you have a jar without a lid, a bag filled in this way can be used as both a lid and a weight. Ensure that the bag is in complete contact with the top of the vegetables.

A Stone
A stone can be effective for well-packed vegetable ferments, but not for whole vegetables, as it will simply

fall to the bottom! Certain types of stone should be avoided, as they may contain elements that could leach into the ferment under the acidic conditions. Do not use limestone because the calcium carbonate will react with the lactic and acetic acid in your ferment and dissolve. If you are using a stone from the garden, sterilize it first by soaking it in Milton fluid according to the instructions and then rinsing thoroughly. Alternatively, you could put it inside a plastic bag.

Nothing

Some people do not agree with the practice of submerging. If you have a casual approach to contamination and discolouration, or if you are just doing a short ferment, feel free to ignore the instructions. It is certainly less important in the vented jars, where an oxygen-free environment is easy to create, or with a short sauce-covered ferment. However, in the case of a Sterilock jar, for example, it is important to submerge the cabbage for a different reason: if it rises in the jar as a result of carbon dioxide production, bits of cabbage could get stuck in the valve and stop it from releasing excess gas.

Using a Starter Culture

As long as you are using fresh vegetables, there is no need to use a starter culture for vegetable fermentation. Recipes suggesting the addition of whey, starter culture sachets or backslopping from previous batches to 'get things going' are missing the point – it will 'get going' all by itself within 24 hours. There is one exception: when you are fermenting cooked vegetables, such as chickpeas.

Using up Odds and Ends

People usually ferment things in quite large quantities – this has arisen traditionally, because if you didn't ferment it you couldn't store it, and also because if you've to wait three weeks for your sauerkraut, you might as well make a big batch. But it doesn't have to

CONTROLLING THE CARBON DIOXIDE AND AIR IN THE JAR

If your ferments are ferociously bubbling away, it is almost irresistible to vent them. Indeed, if the jar is less than sturdy, venting can be essential. This is one of those areas where it is your call – you may prefer to use a self-venting lid, such as on a Sterilock jar, or the bag-of-brine system. To vent a normal jar and lid set-up, turn the lid until you hear a hiss. *Do not* lift it up; just screw it up again very quickly.

To vent a clip-top jar, cover with a tea towel (not one of your best white ones!) and open the catch. Make sure you are pressing down on the lid as you do this, especially with kimchi, which can be rather explosive. Try not to open the jar more than a millimetre or you will let air in. Keep your hand firmly on the top and re-close the catch.

If there is too much room (air) in the jar, use a bag of brine or a scrunched-up piece of greaseproof paper to reduce the volume.

be that way – odds and ends of (fresh) vegetables can easily be chopped and brined in small jars – cauliflower leaves and stems for example that would otherwise just go into the compost, can make a delicious one-serving ferment.

Fermented cauliflower leaves that would otherwise be thrown away – just enough to serve one!

SAFETY

The Definite Don'ts of Fermenting

Many of the safety considerations are the same, whatever fermented foods you are making. However, there are a couple of issues that are specific to wild fermentation. The following is a definitive list of things *not* to do, to negate even the most unlikely risks.

- Don't ferment vegetables without salt.
- Don't ferment fruit and vegetables that are old fridge fodder. They could well be covered with various moulds or stray bacteria from your fridge, which will mean that your ferment could be at risk of growing something it should not. Use fresh vegetables that are likely to be covered with beneficial bacteria, and wash them first.
- Don't use damaged and/or bruised produce, including windfall fruit (use this for jam or compote). Pathogenic bacteria can find their way inside the fruit via fruit flies, birds and maggots, and other wildlife, including strains of *E. coli*. Although both pH and competition with other bacteria can help destroy these, it is best not to take any risks.
- Don't cover your ferments with a layer of any type of oil, in an attempt to create an anaerobic environment. The pH of oil is not low enough to prevent the growth of pathogens including *Clostridium botulinum*, which could become suspended in the oil on particles of food. Instead, use a weight to keep the vegetables submerged under the water, and an airlock system.
- Don't use a tightly sealed (regular) jar without a gasket, a mason jar or a jar with a very tight metal lid for your fermentations without venting. They could explode, due to the gases produced by the microbes while they consume the sugar. It is unlikely, but it is better to be safe than sorry. A Kilner jar with a gasket should allow just enough expansion to prevent a catastrophe.
- Do not open your ferments to check them within 72 hours unless absolutely necessary. The pH will not be low enough to prevent the possible growth of airborne contaminants.

Contaminants in Fermented Foods

To avoid contamination and the growth of any mould, the best bet is to follow guidelines carefully, but sometimes things do go wrong. If that happens, you will have to make a judgement call. There are two major unwanted visitors that can find their way into your ferments: mould and kahm yeast (*see* below for their different characteristics).

Moulds

Some well-respected fermentation gurus have a relaxed attitude to mould and the oft-quoted guide is, 'If it's white it's ok; green, black or blue, throw it out.' However, there are several reasons why the consumption of mouldy ferments is not recommended:

- If mould has grown during an anaerobic fermentation, it is a sign that something has gone awry.
- Unless you are a mycologist, you will not be able to tell anything meaningful about the mould just by looking at it.
- If there is enough oxygen to let mould grow, there may be any number of unexpected metabolites

Mould	Kahm yeast
White, green-blue or black growth	White/very slightly grey
Fuzzy in appearance	No mouldy fuzziness
Often discrete, forming a circular/oval blob	A flat, smooth film or pellicle, sometimes with bubbles of trapped carbon dioxide. Looks like talcum powder on water
May grow beneath the surface	No growth beneath the pellicle

Examples of contaminated foods that should definitely be discarded: top left, an old jar of ruby kraut growing something – probably the result of double-dipping a spoon; top centre, some soya milk kefir that has been overtaken by a growth of kahm yeast; bottom, a sauerkraut where something awful has happened – just throw it out; and, right, kimchi that has started to show signs of bacterial growth after a year or so.

in that jar, making some pretty odd flavours and, potentially, reduced levels of lactic acid.

- Some moulds can produce mycotoxins. (The nastiest of these, aflatoxins, can be removed by *Lactobacillus plantarum*, so you might be OK!)
- Some moulds make their surroundings alkaline so your ferment might have spots that are not acidic enough to inhibit potential pathogens.
- The fungal growth seen on the top is only the tip of the iceberg, and hyphae are likely to have spread throughout the ferment.
- Some people are allergic to moulds, either as inhaled spores or ingested.

Kahm Yeast

Kahm is not one particular yeast – it can be any combination of *Mycoderma*, *Pichia*, *Hansuela* and *Candida*. Kahm can arise for a number of reasons, including insufficient salt concentration, presence of oxygen and temperatures that are too warm (mid-20s). It is commonly believed that kahm may be safely removed and the ferment consumed, but prevention is better than having to make that decision. Sometimes, depending on the species in the kahm, your ferment may have an overly sweet or occasionally cheesy odour. If you have spotted the problem very early on, you may be able to successfully remove traces of it from

the surface of the ferment with a spoon and a piece of kitchen paper.

Preventing Contamination

- Always add the correct concentration of salt.
- Ensure you are using an effective method of oxygen exclusion/submersion.
- Do not open the fermentation vessel for 72 hours, unless you really think it is going to explode. In that case, follow the steps on page 110.
- Keep your ferments in view, or get into the routine of having a quick look at them daily – spotting a hint of kahm that can be easily removed beats discarding the whole batch because it has been taken over.
- For kahm-prone ferments such as red peppers, consider a short room-temperature fermentation, followed by a longer period of ripening in the fridge.

DIFFERENT METHODS FOR FERMENTATION

There are several different methods for fermenting vegetables:

1. Self-brining ferments: when you are fermenting chopped or shredded vegetables, by merely adding

KEEPING FERMENTED FOODS

It is widely believed that fermented foods will last indefinitely, but that is not the case. In fact, it varies according to the vegetables used. The question is how long they remain texturally palatable. Only very rarely will they become mouldy or grow fridge psychrotrophs, but after a few weeks a tomato salsa might be unpleasantly soggy, courgettes wincingly vinegary, and fermented fruits will taste of salty booze. Sauerkraut will last a very long time, because of its fibrous nature, but its probiotic benefit will decrease the longer it is stored. Indeed, this is the case for pretty much all fermented foods. The best keeper is fermented chilli sauce. It will last for years, especially unopened.

To keep foods fresh for as long as possible, as you consume them, put them in progressively smaller jars to keep the air and any potential contaminants out. Very old ferments still might taste good, but as eventually the LAB lose viability, their protective effect diminishes and contamination could occur.

One sure-fire way to put a ferment at risk is 'double-dipping'. Resist the temptation to eat directly from the jar and then put the fork back in – the microbiota in your mouth may contain microbes that could be transferred and soon set to work.

salt, the process of osmosis will draw water out of the plant cells. Before you know it, with a little massaging, you will have created a flavoursome brine, which will be the perfect environment for the microbes. This is suitable for robust vegetables that do not mind being squeezed. Vegetables contain more water than you might realize – for example, red peppers are 92% water.

2. Brined fermentation: sometimes, you will want to maintain the integrity of the vegetables, with pickled gherkins or carrot sticks, for example, or cauliflower florets, which will crumble if squeezed. They can be kept intact by being submerged in a solution of brine.

3. Sauce-based fermentation: kimchi is the main example of sauce-based fermentation, with the vegetables being gently soaked in brine and then wrapped in a thick sauce that melds them together. Submerging these is more difficult, so the fermentation vessel should be chosen carefully.

SELF-BRINING FERMENTS: SAUERKRAUT

Made with just two ingredients – cabbage and salt – and using the cabbage's own water to make brine, sauerkraut has a simplicity that means that

it is the perfect place to start looking at vegetable fermentation.

History of Sauerkraut

Despite Germany's reputation as the home of sauerkraut, it actually all began in China. During the construction of the Great Wall in the seventh century BC, the workers used to live on a diet of cabbage and rice. In the summertime, the cabbage was fresh, but during the colder months they were sustained by supplies that had been preserved and fermented in rice wine. Fresh cabbage is a good source of vitamin C, but the nutritional content is much enhanced in sauerkraut.

Brought from China to Europe by the Tartars, at some point sauerkraut began to be cured with salt instead of rice wine, giving rise to what is known today as sauerkraut, which translates from German simply as 'sour cabbage'. It has been a staple in the Eastern and Central European diet since the 1600s.

In the eighteenth century, sauerkraut played an important part in British naval history. In 1740, Commodore George Anson set off to the Pacific on a mission to disrupt Spanish influence in the region, with a fleet of eight ships and 2,000 men. He returned four years later having lost 90% of the crew to illness,

Sauerkraut may be a staple food in Germany, but that is not where it originated.

notably scurvy. The ship's chaplain recorded the appalling effects of the illness:

> Those affected have skin as black as ink, ulcers, difficult respiration, rictus of the limbs, teeth falling out and, perhaps most revolting of all, a strange plethora of gum tissue sprouting out of the mouth, which immediately rotted and lent the victim's breath an abominable odor.

The terrible losses brought scurvy to public attention. Scottish naval doctor James Lind noticed that those affected by the condition had a very poor diet, and discovered that citrus fruits helped, although he was unaware at the time that vitamin C was the preventive agent. Fermented cabbage was suggested as another solution and, as an experiment, in 1764, Captain Cook set off on a voyage with a large crew and 7,640 pounds of 'Sour Krott'. He returned at the end of the expedition having lost not one crew member to scurvy.

Despite this, the British seem to have lost interest in sauerkraut and it did not become an integral part of Britain's food heritage. It is most definitely prominent in US culture, though, as an essential component of a salt-beef sandwich, or with a hot dog, introduced to the New World by German immigrants arriving there in the eighteenth century.

Germany's national dish. E. MORELAND

In Germany, per capita consumption of sauerkraut has almost halved over the past 40 years, probably due to the globalization of food markets and the prevalence of convenience foods. A similar picture of the loss of traditional eating patterns emerges all over Europe. Nowadays, much of Germany's sauerkraut is pasteurized to make it shelf-stable, so it has no probiotic benefit, although it is still effective as a source of fibre. To be fair, it is traditionally commonly served hot as a side dish or in stews, which effectively pasteurizes it anyway.

There are various different types of sauerkraut: although used as a blanket term, the word usually describes the foodstuff made from white cabbage (*blaukraut* is made from red cabbage and *filderkraut* from pointed cabbage). Savoy and green cabbages can also be used. Generally, these days, the abbreviation 'kraut' is used to describe any ferment with shredded vegetables and cabbage as a base.

Cabbage: The Raw Material

Cabbage, *Brassica oleracea*, is part of a large group of cruciferous vegetables (so called because their four-leaved flowers resemble a cross), which includes cauliflower, kohlrabi, broccoli, kale, Brussels sprouts, spring greens, Swiss chard and rocket. The word is derived from the French *caboche*, a colloquial word for 'head' or in English, perhaps noodle or noggin? We still use the phrase 'a head of cabbage'.

There are at least a hundred different cultivars of cabbage to choose from when making sauerkraut. Although you may be limited by what is available to buy, if you have an allotment you could choose to grow one of the heirloom varieties, such as Brunswick or Golden Acre. The cool British climate is perfectly suited to cabbage cultivation, which started in the fourteenth century. The vegetable is in season all year round and takes between 70 and 120 days to reach maturity. All of these types of cabbage have slightly different qualities.

White or Green Cabbage

The popularity of the very familiar green cabbage has faded recently, to be replaced almost always by white cabbage. Firm, crisp and peppery to the bite,

Chinese, hispi, savoy red and white cabbages in all their unsauerkrauted glory.

this stalwart of sauerkraut requires three weeks' fermentation at room temperature.

Pointed or Hispi Cabbage

A type of green cabbage with loosely packed pointed leaves. It has a softer texture and a sweeter taste. It is much quicker to ferment than the basic white or green cabbage, taking five to seven days to reach a good texture and flavour.

Red Cabbage

The colour of red cabbage is due to the presence of the anthocyanin cyaniclin, which can also be used as a pH indicator; this is very helpful when fermenting. Anthocyanins are known to be a choice food for the gut microbiota and to have antioxidant properties. The flesh of the red cabbage is the most durable of all the varieties and takes several weeks to reach a pleasant consistency (although there are ways of speeding this up in mixed ferments).

Savoy Cabbage

Savoy cabbage is delicious fermented. The outer leaves can take weeks to tenderize through fermentation whilst the inner leaves can be soft within a week.

Napa Cabbage

The stalwart of kimchi, this Chinese cabbage is also a popular ingredient in East Asian cooking. It has a completely different, more lettuce-like texture than the other members of the family. When fermented, the stems retain their structure whilst the leaves wilt to almost nothing. Kimchi made from napa cabbage can be ready to eat within three to five days.

Nutritional Content of Sauerkraut

White cabbage comprises about 90% carbohydrates, approximately one-third as dietary fibre and two-thirds as other carbohydrates, including glucose, fructose, sucrose and raffinose. Glucosinolates give brassicas their characteristic flavours and that slightly sulphurous odour, and there are high levels of vitamin C, especially in red cabbage.

During fermentation, bacterial metabolism alters the composition, resulting in sauerkraut with an increased content of minerals, antioxidants including vitamin C, and also vitamins A, some B6, and K2, folate, iron, organic acids, breakdown products of glucosinolates, sulphorophanes, histamine and tyrosine. In fermented red cabbage there are higher levels of flavonoids and anthocyanins. It also contains an enormous population of potentially probiotic microbes.

Health Benefits of Sauerkraut

Even today, when there is so much enthusiasm for fermented foods, the health effects of sauerkraut consumption on human subjects have not been extensively studied. However, the probiotic and bioactive phytochemical content is undeniable. Below are some of the positive findings.[68]

Antioxidant Action

Sauerkraut contains high levels of free radical scavengers that can protect cells from oxidative stress.[69] In addition, the high levels of vitamin C can reduce levels of C-reactive protein, which is involved in inflammation and atherosclerosis.[70]

Anti-Carcinogenic Properties

Glucosinolate breakdown products have been shown to be involved in detoxification pathways for some environmental carcinogens in rat livers and kidneys. In human breast cell lines, sauerkraut juice was involved in the inhibition of oestrogen production, suggesting a potential protective activity against breast cancer.[71] A case-control study in Polish migrant women in the USA showed that raw or lightly cooked cabbage, and/or sauerkraut consumption, at least three times a week during adolescence and adulthood, was linked with a 72% reduction in breast cancer risk. Breast cancer incidence in these communities had tripled within one generation, pointing to diet as a risk factor.[72]

Anti-Inflammatory Effects

Several bioactive components of sauerkraut are able to inhibit the production of nitric oxide, which is an inflammatory marker produced by activated macrophages, important cells involved in the immune response. Sauerkraut is much more effective than raw cabbage.[73]

WHO IS SAUERKRAUT NOT SUITABLE FOR?

The biogenic amines histamine and tyramine can sometimes be problematic. Anyone who is taking monoamine oxidase inhibitors, often used as antidepressants, should be aware that tyramine can interfere with their action. Equally, anyone who is histamine-intolerant might have a problem – middle-aged or older sauerkraut is better for them, as it seems that L. *plantarum*, which appears in the middle stages of fermentation, actually consumes histamine.

Probiotic Action

It can only be roughly estimated, as it will vary according to culture conditions, but sauerkraut samples have been found to contain in the region of 10^6–10^8 cfu/g lactic acid bacteria. That is 1,000,000 to 100,000,000 per gram, and in a 100-gram serving, 10,000,000 to 1,000,000,000. Up to 15 different types of LAB have been detected in sauerkraut samples.

Mechanism of Sauerkraut Fermentation

Complete fermentation of white sauerkraut takes about 20 days. The microbiota is established very quickly when fermentation begins. The microbes present can vary significantly at the start of the process, depending upon what is present on the vegetables, and LAB may represent only about 5% of the starting population. However, they always make it through and dominate in the final product, which is just as well as they are responsible for producing the organic acids, bacterioicins, vitamins, and volatile flavour compounds that characterize sauerkraut.

The first stage in the process is the initial proliferation of *Leuconostoc mesenteroides*, one of the commonest commensal organisms associated with vegetables. It is able to tolerate the salty conditions and, in the anaerobic environment provided, breaks down the available sugars to produce lactic acid, carbon dioxide and ethanol through heterolactic fermentation. During this time, the number of bacterial species drops rapidly, as production of antimicrobial substances, increased acidity and salt take their toll on undesirable organisms. This alters the environment so that a different organism, *Lactobacillus plantarum*, is able to thrive, and continues to do so for the main fermentation period. At the end, it facilitates an increase in *Lactobacillus brevis*, for 'finishing off' for the last few days. By the end of the period, LAB account for about 90% of the microbes present.[74]

. . . .

SAUERKRAUT (FOR A 1LTR JAR)

If you are new to fermentation, use a glass jar, so that you can see what is going on. This recipe makes about a litre jar of white cabbage sauerkraut, depending on

Ingredients:

900g white cabbage
2% sea salt
Caraway seeds (optional)

Equipment:

Chopping board
Knife
Colander
Bowl
Scales
Fermentation vessel
Jam funnel
Submerging device

its water content.

Method:

1. Make sure your hands, the equipment and your working area are clean and free from possible raw meat or animal contamination.
2. Finely slice the cabbage, and place in colander.
3. Rinse well and drain.

SALT

The recommended level of salt to use for self-brining fermentation is 2%. That is 2g per 100g of vegetables and can be calculated as follows: weight of veg × 2/100.

The only exception to this is the use of 10% for preserved lemons.

4. Place bowl on weighing scales and set to zero.
5. Add cabbage and record weight.
6. Add 2% w/v salt, using the formula weight (g) ×2/100. For 800g cabbage: 800 x2/100=16g.
7. Massage with your hands until a pool of brine is created. The cabbage will change translucency (if you want to keep its end to use as a weight, do not forget to salt it too).
8. If you are adding caraway or other seeds, set the brine to one side in a jug, and then mix the seeds with the cabbage, otherwise they will mostly end up floating about in the brine and might not make it to the jar. The brine can then be used to top up the jars from the jug if needed.
9. Squeeze the cabbage into your vessel of choice, using a jam funnel. Pack it in well, ensuring there are no air gaps to the shoulder height of the jar (but do not forget to leave room for expansion).
10. Weigh down with your device of choice.
11. Ensure that the brine covers the vegetables by at least 1cm.
12. Place your ferment out of direct sunlight at room temperature (18–22°C), sitting on a plate or tray in case the brine spills over.
13. Ferment for 3 weeks at room temperature.
14. Taste. Leave for longer at room temperature for a softer texture/more farmyardy taste.
15. When it is done, refrigerate it, dispensed into clean jars if you want to reuse your fermenting vessel, or in the original.

. . . .

LEFT: **How to cut a cabbage (without cutting your fingers!).**

ABOVE: **Chop the cabbage as you like. Do not waste the cores – just slice them finely.**

ABOVE: **Adding the salt.**

LEFT: **Rinse the cabbage under the tap.**

Squeezing the cabbage to release the brine.

When a pool of brine has formed, it is time to transfer the cabbage to the jar.

ABOVE: **Press down hard with your fingers to fill any gaps.**

LEFT: **Transfer to the jar using a jam funnel.**

Insert a submerging device – for example, a repurposed food-safe plastic disc that has been cut to fit.

Mixed red and white and fennel kraut, just after making and after 3 days – what a difference those microbes make in such a short space of time.

Fine-Tuning the Process

Chopping the Cabbage

It is possible, if you really want to, to ferment whole heads of cabbage. However, this is a specialist task – penetration of the brine to central tissues is essential, but it is difficult to achieve. For these reasons, shredding is highly recommended. The finer the shred, the more efficient both the brine production and fermentation will be, due to the increased surface area.

Hand-Cutting

You will need a large sharp knife for cutting up your vegetables. Quarter the cabbage and remove the core – do not throw it away, but cut it more finely. Chop the cabbage thickly or thinly – or even into squares if you like!

Grating

Grating your cabbage makes quite a difference to the texture and is great if you are looking for a softer final texture, more reminiscent of bought pasteurized sauerkraut.

Food Processing

Use the slicing attachment on your food processor to cut the cabbage in half, then into thirds. Remove the cores to shred separately. Remove three or four outer leaves and roll them up so they will fit into the food processor opening, and place them in rolled edge

How to cut a cabbage: level it off at the bottom. Put a very sharp knife on top and press down on it with your other hand – now your fingers will be safe!

The best way to process cabbage – separate a few leaves, roll up and cut on the rolled side for lovely long strands.

down. Repeat until the rest will just fit in. This makes long shreds that look great when plated up.

Choosing a vessel

As plain sauerkraut requires a full three weeks for all the microbes to play their parts, it is recommended that you use a vented jar (for example, Sterilock), a bag-of-brine stopper with any jar, or a specialist crock. If you do not have any of these, a clip-top Kilner jar with a rubber band and submerging device will do.

Too Much Air in the Vessel

If there is more than about 5cm headroom, the microbes might not be able to produce enough carbon dioxide to displace the oxygen. Your choices are either to use a smaller jar (this is irritating, but, if you have misjudged the quantity, now is the time to transfer it), or use a filler (for example, a bag of brine, or a piece of scrunched-up greaseproof paper around a stone or weight).

Compacting your Vegetables

When transferring your chopped and salted veg to the jar, the idea is to pack it tightly, to exclude as much air as possible and create an anaerobic environment.

However, you do not need to take this too far; a good press with your hands as you pack is good enough. If the vegetables are too compacted in the jar, it will be impossible to get them out again. If there are some visible gaps, stick a knife down the side to fill them with brine.

Signs of Fermentation

If you have a glass jar, within 24 hours (up to 48 if it is cold) you will see air bubbles forming at the sides of the glass, as *L. mesenteroides* start to produce carbon dioxide and lactic acid. The additional gas in the jar may cause the contents to rise and, depending on the vessel, some liquid might escape. If you have used red cabbage, you will notice a colour change (as it contains phenolic compounds that act as pH indicators). It will become a beautiful magenta as the fermentation becomes more acidic, usually within 48 hours. If you have used white cabbage, it will gain a pale translucency. If you are using a stoneware or ceramic crock or a wooden barrel, you will have to wait patiently. After three days, if you were to measure the pH of your ferment it would be at about 3.7, from a starting point of about pH 6, indicating that a lot of acid has already been generated.

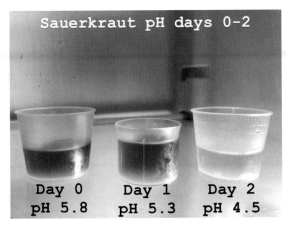

The pH and colour change of sauerkraut at the start and after 2 days.

Sometimes, the brine escapes and the cabbage looks dry. Try not to panic, and do not open the jar unless you absolutely have to.

Troubleshooting

Escape of Brine

Sometimes, as a result of fermentation, the carbon dioxide and heat generated can cause expansion, forcing the brine from the vessel. This can leave the ferment looking dry. It is tempting to open the jar and top it up, but it is not always necessary or advisable. If liquid and air have been forced out, there will be an ideal anaerobic environment inside, which will protect from kahm and mould. Once they have been submerged for a while, the vegetables are usually coated with microbes and the fermentation process should continue unaffected.

It has been reported that the late addition of more brine to a ferment can result in soggy sauerkraut. Once the fermentation period is complete, if you open the lid and press down hard, you will find that the brine is still there! To avoid this happening, try to ensure that you carry out your fermentation as near to 18°C as possible, and leave a little space for the liquid to rise, without being forced out of the jar. Using the bag-of-brine system, which can rise and fall with the volume in the jar, can alleviate this problem.

Development of Mould

If you think that mould is present, follow the advice on page 111.

Taste and Smell

If this is your first time tasting sauerkraut, please do not be put off by the sulphurous smell that will first emerge. This is due to the breakdown products of the glycosinolates, which are extremely important bioactive compounds. Your sauerkraut should also have a vinegary smell that slightly catches at the back of your throat, although it will not be as strong as that of actual vinegar. Tastewise, after three weeks, your cabbage should now be crunchy, squeaky and tangy. If you prefer a softer consistency and more complex flavours, keep it at room temperature, where the process will continue more rapidly than in the fridge. Some people never refrigerate their sauerkraut, preferring an ever-evolving ferment, while others store it near the back of the fridge to slow down any further microbial action.

What to Do with Your Sauerkraut

It is a fact universally acknowledged that sauerkraut goes with everything. Here are the top 5 things to do with it:

1. Use as a condiment with spaghetti bolognese, frittata, dal, falafel, hot dogs, wraps, cheese and biscuits.

Method:

1. Blitz the sauerkraut in a blender, or chop very finely. It should resemble little bits of coconut; you do not want stringy bits of cabbage.
2. Blend the sugar and butter until fluffy.
3. Add the eggs one at a time, alternately with a spoonful of flour.
4. Mix the remaining flour and cocoa powder together, and add alternately a spoonful at a time with the water, vanilla extract and coffee.
5. Place in a deep 8-inch (20-cm) lined cake tin.
6. Cook for 45 minutes at 180°C/160 fan, or until a skewer comes out clean.
7. Top with kefir icing (*see* page 75).

● ●

Additions and Adjustments to Plain Sauerkraut

Adding Flavour: Mixed 'Krauts'

Plain sauerkraut is delicious, but there are good reasons for adding flavour too. You can add an endless array of vegetables, including carrots, onions, garlic, beetroot, other types of cabbage, and fennel, and there are significant additional health benefits. Remember the '30 a week' concept? If you have a mixed kraut with five vegetables and some spices, then every spoonful will provide a variety of five to seven different types.

When making mixtures, the general rule is that the greater the variety, the more rapidly it will ferment. Kimchi, for example, which contains over 10 different ingredients, is often ready for fridge-ripening after just three days. A four- to six-week fermentation for red cabbage on its own can be reduced to about 10 days with the addition of fennel and white cabbage. This speeding up of the fermentation is due to a more diverse source of nutrients from the different vegetables, and an increased number of species of LAB too. Greater diversity also means potentially more biologically active, health-enhancing end products. As a general rule of thumb, consider the recommended

2. Put it in a toastie (*see* recipe for kimcheese toastie on page 163).
3. Mix a spoonful in with some coleslaw.
4. Top with some sesame oil, a touch of soy sauce, toasted sesame seeds, grated ginger and coriander for an oriental-style salad.
5. Make a surprisingly delicious sauerkraut cake (the probiotics will not survive, but it is so intriguing it is worth a try. And it will be full of fibre!).

● ●

SAUERKRAUT CAKE

Ingredients:

100g rinsed sauerkraut
200g sugar
150g butter
3 eggs
280g self-raising flour
75g cocoa powder
1 teaspoon vanilla extract
1 teaspoon coffee
275ml of water

All the colours of the rainbow – a range of mixed ferments that will all be much quicker than plain sauerkraut.

fermentation times of the individual vegetables you are using (based on texture), and check the mixture after the shortest recommended time (*see* page 166).

As an example, a mixed ferment with red cabbage (28 days alone), hispi cabbage (five days), carrot (five days), spring onion (five days), red onion (seven days), chilli and a squeeze of lime juice can be ready to eat in just five to seven days.

Minor Adjustments to Plain Sauerkraut

Additions of tiny amounts of flavouring will not have much impact on fermentation time. A white cabbage sauerkraut can be much enhanced by the addition of herbs and/or spices – for example, chilli; lemon zest, ginger and turmeric; dill and garlic; juniper and clove; cumin, garlic, black pepper;

PROCESS FOR ALL SELF BRINING FERMENTED VEGETABLES

CHOP
WASH
WEIGH
2% SALT
MASSAGE
SUBMERGE
FERMENT

Rules for brine-fermented vegetables.

seaweed; or wild garlic – but fermentation will still take about three weeks.

When following the mixed ferment process, you do not really need to weigh the odd chilli garlic or herb, as they will not make much impact on the salt you need to add.

Rainbow Ferment

One alternative idea is to make a rainbow layered ferment, putting the veggies that will take the longest

Rainbow ferment.

at the bottom and then layering up accordingly. The method varies from the norm only in that the different ingredients are kept separate in order to achieve the 'rainbow' effect.

Suggested ingredients (about 100g of each) are courgettes, white cabbage, grated carrot, sweetcorn, radishes, red pepper and red cabbage.

Method:

1. Wash and weigh the ingredients into separate bowls, adding 2% salt into each.
2. Squeeze the cabbages and carrots to release the brine. Gently toss the other ingredients in the salt.
3. Layer into your jar with the red cabbage at the bottom. Add the rest of the vegetables, top up with the brine and submerge, using the palest brine first to maintain the colour. Over the period of fermentation, the colours will meld a little, but the layers should still be discernible.
4. Try after 5–7 days, and refrigerate when done to your satisfaction.

El Salvadorian Curtido
This lovely zingy creation deserves a mention, as it is an example of how quickly fermentation can proceed when pH-lowering additions are made. In this case, the addition of lime reduces the fermentation time to about three days.

CURTIDO

For a 1ltr jar you will need the following.

Ingredients:

Approx. 1kg hispi cabbage
3 spring onions in slices including greens
3 carrots, grated
Half a garlic clove, crushed
1 hot red chilli, deseeded and finely sliced (or to taste)
Juice of 1 lime
2 tbsp dried or fresh oregano
Salt (2% w/v)

SAUERKRAUTATHON

In 2018, two of the south-west England's premier fermenters, Jo Webster and Katie Venner, organized a successful attempt on the Guinness World Record for the largest vat of sauerkraut ever made. At the so-called Sauerkrautathon, in Wells in Somerset, the two managed to produce a record-breaking quantity of 357kg. Below is the recipe 1kg of the fennel sauerkraut that was used for the challenge:

FENNEL SAUERKRAUT

Ingredients:
Approx. 500g white cabbage
200g red cabbage
100g fennel
1 tbsp fennel seeds
Sea salt (2%)

Carrots and Ginger
Avoid overly sweet and watery carrots as they will turn to mush rapidly. You might also prefer to 'julienne' them instead of grating, which gives a little more texture, although it is time-consuming. For 1kg of carrots (peeled if they are grubby, and grated), add 25g of ginger (grated) and 2% sea salt. Ferment for four to seven days.

Kohlrabi, Celeriac, Apple and Mustard Seed Kraut
This kraut is a fabulous way to use that most underrated brassica, kohlrabi. Ferment for seven to 10 days. For a litre jar use 400g kohlrabi, use 400g celeriac, 200g apple, half a tablespoon of mustard seeds and 2% sea salt.

PICKLED LEMONS

Pickled lemons are a staple of Middle Eastern cuisine, with a very distinctive flavour. For most fermenters

who have discovered them, no fridge is complete without a jar. There is a belief that they are a probiotic powerhouse, but this is not backed up by firm scientific evidence. Two sets of Moroccan researchers found that microbial production of carbon dioxide was pronounced during the first few days of fermentation, but after about 10 days it dropped off rapidly, probably due to the extremely low pH killing the LAB. After four weeks, there were no LAB remaining, although some yeasts associated with lemons could tolerate 15% salt concentrations.[75] Still, fermented lemon peel is rich in flavonoids, hesperidin, which is a compound that might have anti-allergenic effects, and organic acids – so pickled lemons are still good for you![76]

The traditional way of making pickled lemons is to pack them in 10–15% salt, which draws juice out of the lemon by osmosis. This allows diffusion of fructose, glucose and sucrose in almost equal amounts into the medium, which also contains about 40% citric acid. It seems that the citric acid is metabolised in preference to the sugars and that, even after many months, some sugars will be left in the jar.

Fermented lemons are the most acidic fermented food (in terms of pH), even more so than kombucha. After a month or so, they will be effectively salt-cured and will last for a very long time.

When choosing lemons, it is definitely an advantage to go for unwaxed fruit, the more fragrant the better.

Whole Fermented Lemons

In this method, adding some extra lemon juice will help things along, although this is not strictly speaking necessary. You can wait until the lemons have released some of their own juice and then rearrange them, but really, the less often you open the jar, the better.

WHOLE FERMENTED LEMONS

Ingredients:

Enough whole lemons to fill your jar
10% sea salt
Spare 2 or 3 lemons, if extra juice needed

Method:
1. Weigh lemons and juice.
2. Weigh out 10% salt.
3. Cut lemons in quarters four-fifths of the way through, but do not separate into pieces.

4. Sprinkle salt inside the lemons, sharing roughly equally.
5. Squeeze lemons into the jar as tightly as possible. Cut some into halves to fill in the gaps if necessary.
6. Pour over lemon juice, assessing how much you have added.
7. Add 10% salt for the quantity added – so 5g if you add 50ml.
8. Add submerging device and leave for 1 month at room temperature.

The principle of preserving lemons in this way applies to all citrus fruits, and you can also mix and match. If you are fermenting limes alone, though, be aware that the skins are often quite tough, so covering with extra lime juice really will help. Limes can take months longer to reach the same consistency as lemons and oranges, but will catch up eventually.

Quick and Easy Lacto-Fermented Lemons

This is a highly practical and quick method to produce a kitchen staple. They can be ready in 10 days.

Method:
1. Slice lemons finely, about 3–5mm thick, and pick out the pips.
2. Weigh into a bowl.
3. Calculate 10% salt, add and stir in.
4. Compress into a jar – the lemon juice will easily cover the lemons.
5. Submerge them using the device of your choice.

6. Leave at room temperature for about 10 days.
7. Refrigerate.

FERMENTED SAUCES

Using Chillies and Peppers

Most chillies and all red pepper varieties are part of the genus *Capsicum annuum*. The anti-cholesterol, anti-hypertensive, anti-diabetic and anti-obesity effects of various chillies and peppers have been noted in various experiments, and, in one human trial, eating fermented red pepper paste for 12 weeks had a cholesterol-modulating effect, compared with a placebo group. Probiotic microbes and colourful carotenoids would help to enhance this effect.[77]

As you will be having only a spoonful or two of the fermented sauce, the nutritional effects will not be huge, but it will pack a huge punch flavour-wise – indeed, there are entire books and online forums dedicated to their creation.

If you have a glut of home-grown chillies, they can be used in any combination according to how hot you would like your sauce. The fermentation process rarely mollifies the heat of a hot chilli, so what you start with largely reflects what you will end up with. If you do not have your own supply and are baulking at the cost of buying a kilo of chillies, use red peppers and a few very hot chillies to achieve a similar effect. You can also use dried chillies, but they might take up to three weeks to be fully fermented and reconstituted. They will also need some real vegetables in there as well, to ensure

Mash Ferment vs Brined Ferment Pros and Cons

Mash Ferment	Brined Ferment
'Funkier', more complex taste	Cleaner, more predictable taste
Easier to judge final heat, by tasting before fermenting	Trickier to judge how hot it will be, as chillies added separately
Very simple: mash and leave	Requires straining and blending
Can be an unpredictable ferment	Well-behaved fermentation
Hard to alter consistency	Consistency may be adjusted

CHILLIES

Capsaicin, the active hot component of chilli peppers, is a phytochemical produced by the fruits, probably as a deterrent to animals and pathogens. It is present in highest quantities in the white pith inside, called the placenta, not in the seeds, as most people think. The capsaicin mixes with saliva in the mouth and binds to special receptors, or TVRP1s, on the tongue, which are actually there to detect physical heat. The receptors are activated and send a signal to the brain, which identifies a burning sensation. Birds, unlike mammals, do not have TVRP1 receptors, which allows the dispersal of chilli seeds and the spreading of the species across parts of the world.

Human responses to eating chilli include dilation of the pupils and a release of adrenaline. Hard-core chilli eaters even claim that it can lead to the production of endorphins.

Chilli 'heat' is measured in Scoville units, on a scale developed by Wilbur Scoville in 1912. At first, the rating was done simply by taste, but now high-pressure liquid chromatography (HPLC) is used. Those chillies that are easily available in the shops, with a 'two pepper' rating, are usually about 500SHU. The hottest chilli in the world, the Carolina Reaper, comes in at 1,570,000SHU. Eating one of these has caused serious acute damage, but even so, people still regularly post videos of themselves online.

Chillies and peppers frequently contain as part of their natural flora many of the usual beneficial bacterial suspects, including *Leuconostoc mesenteroides*, *Lactobacillus plantarum*, and *Weisella* sp.

that there are enough viable LAB to get the process started.

There are two methods for producing a fermented chilli or pepper sauce: the first involves making a mash (*see* below), which requires only vegetables and salt; the second is brine-fermenting whole vegetables (*see* page 149). Curiously, the taste does differ according to the method used, probably relating to the surface area of the substrate and how nutrient availability affects the fermentation. *See* opposite for a comparison to help you choose (although it is always worth trying both).

Mash Ferment

Choosing the right vessel for mash fermenting can be a challenge, as the pepper or chilli mash is mixed up with its own brine and cannot easily be submerged. As a fairly explosive ferment it also does better in an environment where the carbon dioxide can escape. A clip-top jar will need regular venting, or securing with a rubber band instead of the clip. One good option is a vented jar, with a circle of baking parchment placed on the top to prevent the mash getting stuck in the valve. Alternatively, you can forget the venting altogether and use a bag of brine seal with a normal jar, or a sturdy ziplock bag, and open the corner of it to vent.

For a mild sauce, use mostly red peppers and about three jalapeños. For a hotter sauce, increase the number of chillies or use mostly red peppers and three or four bird's-eye chillies. One of the joys of this method is that you can taste the mash to gauge the heat, and amend if necessary *before* you start fermenting.

If you are using mostly bell or Ramiro peppers, a good way to intensify their flavour is to grill three-quarters of them and let them cool. This might sound like cheating, but it is strongly recommended, as the more concentrated flavour really does help. You can remove the blackened skins before adding them in, to avoid spoiling the colour of the finished sauce. As long as you have predominantly fresh ingredients in the jar, and remember to cool the peppers first, fermentation will still continue with gusto.

PEPPERS

Red peppers have been left the longest to ripen on the vine and contain more than 10 times the beta carotene and more vitamin C than green peppers. A rumour exists that all peppers are exactly the same variety, in different stages of ripeness. This is not the case, although all yellow, red and orange peppers do begin as green peppers.

• •

FERMENTED CHILLI AND PEPPER SAUCE

Fermented chilli sauce packs a punch and lasts for months and months in the fridge.

Ingredients:

800g red peppers and chillies in any combination, chopped; stems removed (and pith and pips from peppers)
100g chopped pineapple
1 large bulb of garlic, peeled
2% sea salt (20g/kg)

Method:

1. If using: grill 600g of bell peppers until their skins are black. Place in a covered bowl to cool (this helps the skins to loosen). Remove skins.
2. Wash and weigh all ingredients including cooked peppers, and record weight.
3. Add 2% salt.
4. Blitz all ingredients in a blender until a thick paste is formed.
5. Taste to assess heat and flavour, then pour into vessel of choice.
6. Leave at cool room temperature for 7–10 days. If it tastes sweet and tangy, it is ready. If the weather is warm, 7 days at room temperature will be enough, and fridge-ripening is recommended, either before or after bottling.
7. Avoiding opening for 7 days, to reduce risk of kahm yeast.
8. When you like the flavour, you can either bottle it as it is, blitz again in the blender to make it smoother, or strain out any seeds and skins with a fine sieve for a perfectly smooth sauce.
9. Decant with a funnel into 'dishwasher-clean' bottles, and refrigerate.

It will last for months, and will improve with keeping.

• •

Troubleshooting

Mash Separates During Fermentation

This is quite normal and makes no difference to the fermentation – the carbon dioxide generated by the LABs gets trapped in the vegetable matter and makes it float to the top. As long as a self-venting valve is not blocked through the movement of the mash, do not open it for seven days. After this time, you can give it a stir if you like.

Lack of Flavour

If the sauce seems to lack flavour, put it at the back of the fridge and forget about it for three months, then try it again. You may be pleasantly surprised!

Chilli saucegate – it can be a feisty ferment. It might be better to repurpose a pour and store bag.

Appearance of Kahm Yeast

If there is a thin film of kahm yeast, it can be removed with a spoon. If it is a thick pellicle, the ferment should be discarded. Next time, keep your ferments where you can see them, so that you can spot the early appearance of kahm.

LACTO-FERMENTED PULSES AND LEGUMES

Pulses – chickpeas, haricots, broad beans, peas, borlottis, butter beans, and so on – are the seeds of plants of the *Leguminosae*, hence their common name, legumes. After grains, they are the next most important food source in the world: tiny nutritional powerhouses, full of minerals, prebiotic oligosaccharides, resistant starch, proteins, B vitamins, and up to a hundred phytochemicals. There is a great deal of interest in pulses as sustainable crops for the future. As they grow, they fix nitrogen into the soil, decreasing the need for additional fertilizers and thus reducing greenhouse emissions associated with their use.

The downside of pulses is that they also contain phytic acid, which serves a purpose to the legume as the major storage form of phosphorus, but is known as an 'anti-nutrient' for humans. It binds to minerals such as calcium, iron and zinc, and stops them being absorbed in the human gut. Soaking, cooking, sprouting and fermenting legumes are all ways of reducing the phytic acid content. Adding some vitamin C can also have the same effect, which is why it is common to add a squeeze of lime or lemon juice to dahl before eating it. After soaking and cooking, legumes become much more digestible and nutritious; fermenting takes it one step further, and turns them into a vehicle for the delivery of a healthy dose of probiotics.

Before fermenting, legumes must be cooked first. This will kill the LABs that are needed for the fermentation process, so you will have to add some. Fermenting cooked foods is the only circumstance in which you will need to add a starter culture to provide some LAB. There are two potential sources: either fresh (probiotic-rich) vegetable fermentation brine or strained kefir whey. A couple of spoonsful of starter will introduce several million microbes into the pot.

Salt must still be added, even though the substrate is cooked. Some bacteria can form resilient spores (such as *Clostridium botulinum*, *Bacillus cereus*), which can withstand cooking, and salt provides protection until the lactic acid production kicks in.

You can very successfully use tinned or tetra-packed pulses, but if they have added preservatives fermentation simply will not work. This is understandable, as the additives (often sulphites) are added to ensure that the product lasts and does not soften. Those without additives, including organic varieties, which usually contain just water, will be fine. In fact, in comparison with home-cooked chickpeas, it is more or less impossible to tell the difference.

The fermentation of legumes is further complicated by the presence of their thick waxy seed-coat or testa, which is pretty impenetrable for the LABs. The easiest way around this is to purée or at least roughly crush the legumes, to help the process get started.

● ●

LACTO-FERMENTED HUMMUS

Ingredients:

500g of your pulse of choice; either home-cooked and cooled, or canned and rinsed (in water only)
50ml old brine/milk kefir whey
1 garlic clove (crushed; optional)
2% salt (so approx. 20g)
20ml lemon juice (optional)

Method:

1. Weigh all ingredients together, calculate 2% salt and add.
2. Mix all the ingredients, crushing with a potato masher for a rough texture, or blitzing in a food processor for a smoother paste.

3. Pack firmly into a jar, leaving just a small amount of headroom. With such a short fermentation time, the inclusion of a starter culture, and the thickness of the paste, contamination problems are unlikely.

4. Ferment at room temperature for 3 to 4 days. With the starter brine it tends to get going rapidly and air pockets should be visible within 24 hours.

5. After 3 or 4 days, it should smell and taste pleasantly vinegary.

6. Refrigerate. It will keep for months and can be readily mixed with tahini, olive oil and any other flavourings for almost-instant hummus.

Note: do not put oil or tahini in before you ferment the legumes, just in case pockets of oil form, which would not ferment properly. It is extremely unlikely, but it might happen.

CHAPTER 8

BRINED FERMENTATION

In brined fermentation, the vegetables will be kept intact and recognizable, as a brine solution is added to them, rather than being extracted from them. The end product will be perfect for side dishes and for providing an instant probiotic snack, and the process is simple enough to do almost daily. It can also be scaled up or down, to suit the smallest or the largest pile of ingredients or vessel.

HOW MUCH SALT?

A debate rages on online fermentation forums about the 'correct' brine concentration to use for vegetables prepared in this way. As with every method, salt is very important. The most commonly cited brine concentration is 3.5%, but there is a reason why that is not always efficient or accurate. Remember, for self-brining ferments, the concentration is 2% salt.

To think about calculating the amount of salt needed, imagine a large jar of 1ltr capacity, with 500g carrots, topped up with 500ml of a 3.5% brine solution (35g/ltr). The jar will contain 17.5g of salt, 500g of water and 500g carrots. This gives a final salt concentration of 1.75%.

Then imagine the jar is crammed with 800g carrots, leaving space for only 200ml of 3.5% brine. That will give 7g of salt (in 200ml of 3.5% brine there are 200/1000 x 35g = 7g of salt) in the jar. Considering the total weight of water and carrots, 1,000g, this gives a final salt concentration of just 0.7%.

A salt concentration of 0.7% is not high enough. (When making some self-brining sauerkraut, for example, for 800g of cabbage, there would be 16g of salt in the same jar, at a concentration of 2%.) At just 0.7%, there is no guarantee that the LAB will be able to outcompete other less desirable species. It could result in soggy ferments and the formation of kahm yeast. It is not enough salt to make the vegetables taste nice either.

To avoid these problems, simply add 2% salt to account for the weight of everything in the jar, whether water or vegetable, as follows:

1. Zero the jar on the scales.
2. Put vegetables in the jar.
3. Top up with water to shoulder height.
4. Note the total weight and calculate 2%. For example, if the total weight is 960g, the salt required to make 2% solution = 960 × 2/100 = 19.2g. (Strictly speaking, you should now remove 19.2ml of water from the jar to make the w/v ratio correct, but this level of precision is not vital.)
5. Now, either add the salt directly to the jar if there is room to stir it in, or tip some of the water out of the vessel into a jug, dissolve the salt in it by stirring, then tip it back.

TORSHI (MIXED PICKLED VEGETABLES)

Mixed brined vegetables have their origins in ancient traditions in the East, and many countries have their own version, to which vinegar or lemon juice may also be added. They are widely known as 'torshi', from the Persian word *torsh*, meaning 'sour', and have a number of slightly different names in different regions – for example, *tursu* in Turkish, or *turshiya* in Bulgarian. They are usually served as a starter, meze or side dish.

Golden and choggia beet kvass with the leftovers.

calculating the salt, they will stay crispy in their brine for several weeks. You can even include some of the more difficult to ferment vegetables, such as chopped kale or spring greens.

Torshi Shoor Method

This is more of a method than a recipe, any combination of vegetables and spices can be used, but the one below is fairly typical. Depending on the variety, the dark purple of the aubergine skin can sometimes make the whole ferment a very pretty pink! Ensure that dense vegetables are cut so that no surface is thicker than about a centimetre, which will help with osmosis and salt transfer, important for flavour and fermentation.

Recipes often include the addition of vinegar, but it is recommended that you let nature alone take its course. Although LAB do produce some acetic acid themselves, high concentrations can inhibit them and adding more could potentially interfere with the probiotic balance of the ferment. You could use some lemon juice instead; some LAB can even convert citric acid to lactic acid.

Almost all vegetables are suitable for mixed brine-fermenting and, if you use the suggested method for

Ingredients:

Half a cauliflower, cut into teaspoon-sized florets, including stems
Aubergine, cut into chunks or fat slices
1 courgette, cut into semi-circles
5 cloves of garlic
1 firm red pepper, cut into chunks or strips
1 stick of celery, sliced
Coriander seeds
Bay leaf
Peppercorns
Salt

Method:

1. Rinse and prep the vegetables.
2. Weigh them into a mason jar with the seasonings.
3. Fill with water to shoulder height.
4. Weigh and calculate 2% salt of total.
5. Use longer pieces of vegetable to rest under the shoulders of the jar to keep others submerged (you could improvise with a celery 'gate'). Weights will not work unless the jar is very well packed, as they will just fall to the bottom.
6. Leave at room temperature for 5 days, then taste; leave for longer if desired.

Torshi shoor – any combination of vegetables seems to give delicious results!

Refrigerate. They will keep well for several weeks.

Cloudiness and the formation of a sediment are completely normal.

Signs of Fermentation

For all brined vegetable ferments, after a few days, you will notice that the brine is cloudy and that the chlorophyll of the green vegetables has faded, as those vibrant vegetable greens are broken down in acid environments. These are completely normal signs of fermentation. Over the next few days, bacterial cells, plant matter, yeasts and phytochemicals that are visible in the brine will eventually settle into a sediment at the bottom. This is also completely normal and it can be a few millimetres thick in a jar of pickles.

Green Brine-Fermented Chilli and Pepper Sauce

This is the brine-fermented method for chilli sauce and pepper sauce, an alternative to the mash method described on page 141. For this recipe, add in a couple of yellow peppers, as they are much sweeter than green ones. The colour will still be green-ish overall, but will lose its vibrancy

during the process. This is a much easier ferment to look after, as it is not as explosive as a pepper mash, so is recommended if you are too busy to be attentive.

● ●

GREEN BRINE-FERMENTED CHILLI AND PEPPER SAUCE

Ingredients:

About 800g of any combination of green/ yellow peppers and chillies
2 shallots
2 lemongrass stalks, chopped
8 garlic cloves, peeled
1 inch of ginger, chopped
1 inch of galangal, if available

Method:

1. Wash and weigh all ingredients into a 1ltr jar. (You will need to gauge the heat of the chillies, as you will not have a homogenized mash to taste. Remove the stems, seeds and pith from the peppers, and the stems from the chillies.)
2. Cover with water and note final weight.

Green chilli and pepper sauce when first set up; (top left) after 10 days at room temperature, when the brine has gone cloudy and the vegetables have faded; and (below) with roasted butternut squash.

3. Add 2% salt for the total weight of the jar.
4. After 10–14 days, the brine will have become cloudy and the green peppers and chillies will have faded. Check the jar for a spicy vinegary smell, and then taste.
5. Strain the contents of the jar through a sieve into a jug. Keep the brine.
6. Remove the lemongrass and blitz the vegetables in a blender or food processor.
7. Add in a little of the brine to achieve your desired consistency.
8. For a completely smooth sauce, strain or mill it before bottling.
9. Place in dishwasher-clean bottles.

Refrigerate. It will keep for months.

• •

Gherkins with their flowers attached. It is advisable to cut off the flowering ends, just in case there are detrimental enzymes present.

Brine-Pickled Cucumbers or Gherkins

Without a well-established culture of fermentation, it is hard to imagine pickled cucumbers as anything other than those deliciously sweet, tart, yet lifeless creations in jars on supermarket shelves. They are completely dead, of course, as they have been pasteurized for storage purposes. A large gherkin or pickled cucumber contains approximately half a teaspoon of sugar, so it makes a nice sweet snack.

There is, however, another way: brine-pickling gherkins has been popular in Eastern Europe for centuries, and spread to the USA with the arrival of Polish immigrants in the 1880s. They are known as half or full sour pickles, or kosher dill pickles, and are a speciality in many a New York delicatessen.

The difference between a large gherkin and a small cucumber is sometimes hard to spot. They are both varieties of *Cucumis sativus*, but you should always try to use a pickling variety if you have any choice, as they are bred to have denser flesh, with smaller pips and less bitter skins. They can be either rough or smooth, depending on the variety.

The process of brine-fermenting cucumbers has a reputation for being tricky, but there are a number of ways of increasing your chances of success:

1. Always use very fresh fruits; if you can harvest them yourself, that is even better. Do taste them before you start. Remember, you cannot ferment away bitterness.
2. Remove the flowering end of the cucumber. Enzymes sometimes present in the flowering ends can break down the pectin and cellulose cell walls and make them soggy.
3. Add a source of tannin that can inhibit the enzymes – vine, oak, horseradish or tea leaves or a teabag will suffice. Even a teabag will have little impact on the flavour.
4. A lower temperature and a slower fermentation seem to produce the best results, so do not attempt the process if it is 30 degrees outside, unless you have a contingency plan for keeping them cool. Putting them in a cool box with a jug of cold water works well. In Romania, they bury brined cucumbers in the ground from August to October, to protect them from the heat!
5. Use a jar with an airlock. Sometimes the carbon dioxide that is formed displaces the insubstantial seed tissue in the middle of the cucumbers and they end up being hollow. This seems to happen especially if the gas cannot escape.
6. Prick the cucumbers with a pin. Sometimes after 5 days, the brine will not have reached the

middle of the cucumber, so fermentation will be incomplete and patchy. Pricking them helps this along, and ensures that the process occurs as quickly as possible, before any sogginess can take hold.

Before and after brine-pickled gherkins.

BRINE-PICKLED GHERKINS

Ingredients (for a 1ltr mason jar):

800g gherkins, fresh as possible, washed and scrubbed to remove any hairs
5 garlic cloves, sliced
1 stick of celery, sliced (optional)
2–3 tablespoons of pickling spice (or coriander, peppercorn, fennel)
Large handful of fresh dill
2 or 3 vine, oak or horseradish leaves, or a teabag
Sea salt

When they are completely translucent on the inside, pop them in the fridge, where they will ripen over the next 3 weeks or so. They should keep for many months without deterioration.

Method:

1. Cut the flowering ends off your cucumbers. If you are not sure which end this is, cut off both ends just to be on the safe side. Decide whether you are going to cut your cucumbers into slices, strips, or leave them whole.
2. Place the vine leaves in the bottom of the jar with the spices.
3. Weigh the cucumbers into the jar.
4. Add water to shoulder level.
   Note total weight and calculate 2% salt, then add.
5. Use a suitable device to keep the cucumbers under the brine (for example, a cucumber that rests across the top and under the shoulders, or a repurposed plastic lid).
6. Leave somewhere cool for 3 days then remove one to examine it. Smell first, for signs of vinegariness, then cut a small piece off. Inside should be translucent, without any pale patches. If it is not ready, leave for another 48 hours before checking again.

It is very simple to ferment sprouts and the process adds a delicious vinegary note that covers up their taste, which is sometimes described as a bit 'worthy'.

FERMENTED SPROUTED SEEDS AND PULSES

A germinating seed is in a highly active state of nutritional excitement and full of phytochemicals. Sprouting legumes, pulses and seeds is also one of the best ways of reducing their phytic acid content and making them more digestible. You can sprout your own (always use seeds specifically designed for home sprouting) or purchase some fresh from a reliable source. To increase their nutritional impact even further, fermenting them makes them probiotic, can remove even more phytic acid, and potentially negate the minor risk of pathogenic bacteria being present in them. The process could not be simpler, using the standard brine calculation and method. Flavour can be added by mixing in with the sprouts before putting them in the jar.

• •

CURRIED FERMENTED SPROUTS

Ingredients (for a ½ litre jar):

500g sprouted seeds/legumes/pulses
1 tsp curry powder
1 tsp turmeric powder
½ tsp black pepper
2 tsp grated ginger
½ crushed garlic clove
Sea salt

Method:
1. Weigh all ingredients into the jar.
2. Add water to cover, to shoulder of jar.
3. Add sea salt (2% total weight of water and sprouts).
4. Submerge and leave to ferment for 5 days at room temperature.

• •

A Russian truck selling rye bread kvass.

KVASS

Kvass, perhaps even more so than vodka, is Russia's national drink, with origins stretching back 1,000 years. Yellow kvass tanks can be found street-side and it is a huge commercial business today, with the huge multinationals Pepsi and Coca-Cola in on the action. Traditionally, it has been made by fermenting rye bread with added yeast, herbs and spices, and contains about 2.5% alcohol. It has for many years been given to children from a young age, and a recent article has suggested that this practice could be a contributory factor in the incidence of chronic alcoholism in Russia.[78]

The recipe below is for the poor relation of bread kvass – beet kvass. Despite not having made the big time, beet kvass has remained a staple of Russian home cooking. Indeed, it is said that, when harvests were poor, it kept whole villages alive.

Research has shown the potential of beet kvass as a powerful health tonic, with improved clinical outcomes for pathologies including hypertension, type 2 diabetes and even dementia.[79] Beetroot is a particularly nutrient-dense vegetable, rich in vitamin C and phytochemicals, while its colourful pigments contain potent antioxidants and anti-inflammatories, as well as food for gut microbes. It contains high levels of inorganic nitrates, which can be converted in the body to nitric oxide, a very important messenger molecule. 'In vitro' anti-cancer activity has also been

The original and best, with the most concentrated pigments for a nutrient-dense tonic.

Refrigerate and either drink straight away, or leave to develop for up to a month. If you place it in a suitable bottle, over this time it might well become deliciously carbonated, although usually not explosively fizzy. Kvass is usually taken as a shot in the morning and/or evening. Using choggia or golden varieties of beetroot will produce a much sweeter drink, which some would describe as more palatable. However, it will not have the benefit of the higher concentration of phytochemicals in red beets.

demonstrated with gastric cancer cells.[64] Fermentation conserves levels of phytochemicals even during storage, and kvass aficionados often say it improves with age. Add this to the additional benefits of the probiotic LAB, and other bioactive compounds, and it could be that kvass out-does all other fermented drinks! It does not have a high alcohol content.

• •

BEET KVASS

Ingredients (for 1ltr mason jar):

250–300g of washed, diced beetroot (not grated, as that would mean too much sugar in the end product), or red carrots, or a mixture of the two
Several peppercorns and a bay leaf
Salt (2%)
Water

The beauty of a choggia beet cannot be denied, and the kvass produced from it is delicious, even though it is less nutritious than the other types.

Method:

1. Weigh vegetables and aromatics into jar.
2. Cover with water.
   Note total weight and calculate 2% salt.
3. Add salt and stir.
4. Leave to ferment for 5–7 days at room temperature.
5. Strain to remove beets and ripen the kvass in the fridge. You can eat the fermented beets too!

• •

PROCESS FOR ALL BRINED FERMENTS

PREP VEG
WASH
WEIGH INTO VESSEL
ADD WATER
NOTE TOTAL WEIGHT
CALCULATE 2% SALT
TIP WATER INTO A JUG AND MIX WITH SALT
TIP BACK INTO VESSEL
SUBMERGE VEGETABLES
FERMENT

The process for making brined ferments.

CHAPTER 9

KIMCHI AND OTHER PASTE-WRAPPED FERMENTS

The final method for lacto-fermentation applies to relatively few named ferments, but can be easily adapted to your own ideas. Coating vegetables in a sauce is an excellent way of recreating a more relish-like consistency and transferring flavour to every component, while ensuring that a rich mixture of nutrients is available for every microbe. These ferments happen quickly, usually within three days. Heavy on the ingredients, they are also heavyweights in the diversity-diet stakes. Every mouthful will provide numerous different sources of fibre for your gut microbes.

KIMCHI

Kimchi is the king of the ferments. First, its influence has been significant enough to define the culinary heritage of Korea; second, if it is made in the authentic way, it does not quite follow the rules; and, third, its taste is quite unique. People either love or hate it, but few are unmoved by it. A fiery mixture of vegetables, red pepper powder, ginger, garlic and often seafood in a starchy paste, it reaches the parts other ferments cannot reach, with umami, salt, sweet, sour, spicy flavours all at once.

Korean Origins

Cultural appropriation is sometimes an issue with the widespread dissemination of foods that have an emblematic status in their territory of origin. The South Korean government is seemingly delighted that kimchi is now firmly on the world food map, but it is important to take it as seriously as it is taken in that country. There is a dedicated research centre – the World Institute of Kimchi – and in 2013 UNESCO added South Korea's 'Kimjang: Making and Sharing Kimchi' to its World Intangible Cultural Heritage list. According to that text, 'late autumn is Kimjang season, when communities collectively make and share large quantities of kimchi to ensure that every household has enough to sustain it through the long, harsh winter'.

The annual kimchi-making festival came about because of a naturally occurring cycle: spring was the season of fermenting seafood, in late summer, the gochu peppers were harvested, and in early autumn, the cabbages and daikon radish would be ready. These days, when everything can be available all year round, the timing is less important, but the tradition still stands, and kimchi is still stored in pots (known as onggi) on roofs and in gardens throughout the winter.

Winters in Korea are cold and harsh, and kimchi probably has its origins in a time when planning

Korean pots, or onggi, that have traditionally used for storing kimchi.

KIMCHI ETYMOLOGY

Kimchi is the Korean name for seasoned preserved vegetables, possibly derived from *gimchi* and previously *chimchae* in an ancient Korean language. In Korean, it looks like this:

김치

nourishment and the storage of food through the season was essential for survival. It can be traced back to the era of the three kingdoms of Korea, around 2,000 years ago, when it was observed that cabbage lasted longer when mixed with red pepper powder. The recipe for kimchi has been passed down via verbal communication for generations. These days there are at least 200 different named varieties, as well as countless home-made variants.

Today, kimchi remains an essential part of every Korean meal, transcending class and regional differences. It is not unusual for Koreans to consume 200–300 grams daily. It does not even need to be fermented, although the health benefits of doing so are unquestionable.

Baechu Kimchi

Kimchi is a mixed ferment that is a winner in terms of dietary diversity, as each mouthful contains an extraordinary variety, with as many as 10 different vegetables. The traditional baechu (cabbage) kimchi is a good ferment to use as an example, as this is the version that is most commonly eaten and made in both Korea and the UK. Each variety also has its own subdivisions; in baechu kimchi, these subdivisions are categorized according to how the cabbage is cut. For long storage, for example, the cabbage is cut into wedges, with a smaller cut surface area; for more rapid consumption, a 'table kimchi' of chopped cabbage can be made.

Making kimchi requires three stages, but that should not deter you, as they can interweave quite nicely.

Ingredients for Kimchi

Napa Cabbage

Napa cabbage, or Chinese leaf lettuce as it is often called in the UK, has been a staple of Korean agriculture for centuries. Although it looks like a lettuce, it is actually part of the *Brassica* family, with surprisingly robust stems, yet easily wilted leaves.

Gochugaru

The element of kimchi that imparts its unique taste is Korean red pepper powder, gochugaru. Korean peppers (gochu), are members of the species *Capsicum annuum*, which also includes paprika and Sichuan pepper. Gochu pepper has a rating of usually <1,500 on the Scoville heat unit scale (very mild in comparison with bird's-eye chilli, for example). It is spicy with notes of paprika (especially when you smell it), without being excessively hot.

All the plant-based components of your kimchi – add fish sauce, fermented shrimp or seaweed if you like.

There is some debate over whether the gochu pepper was introduced in 1592 during the Japanese invasion of Korea, from Mexico, or whether it was already in cultivation in the three kingdoms, centuries earlier. The evidence suggests that it has always been part of kimchi – had it been introduced later, perhaps 'red kimchi' would have been differentiated from an earlier 'white kimchi', but this does not seem to have occurred in the literature. White kimchi seems to be mentioned only in the context of distinguishing it from normal kimchi.[80] Unfortunately, research on the matter is somewhat stymied by the lack of a written Korean language before 1443.

A close-up of gochugaru, the Koren red pepper powder that is the defining element of kimchi as it is known in the UK. Nothing smells or tastes quite like it.

Daikon Radish

Daikon radishes, or mooli, have been cultivated in Korea since the time of the three kingdoms. In the UK, it is common to find enormous specimens in the greengrocers, sometimes up to 15 inches (nearly 40cm) long. These are not quite the same as the Korean *mu*, which tend to be shorter and pale green at the top, with denser flesh, but they are almost interchangeable. It is usually best to go for smaller ones, as they do become more woody in texture the older and bigger they are. If you cannot find daikon radishes, normal English radishes will do. They are a bit more watery, so you might like to salt them with the cabbage, to extract some of the water.

Kimchi Mode of Action

Red pepper powder not only provides the taste that typifies kimchi, it is also an essential part of the fermentation pathway. Fermentation begins in a similar way to sauerkraut, with populations of *Leuconostoc mesenteroides* dominating at first, utilizing readily available glucose and fructose to make carbon dioxide and lactic acid. During the next phase, LAB increase in number, as do – in the presence of red pepper only – certain *Weissella* species, including *W. koreensis*. This may be because these microbes can utilize capsaicins in the pepper powder. Gochugaru also slows the fermentation process, especially at the start, and influences both microbial succession and the metabolites formed from the ingredients.[81] The variation of substrates provided by different vegetables

and gochugaru and rice paste, coupled with the different types of bacteria present (of which there may be as many as 20), results in a rich and rapid generation of bioactive compounds, from secondary pathways of metabolism. Lactic and acetic acids and ethanol are also produced, and a good amount of mannitol, which adds a refreshing taste to the end product.

The bioactive components will alter depending upon whether there is fish sauce, saujeot or fish paste in your kimchi; fish components will include protein that can be broken down into amino acids. It is also heavily influenced by seasonal variations in vegetables. If arginine is present, it can be utilized by *W. koreensis* to make ornithine as a secondary metabolite, which could potentially be beneficial. In the absence of fish, it could be a good idea to substitute a little seaweed, as this is also high in arginine.

Weissella sp. are psychrophilic, which means that they are able to thrive at low temperatures, even down to zero degrees. That is why kimchi will continue to ripen in the fridge and may soften within a few weeks, especially with chopped table kimchi.

Temperature

In many Korean recipes, fermentation at 5–10 degrees is recommended. In the UK, room temperature is normally used, although in warmer weather kimchi can reach the optimal pH of 4.3–4.5 in about 48 hours.

Three to four days is more usual in spring and autumn, which are are the ideal seasons. After a short time at room temperature it is then removed to the fridge for 'ripening'.

Seafood Flavourings

In Korea it is extremely common to include fish sauce or fermented shrimp in kimchi, but in the UK it is often omitted. This is perhaps because the UK is rather behind Korea in terms of fermenting vegetables, and fermented fish is not yet on the menu! There is also a significant move towards veganism in the UK, alongside an increased interest in experimental and fermented foods, which has led to a rise in the popularity of 'vegan' kimchis. In these, it is common for kelp, or other green leaves, to be added to provide the taste of the sea.

Nutritional Content of Kimchi

With its wide variety of ingredients, kimchi is a nutritional powerhouse even before it has been fermented. Indeed, it is common in Korea to eat it fresh too. Kimchi contains vitamins A, B and C, 34 amino acids, 10 minerals, carotenoids, polyphenols, dietary fibre and myriad other plant phytochemicals.

Potential Health Benefits of Kimchi

In a rare human crossover study, fermented kimchi (as opposed to fresh kimchi) was found to reduce body weight and improve metabolic parameters in overweight and obese patients.[82] The portion size was 100g with every meal – that is 300g a day, or a whole jarful! This is thought to be the result of the ability of *W. koreensis* to make a compound called ornithine, which prevents intracellular lipid accumulation and accelerates the basal metabolic rate.[83] There also seems to be a role for capsaicin, which is present in the red pepper and has been proposed to enhance fat digestion.[84] In another study, obese subjects were given kimchi capsules, which had a similarly beneficial effect.

Several animal studies have identified possible anti-carcinogenic properties in kimchi, which seem to be due to the regulation of apoptosis (death) of cancer cells, and an ability to reduce inflammation.

Kimchi also contains high levels of lactic acid bacteria (about 107–108cfu/g).[85]

In short, in line with the other fermented foods described here, kimchi seems to offer significant health benefits, despite its salt content. Its functionality seems to include anti-cancer, anti-obesity, anti-oxidative and anti-ageing effects when it is consumed in moderate quantities, through mechanisms that are currently being further elucidated. Some of these will be due to the bioactive molecules resulting from the fermentation process, while others are likely to be stimulated by the probiotics themselves.

• •

BAECHU KIMCHI OR CUT CABBAGE KIMCHI

Ingredients (for a 1ltr jar):

1 large Chinese leaf lettuce or napa cabbage approx. 600g chopped into 2cm slices
1 pak/bok choi, chopped into 2cm slices
50g sea salt (for example, Maldon, for 5% brine; or 10% for a shorter time)
1 litre of water, to cover the cabbage
250–300g daikon radish (mooli), cut in strips or triangles
3 spring onions cut into diagonal 1cm chunks
1 large handful of spinach (50g)

For the rice flour base and the marinating paste:

50g Korean red pepper powder (gochugaru)
20g rice flour
10g sugar (for the microbes, not for you)
100ml water
8 cloves of garlic, minced
1cm of fresh ginger, grated
5cm of leek, finely chopped
½ Asian pear/normal pear or apple grated
Optional: 1 tbsp fish sauce or kelp powder and/or 1–2 tsp shrimp paste

Method:

1. Make a 5% salt solution (50g salt in 1ltr of water) in a large bowl and stir until dissolved.

2. Chop cabbage and pak/bok choi into wide slices (about 2cm) and add to bowl. Leave to soak for 6–12 hours (or with 10% salt for 3–4 hours).

3. To make the marinating paste: in a saucepan heat the rice flour, sugar (optional) and water and boil for 3–5 minutes until it makes a thick gloopy paste. Leave to cool.

4. In a blender, or having separately grated/chopped the components, mix together the garlic, ginger, leek, and pear or apple (and fish sauce, kelp powder or shrimp paste, if using).

5. Periodically, check the cabbage until a piece of stalk can be bent in two. Bite into a piece of the stem – it should be plump, juicy and delicious.

6. When the cabbage is ready, drain and rinse in water for a minute or so if the salt concentration is 5%; 10% salt will need a longer rinsing time. Taste another piece of cabbage stem – it should be salty, but not unpleasantly so. Squeeze the cabbage gently to remove excess water, but do not overdo it.

7. Add everything else – daikon, spring onion, spinach, gochugaru, rice flour base – and with your hands (gloved, if you have sensitive skin or if you do not want them to be stained orange), mix about two-thirds of the marinating paste into the vegetables. Assess coverage and add more paste if you would like. The amount will depend on how much the vegetables have wilted, and how much sauce you want. If there is any left over, freeze it, or use with some other vegetables.

8. Transfer to a Kilner jar, pushing the vegetables down gently – it is not critical to cram them in tightly for this quick ferment. Leave space at the top of the jar to allow for expansion as carbon dioxide is created.

9. Leave for 3 days at a cool temperature (approx. 18°C). At this point your kimchi will have reached a pH of about 4.3–4.5.

10. Taste to check that it is delicious (it will be) and transfer to fridge; it should be kept at the back where temperatures are lowest.

The kimchi will last for many weeks but will eventually go soft. When it reaches this stage, it is still edible, but its texture may be less appealing. It can still be used to add a flavour kick to soups, stews or mayonnaise. If it is added to hot foods, the beneficial bacteria will not survive, but it will still be a rich source of fibre and heat-stable bioactive compounds.

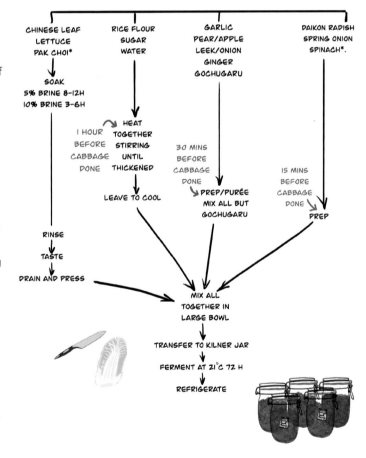

The process for making kimchi (*denotes optional ingredients).

SALTING THE CABBAGE

Using 50g Maldon or other flaky sea salt per litre of water just for wilting the cabbage may seem excessive and wasteful, but the Koreans do it for a good reason. In an experiment comparing kimchi made with cabbage in four different ways – soaked in 5% brine for 12 hours, soaked in 10% brine for 3 hours, wilted, with 5% salt directly, added for 1 hour, and squeezed with 5% salt – the results were interesting. (A higher than usual concentration of salt was used for direct wilting, because in kimchi only the cabbage is salted, not the other ingredients, and you want to end up with approx. 2–2.5% overall concentration.) At the end of the experiment, both saltwater-soaked cabbage pieces were plump, juicy and sweet, while the directly brined ones were flat and slightly bitter in comparison.

Napa cabbage salting experiment: the middle two pieces, left in brine for some hours, are plump and juicy; the rest of the cabbage, subject to the direct salting method, is flat and floppy.

So, it is recommended that you leave time to soak your cabbages if you can. If you do not have time, wilting them in salt will suffice – they might just lack a little sweetness and texture. You could also leave them overnight – 5% salt is ideal for this.

After rinsing the cabbage pieces, you have two options: either leave them to dry off a little naturally by draining in a colander for an hour, or gently press down to remove excess moisture. For the best texture, do not press too hard.

Prepping the cabbage: chopping; using everything except the very end of the stalk; soaking; checking the texture.

Variations

Cutting the Daikon

There is room for a little self-expression in the cutting of the daikon. Fine matchsticks, or julienned daikon pieces are common when making poggi (wrapped, or uncut) kimchi, but when making a cut kimchi, pieces tend to be larger. You might prefer to cut sticks about half a centimetre square and 3–5 cm in length, or wedge-shaped pieces. For special occasions, you can even make stars or hearts with mini cutters! Do make sure to remove any hairs – they can look rather human when they are in the jar.

Mixing the Paste

Some prefer to mix all the elements of the paste together, while others prefer to add the gochugaru separately because it makes the paste very stiff and hard to manage. It will all be mixed together in the end, anyway.

Selecting the Correct Jar

Kilner jars are excellent for kimchi as it will be ready for fridge-ripening after about three days at 18°C, and probably only two days above 23 degrees. Be sure not to over-fill the jar – when the microbes start to metabolise, they will produce vast amounts of carbon dioxide and expansion will occur. Fill to the shoulder, leaving at least 5cm between the top of the kimchi and the top of the lid. The kimchi should be lightly tamped down by

Prepping the daikon and spring onions: cut vertically into the vegetables to make pie-shaped pieces, then cut horizontally across in thin slices. Alternatively, make sticks or stars.

Mix everything together with gloved hands. You could use a wooden spoon, but why not embrace the Korean principle of *son-mat*, literally 'the taste of one's hands', putting something of yourself into the food you prepare.

about an explosion, you can replace the metal clip with a rubber band. If your kimchi is very lively, when it is done you will need to take care when opening the jar. Cover the jar with a tea towel (bear in mind it might get stained), and press down hard with one hand whilst reaching below to release the clip with the other.

hand, not firmly squeezed as with sauerkraut, and there is no need to try to submerge the vegetables below the paste – there is not likely to be enough brine and the red pepper powder gives additional protection again kahm yeast and mould growth anyway.

Is it Working?

Despite having tamped down the kimchi, within 24 hours you are likely to see large air pockets forming in the jar, and you might hear squeaks and hisses as carbon dioxide escapes from the gasket. If you are worried

Upon opening the lid, the kimchi nearly escapes from the jar!

Tasting the Kimchi

Unless you have an electric pH meter it is going to be difficult to check the pH of your kimchi – because of the colour, indicator paper is completely useless. A pH of 4.2–4.5 is almost always achieved after two to three days at room temperature, but you will have to rely on your nose and taste buds. It will taste spicy and tangy, and the onion flavours might be quite prominent. After a few days in the fridge, this will have mellowed and the ginger will stand out more.

Storing the Kimchi

With its large cut surface area, table kimchi can soften within a few weeks, even in the refrigerator, as fermentation slowly continues. To retard this, keep it at the back, where temperatures are lower. In Korea it is not unusual to have a special 'kimchi fridge' at 0 degrees for this purpose.

What to Do with Your Kimchi

Of course, one way to eat kimchi is straight from the jar! However, you want to avoid introducing mouth bacteria and enzymes to your store, as this could hasten its degradation. Always decant before tucking in.

Below are five more things to do with it:

- Cheese has not historically been part of the Korean diet, but, curiously, the pairing of kimchi and cheddar is quite spectacular! (*See* below for the recipe for a kimcheese toastie.)

- Use as a condiment; a spoonful on the side of almost any dish adds colour and variety and it goes especially well with eggs, so is perfect in an omelette.
- Use some of the juice to make a spicy and delicious kimchi mayonnaise. Just stir in a little of the juice from the bottom of the jar, or use in place of vinegar if making your own.
- If you have not put fish sauce in, use in rice 'summer rolls' with prawns.

As it ages and softens, it can be turned into a cooking ingredient, adding a delicious and surprisingly un-kimchi-like tang to soups, stews, mayonnaise, butter and sauces (*see* below for the recipe for kitchen sink soup). Remember, if it is cooked, it will lose its probiotic microbes.

Preparing a kimcheese toastie.

- -

THE KIMCHEESE TOASTIE

This toasted sandwich was named by Lisa Cadd, the FussFreeFoodie.

Ingredients:

Two slices of sourdough bread
60–80g decent Cheddar cheese, grated
Butter
Two spoonfuls of kimchi
1 tsp oil for the frying pan (optional)

Method:
1. Heat the frying pan while you prepare the ingredients: add oil if the pan is prone to sticking.
2. Sprinkle half the cheese on to one of the slices of bread.
3. Spoon the kimchi on top, and finish with the rest of the cheese.
4. Top with the other slice of bread.
5. Butter the top (the outside surface that will touch the frying pan).

6. Invert the sandwich into the hot pan, so the buttered side is face down and cook over a low-medium heat for 3 or 4 mins.
7. While it is frying, butter the top slice of bread.
8. When the cheese starts to melt, turn the sandwich over and cook the other side for a couple of minutes.

- -

KITCHEN SINK SOUP

Served with kimchi, this soup provides the complete gut-healthy lunch, with up to 19 different vegetables in one sitting!

Ingredients (serves 6):

450g sweet potatoes, peeled (optional) and cubed
2 onions (red and/or white), chopped
2 garlic cloves, whole, peeled
1 celery stalk, chopped
1 carrot, chopped
1 red pepper, chopped
1 cup red lentils
Tin of tomatoes
Large spoonful of kimchi
½ block coconut cream
Stock cube (vegetable or chicken)
Salt/pepper to taste
Large handful of coriander, chopped

Kitchen sink soup. PAREIDOLIA

Method:

1. Roast the sweet potatoes, onions, garlic, celery, carrot and red pepper for about 1 hr at 180°C (fan) in a covered pot or tray until softened (onions slightly caramelized).
2. Transfer to a pan on the hob and add the lentils, tomatoes, kimchi (used here for flavour rather than for its probiotic qualities) and stock cube.
3. Add water to cover, to just above the level of the vegetables.
4. Simmer over a low heat for a further 15 mins or until the lentils are cooked through
5. Blend with a stick blender, adjusting consistency by adding more water if necessary
6. Season with salt/pepper as required and sprinkle with coriander before serving.

PICCALILLI

The same principles of sauce wrapping can be applied to make a fermented piccalilli. The process is largely the same, but it is much quicker to make than kimchi.

PICCALILLI

Ingredients:

800g of the following, in any combination: cauliflower (around 500g for the best balance), carrot, leek, courgette (avoid big seeds if there are any, use firm flesh), green beans, red/yellow/green pepper
2% salt

For the sauce:

20g rice flour
80g water
10g honey
Large pinch of salt

Spice mix:

2 tsp English mustard powder
2 tsp turmeric
1 tsp coriander seeds
½ tsp fenugreek
1 tsp nigella seeds
1 tsp cumin seeds

Method:

1. Chop the vegetables into small pieces about 1cm square. Break the cauliflower into small florets and cut up any thick pieces of stem.
2. Rinse in a colander.
3. Weigh vegetables into an empty bowl and record the weight.
4. Calculate 2% salt.
5. Mix the salt and vegetables together, taking care not to break up the cauliflower florets, and set aside. The salt will begin to draw water out of the vegetables, which will help to keep them crispy.
6. Boil the rice flour, honey and water in a saucepan until it forms a thick gloopy sauce, adding a pinch of salt (approx. 2%). Leave to cool.
7. Make up the spice mix.
8. Add the cooled sauce and the spice mix to the vegetables and stir in with a wooden spoon – or

As long as piccalilli is not over-fermented at room temperature, it will remain deliciously crispy for several weeks in the fridge.

your hands if you do not mind them being temporarily turmeric-coloured.

9. Pack the piccalilli mixture into your chosen jar (a Kilner jar would work, or a mason jar with an airlock), leaving about 6cm of headroom and eliminating air pockets as you go. Alternatively, use a ziplock bag.

10. As there is no brine, it is difficult to submerge the vegetables, but for this short time there is no need to worry.

11. Ferment for approximately 3–4 days at room temperature. Pockets of carbon dioxide will form. Try to resist opening the jar until the time is up, then smell and taste before refrigerating. The piccalilli can then be left to develop its flavour for several more days.

A FAST FERMENT: TOMATO SALSA

Another very quick ferment, once more wrapping the vegetables in a sauce as a great way of transferring flavour. However, it is perhaps not one to keep for a long time when made with red tomatoes, as these can quickly turn to mush. It is ideal for when you can plan a day or two in advance to catch it at its best. If, however, you substitute green tomatoes and yellow and green peppers for the red ones, you will have a ferment that will retain its texture for longer and be even more flavoursome. Leave out the tomato purée if you want to keep the colour vibrant green/yellow – curiously, the green tomatoes keep their colour quite well.

TOMATO SALSA

Ingredients:

250g red tomatoes (firm and not too ripe), chopped
1 red chilli, chopped
1 green chilli, chopped
2 peppers, 1 green, 1 red/yellow/orange
2 garlic cloves
Zest and juice of 1 lime
1 small red onion, finely chopped
Handful of chopped coriander
¼ tsp crushed cumin seeds or cumin powder
Squeeze of tomato purée (optional)
Sea salt

Method:

1. In a food processor, pulse the garlic, chillies, lime, half of the onion, half of the peppers and the tomato purée (if using) to make a thick lumpy paste.

2. Weigh all ingredients into a bowl including the sauce.

3. Add 2% sea salt

4. Place in your fermentation vessel of choice at room temperature for two to three days.

The salsa can now be used as a base to invigorate any number of different vegetables, or to mix with avocado, sweetcorn, grilled aubergines or courgettes.

Green tomato salsa lasts much longer than its red relative.

APPENDIX: THE VEGE-TABLE

Vegetable (or fruit)	Method	Fermentation Time	Notes
Apples	Skins and peels for apple cider vinegar. Excellent in krauts	6 weeks (Vinegar) 5 days (Fresh in krauts)	
Artichoke, Jerusalem	Scrub skins, slice if very thick Brine ferment	7 days	Fermentation seems to limit the wind factor! Surprisingly delicious
Asparagus	Brine ferment	5–8 days	Excellent as a snack
Aubergine	Brine ferment/sauce ferment	5–10 days	Texture does not really change however long you leave it. Spongy in a good way
Avocado	Best in mixed ferments Fresh into a fermented salsa to serve	3 days	Goes brown very quickly. Better mixed
Beans, broad	Remove coats and ferment in brine or cook and mash	7 days	Better as a mash
Beans, green	Brine ferment	3 days	Ripen in fridge. If they are not fresh enough, they can end up tough and stringy. They should 'snap'
Beans, runner	Brine ferment	3–5 days	Can be very stringy; check that they 'snap' before using
Beans, cooked cannellini, borlotti, black, haricot, butter, kidney, black-eye	Mix with whey or sauerkraut brine as a starter	3 days	Mash first, or remove seed-coats and use in mixed ferments
Beetroot	Sliced for kvass In mixed ferments Choggia/ golden	5–7 days 5 days 7–10 days	Choggia or golden can be sliced and used alone
	Note: Red beetroot is not recommended grated alone as it becomes too alcoholic		
Broccoli, tender-stem	Brine ferment	5–7 days	Florets will go soggy
Brussels sprouts	Brined	2–3 weeks	Ferment better when opened out with a cross
Cabbage, white/green	Self-brining Quicker in a mixture	3 weeks 5–10 days	
Cabbage, red	Self-brining Quicker in a mixture	3–6 weeks 10 days	

Vegetable (or fruit)	Method	Fermentation Time	Notes
Cabbage, hispi/sweetheart		5–7 days alone, 3 days in mixed	Wilts to nothing!
Cabbage, napa/Chinese	Fantastic for kimchi	3 days, but can go longer in non-kimchi ferments	
Cabbage, Savoy	Old leaves/inner leaves	Up to 6 weeks/1 week	The difference in fermenting time between outer and inner leaves can be a problem!
Carrots	Sticks in brine / Grated with ginger	5 days / 3–5 days	Avoid cheap over-sweet carrots
Cauliflower	In small florets as brine ferment, or mixed kraut, or piccalilli	3 days mixed; 5–7 days alone	Very versatile. Cut stems into smaller pieces
Celery	Good for torshi	5–7 days	
Celeriac	Self-brining or brined. Mixed ferments	7–10 days According to mixture	Good spiralized for remoulade
Chickpeas	Mash method	3 days	Good hummus base
Collard greens	Use shredded in mixed fements	According to mixture	Tricky alone
Courgettes	Diced, mixed torshi/shredded, sauce ferment	5–7 days/ 3 days	Can taste slightly chlorine-like alone
Cucumber	Sauce ferments	3 days	Can be used in place of napa cabbage in kimchi – salt in the same way
Fennel	Torshi brine ferment, mixed krauts	5–7 days	Softens surprisingly quickly
Ginger	Brine ferment	2 weeks	
Garlic	Peel, ferment in brine	14 days	
Daikon	Apart from kimchi, mixed brine ferment in sticks, or self-brining with other vegetables	5 days	
Kohlrabi	Spiralized or grated: in mixed self-brining ferments, or brined sticks	3 days	Delicious and much under-rated!
Leeks	Cut in sticks	3–5 days	
Lemons	Whole/sliced	4 weeks/ 10–14 days	10% salt
Lime	Whole	8 weeks	10% salt
Kale	Use in mixed krauts	According to mixture	Does not reach low pH alone and smells horrible. Not recommended
Onions (red)	Cut in rings/whole, for pickling	5–7 days/ 3–4 weeks	Put with other vegetables to facilitate fermentation – carrot sticks are ideal
Pak/bok choi	Treat like napa cabbage	3 days	

Vegetable (or fruit)	Method	Fermentation Time	Notes
Parsnips	Julienned, self-brining, mixed torshi	7–10 days, 5–7 days	Cut quite finely
Pears	Good in mixed self-brining ferments	According to mixture	
Peas	Use a few in a mixed self-brining ferment	According to mixture	Not ideal whole
Peppers	Brined ferments / mashes	3–5 days / 10–14 days	Can be self-brining but go a bit slimy
Pumpkin	Diced in brine	14–21 days	
Radishes	Whole radish bombs (brined) / sliced (self-brining)	7–12 days / 5–7 days	
Samphire	Use in mixed ferments, avoid woody stems	According to mixture	Beware if picked wild; may go black and pH may not fall below 5.5
Spinach	Best in mixed self-brining ferments. Alone, self-brining	According to mixture. 3–5 days	Goes to almost nothing but tastes good
Sprouted seeds	Brined ferment	5–7 days	
Squash, butternut	Brined ferment	7–10 days	
Swede	Cubed, brined. Grated in mixed ferments	10–14 days. According to mixture	
Tomato, green	Self-brining ferment	3–10 days	Depending on how green they are
Tomato, red	Self-brining ferment/whole cherry tomatoes, brined	2–3 days / 7 days	Can go mushy very quickly. Whole ones can go fizzy
Turnip	Cut into chunks and brined,	3–5 days	Good in torshi
Watercress	Best in mixed self-brining ferments. Alone, self-brining	According to mixture. 3–5 days	
Watermelon	Brine fermented	5 days	Remove skins, and ferment the white part too
Wild garlic	Best in mixed self-brining ferments. Alone, self-brining	According to mixture	May be difficult to achieve a safe pH

Vegetables that don't ferment easily

The following vegetables, for various plant physiological reasons, are more difficult to ferment: kale, collard greens, samphire, wild garlic and seaweed. In fact, all of these are strongly flavoured dark green vegetables. In the table above vegetables are highlighted that could be a cause for concern and do not in tests reach pH 4.5 or below within three days. These can, however, be safely mixed in with cabbage and other mixed ferments. Spinach and watercress are more adaptable.

GLOSSARY

Aerobic microbes   Microbes that require oxygen in order to metabolise.

Anaerobic microbes   Microbes that thrive in the absence of oxygen.

Antioxidants   Compounds that inhibit oxidation, which is a chemical reaction that can produce free radicals, leading to chain reactions that can damage human cells. Antioxidants such as ascorbic acid can terminate these chain reactions.

Colony Forming Units (CFU)   A way of counting viable (living) bacteria in a laboratory. If a bacterium can form a colony, it is viable. You can count single colonies.

Commensal   An older term used to describe bacteria that exist in a person's microbiota that do not harm them, but do not necessarily benefit them. Still used today, although it is now known that the relationship is symbiotic.

Digesta   The bulk of dietary fibres that is digested in the GI tract.

Disaccharide   A sugar consisting of two simple sugar molecules joined together, for example, lactose (glucose and galactose) and sucrose (glucose and fructose).

Dysbiosis   An imbalance in the types of organism present in a person's microbiota, especially the gut, which may contribute to a range of health conditions.

Epiphytic   Describes bacteria that exist non-parasitically on plant surfaces including leaves, seeds, roots, flowers, buds and fruit.

Epithelium   Made up of cells that line the outer surfaces of the body. The gut is lined by gut epithelial cells.

Facultative aerobe/anaerobe   An organism that is able to grow in the presence/absence of oxygen, even if it prefers not to.

Functional foods   Foods that have a potentially positive effect on health beyond basic nutrition.

Heterofermenter   A fermentation resulting in a number of end products, for example, lactic acid bacteria that ferment carbohydrates to volatile acids and carbon dioxide as well as lactic acid.

Homofermenter   A fermentation resulting in a single end product, for example lactic acid bacteria that ferment carbohydrates to lactic acid.

Mesophilic   Describes microbes that grow best within a moderate range, 18–40°C.

Metabolism   The entire set of chemical reactions that organic molecules undergo in living cells.

Microbial symbiosis   The co-existence of microorganisms in an intimate associate that sees all benefit.

Microbiota-accessible carbohydrates (MACs)
Carbohydrates that are resistant to digestion by a host's metabolism, but can be fermented by the microbiota. Includes inulin, resistant starch and fructooligosaccharides.

Organic acid   An organic compound with acidic properties (the chemical definition of 'organic' means it contains carbon). Many of these are beneficial to human health, for example, ascorbic acid (vitamin C).

Pathobiont   Some bacteria normally considered as commensals can become pathogenic when they start to overgrow and take over.

Phytochemicals   Chemical compounds produced by plants, to help them thrive or thwart competitors, predators or pathogens. The name comes from Greek meaning 'plant'.

Polyphenols   A large class of phytochemicals comprising flavonoids and phenolic acids, which give foods their colours and seem to be beneficial to human health.

Prebiotics   Describes a substrate that is selectively used by host microorganisms, conferring a health benefit.

Probiotics   Live bacteria and yeasts that, when administrated in adequate (viable) amounts, are beneficial to human health. Found in functional foods and may be taken as dietary supplement.

Short chain fatty acids   Derived from intestinal microbial fermentation of indigestible foods, SCFAs are the main energy source of colonocytes (gut epithelial cells), making them crucial to gastrointestinal health.

Species/strain   Basic units of the biological classification system and taxonomic ranks. The full classification is: kingdom, phylum, class, order, family, genus, species/strain.

Stool sample   Medical term for poo sample.

Thermophilic   Describes microbes that thrive at high temperatures, over 40°C.

RECOMMENDED SUPPLIERS

Kefir Grains	Every Good Thing	everygoodthing.co.uk, info@everygoodthing.co.uk
Kombucha SCOBYs	Happy Kombucha	happykombucha.co.uk
Sterilock jars	Sterilock	sterilock.co.uk
Boyajian Lemon Oil	King's	www.kingsfinefood.co.uk
Good Grips funnel and strainer set	Oxo	amazon.co.uk (not available elsewhere in UK)
pH meter suppliers	Hanna Instruments	hannainstruments.co.uk
Ceramic fermentation crocks	Mark Campbell Ceramics	etsy.com/uk/shop/MarkCampbellCeramics
The best greengrocer in Bristol	Hugo's Greengrocer & Deli	72A North Street, Bedminster, Bristol
Yoghurt cultures	Freshly Fermented	freshlyfermented.co.uk

REFERENCES

1. Sudo, N. et al. Postnatal microbial colonization programs the hypothalamic-pituitary-adrenal system for stress response in mice. J. Physiol. (2004). doi:10.1113/jphysiol.2004.063388

2. Donaldson, G. P., Lee, S. M. & Mazmanian, S. K. Gut biogeography of the bacterial microbiota. Nature Reviews Microbiology (2015). doi:10.1038/nrmicro3552

3. Hehemann, J. H. et al. Transfer of carbohydrate-active enzymes from marine bacteria to Japanese gut microbiota. Nature (2010). doi:10.1038/nature08937

4. Rafii, F. The role of colonic bacteria in the metabolism of the natural isoflavone daidzin to equol. Metabolites (2015). doi:10.3390/metabo5010056

5. Tamburini, S., Shen, N., Wu, H. C. & Clemente, J. C. The microbiome in early life: Implications for health outcomes. Nature Medicine (2016). doi:10.1038/nm.4142

6. Goodrich, J. K., Davenport, E. R., Waters, J. L., Clark, A. G. & Ley, R. E. Cross-species comparisons of host genetic associations with the microbiome. Science (2016). doi:10.1126/science.aad9379

7. Schloss, P. D., Iverson, K. D., Petrosino, J. F. & Schloss, S. J. The dynamics of a family's gut microbiota reveal variations on a theme. Microbiome (2014). doi:10.1186/2049-2618-2-25

8. Fransen, F. et al. The impact of gut microbiota on gender-specific differences in immunity. Front. Immunol. (2017). doi:10.3389/fimmu.2017.00754

9. Spector, T. I spent three days as a hunter gatherer to see if it would improve my gut health. Available at: https://theconversation.com/i-spent-three-days-as-a-hunter-gatherer-to-see-if-it-would-improve-my-gut-health-78773. (Accessed: 1st October 2019)

10. Markowiak, P. & Iizewska, K. Effects of probiotics, prebiotics, and synbiotics on human health. Nutrients (2017). doi:10.3390/nu9091021

11. Monteagudo-Mera, A., Rastall, R. A., Gibson, G. R., Charalampopoulos, D. & Chatzifragkou, A. Adhesion mechanisms mediated by probiotics and prebiotics and their potential impact on human health. Applied Microbiology and Biotechnology (2019). doi:10.1007/s00253-019-09978-7

12. Berry, S. et al. Predicting Personal Metabolic Responses to Food Using Multi-omics Machine Learning in over 1000 Twins and Singletons from the UK and US: The PREDICT I Study (OR31-01-19). Curr. Dev. Nutr. (2019). doi:10.1093/cdn/nzz037.or31-01-19

13. Zeevi, D. et al. Personalized Nutrition by Prediction of Glycemic Responses. Cell (2015). doi:10.1016/j.cell.2015.11.001

14. García-Cano, I. et al. Lactic acid bacteria isolated from dairy products as potential producers of lipolytic, proteolytic and antibacterial proteins. Appl. Microbiol. Biotechnol. (2019). doi:10.1007/s00253-019-09844-6

15. Chai, E. et al. Botulism associated with home-fermented tofu in two Chinese immigrants - New York city, March-April 2012. Morb. Mortal. Wkly. Rep. (2013).

16. Morse, D. L., Pickard, L. K., Guzewich, J. J., Devine, B. D. & Shayegani, M. Garlic-in-oil associated botulism: Episode leads to product modification. Am. J. Public Health (1990). doi:10.2105/AJPH.80.11.1372

17. Wolkers-Rooijackers, J. C. M., Thomas, S. M. & Nout, M. J. R. Effects of sodium reduction scenarios on fermentation and quality ofsauerkraut. LWT - Food Sci. Technol. (2013). doi:10.1016/j.lwt.2013.07.002

18. Pozdnyakova, M. Love for Kefir. The secret of the

drink of the highlanders. Available at: https://www.aif.ru/food/products. (Accessed: 16 September 2019).

[19.] Danone. Danone History. Available at: https://www.alliedmarketresearch.com/yogurt-market. (Accessed: 14th September 2019)

[20.] www.dairyreports.com/article/2014/06/23. (Accessed: 20 August 2019

[21.] Guarner, F. et al. Should yoghurt cultures be considered probiotic? Br. J. Nutr. (2005). doi:10.1079/bjn20051428

[22.] Desobry-Banon, S., Vetier, N. & Hardy, J. Health benefits of yogurt consumption. A review. International Journal of Food Properties (1999). doi:10.1080/10942919909524585

[23.] Šednika-Tober, D. et al. Higher PUFA and n-3 PUFA, conjugated linoleic acid, -tocopherol and iron, but lower iodine and selenium concentrations in organic milk: A systematic literature review and meta- and redundancy analyses. British Journal of Nutrition (2016). doi:10.1017/S0007114516000349

[24.] Quigley, L. et al. The complex microbiota of raw milk. FEMS Microbiology Reviews (2013). doi:10.1111/1574-6976.12030

[25.] www.milkfacts.info. (Accessed: 19 September 2019

[26.] Dannenberg, F. & Kessler, H. G. Reaction Kinetics of the Denaturation of Whey Proteins in Milk. J. Food Sci. (1988). doi:10.1111/j.1365-2621.1988.tb10223.x

[27.] Marcó, M. B., Moineau, S. & Quiberoni, A. Bacteriophages and dairy fermentations. Bacteriophage (2012). doi:10.4161/bact.21868

[28.] Lee, W. J. & Lucey, J. A. Formation and physical properties of yogurt. Asian-Australasian Journal of Animal Sciences (2010). doi:10.5713/ajas.2010.r.05

[29.] Tamime, A. Y. Fermented milks: A historical food with modern applications – a review. Eur. J. Clin. Nutr. (2002). doi:10.1038/sj.ejcn.1601657

[30.] Rosa, D. D. et al. Milk kefir: Nutritional, microbiological and health benefits. Nutr. Res. Rev. 30, 82–96 (2017).

[31.] Richard, B. A Whole New Generation of Milk Kefir Grains Formed from Freeze-dried Starter Cultures A Fascinating Insight Into a Hidden World.

[32.] Prado, M. R. et al. Milk kefir: Composition, microbial cultures, biological activities, and related products. Frontiers in Microbiology (2015). doi:10.3389/fmicb.2015.01177

[33.] Dobson, A., O'Sullivan, O., Cotter, P. D., Ross, P. & Hill, C. High-throughput sequence-based analysis of the bacterial composition of kefir and an associated kefir grain. FEMS Microbiol. Lett. (2011). doi:10.1111/j.1574-6968.2011.02290.x

[34.] Witthuhn, R. C., Cilliers, A. & Britz, T. J. Evaluation of different preservation techniques on the storage potential of kefir grains. J. Dairy Res. (2005). doi:10.1017/s0022029904000652

[35.] Liu, J.-R., Wang, S.-Y., Lin, Y.-Y. & Lin, C.-W. Cancer Antitumor Activity of Milk Kefir and Soy Milk Kefir in Tumor-Bearing Mice. Nutr. Cancer (2002). doi:10.1207/S15327914NC4402_10

[36.] Tu, M. Y. et al. Short-Term Effects of Kefir-Fermented Milk Consumption on Bone Mineral Density and Bone Metabolism in a Randomized Clinical Trial of Osteoporotic Patients. PLoS One (2015). doi:10.1371/journal.pone.0144231

[37.] Marshall Ward, H. The ginger-beer plant, and the organisms composing it: a contribution to the study of fermentation-yeasts and bacteria. Philos. Trans. R. Soc. London. 183, 125–197 (1892).

[38.] Lutz, L. Recherches biologiques sur la constitution du Tibi. Bull. Soc. Mycol. Fr. 15, 68–72 (1899).

[39.] Godoy Augusto, Herrera Teófilo, U. M. Más allá del pulque y del tepache. Bebidas alcohólicas no destiladas indígenas de México. Ediciones UNAM. México. 2003. a b. (Ediciones UNAM. México., 2003).

[40.] Fiorda, F. A. et al. Microbiological, biochemical, and functional aspects of sugary kefir fermentation – A review. Food Microbiology (2017). doi:10.1016/j.fm.2017.04.004

[41.] Laureys, D., Aerts, M., Vandamme, P. & De Vuyst, L. Oxygen and diverse nutrients influence the water kefir fermentation process. Food Microbiol. (2018). doi:10.1016/j.fm.2018.02.007

[42.] Miguel, M. G. da C. P., Cardoso, P. G., Magalhães, K. T. & Schwan, R. F. Profile of microbial communities present in tibico (sugary kefir) grains from different Brazilian States. World J. Microbiol. Biotechnol. (2011). doi:10.1007/s11274-010-0646-6

[43.] Marsh, A. J., O'Sullivan, O., Hill, C., Ross, R. P. & Cotter, P. D. Sequence-based analysis of the microbial composition of water kefir from multiple sources. FEMS Microbiol. Lett. (2013). doi:10.1111/1574-6968.12248

44. Gulitz, A., Stadie, J., Wenning, M., Ehrmann, M. A. & Vogel, R. F. The microbial diversity of water kefir. Int. J. Food Microbiol. (2011). doi:10.1016/j.ijfoodmicro.2011.09.016

45. Verce, M., De Vuyst, L. & Weckx, S. Shotgun metagenomics of a water kefir fermentation ecosystem reveals a novel Oenococcus species. Front. Microbiol. (2019). doi:10.3389/fmicb.2019.00479

46. Alsayadi, M. et al. Evaluation of Anti-Hyperglycemic and Anti-Hyperlipidemic Activities of Water Kefir as Probiotic on Streptozotocin-Induced Diabetic Wistar Rats. J. Diabetes Mellit. (2014). doi:10.4236/jdm.2014.42015

47. Alsayadi, M., Al Jawfi, Y., Belarbi, M. & Sabri, F. Z. Antioxidant Potency of Water Kefir. J. Microbiol. Food Sci. (2013).

48. Lindau. Über Mesudomyces gisevii, eine neue Gattung und Art der Hefepilze. Beriche der Dtsch. Bot. Gesellschaft 31, (1913).

49. Chakravorty, S. et al. Kombucha tea fermentation: Microbial and biochemical dynamics. Int. J. Food Microbiol. (2016). doi:10.1016/j.ijfoodmicro.2015.12.015

50. Marsh, A. J., O'Sullivan, O., Hill, C., Ross, R. P. & Cotter, P. D. Sequence-based analysis of the bacterial and fungal compositions of multiple kombucha (tea fungus) samples. Food Microbiol. (2014). doi:10.1016/j.fm.2013.09.003

51. Sinir, G. Ö., Tamer, C. E. & Suna, S. Kombucha Tea: A Promising Fermented Functional Beverage. in Fermented Beverages (2019). doi:10.1016/b978-0-12-815271-3.00010-5

52. Bellassoued, K. et al. Protective effect of kombucha on rats fed a hypercholesterolemic diet is mediated by its antioxidant activity. Pharm. Biol. (2015). doi:10.3109/13880209.2014.1001408

53. Chu, S. C. & Chen, C. Effects of origins and fermentation time on the antioxidant activities of kombucha. Food Chem. (2006). doi:10.1016/j.foodchem.2005.05.080

54. Deghrigue, M. et al, Antiproliferative and antimicrobial activities of kombucha tea. African J. Microbiol. Res. (2013). doi:10.5897/AJMR12.1230

55. Aloulou, A. et al. Hypoglycemic and antilipidemic properties of kombucha tea in alloxan-induced diabetic rats. BMC Complement. Altern. Med. (2012). doi:10.1186/1472-6882-12-63

56. Leal, J. M., Suárez, L. V., Jayabalan, R., Oros, J. H. & Escalante-Aburto, A. A review on health benefits of kombucha nutritional compounds and metabolites. CYTA - J. Food (2018). doi:10.1080/19476337.2017.1410499

57. Lavasani, P. S., Motevaseli, E., Sanikhani, N. S. & Modarressi, M. H. Komagataeibacter xylinus as a novel probiotic candidate with high glucose conversion rate properties. Heliyon (2019). doi:10.1016/j.heliyon.2019.e01571

58. Greenwalt, C. J., Steinkraus, K. H. & Ledford, R. A. Kombucha, the fermented tea: Microbiology, composition, and claimed health effects. Journal of Food Protection (2000). doi:10.4315/0362-028X-63.7.976

59. Malbaša, R., Lončar, E., Djurić, M. & Došenović, I. Effect of sucrose concentration on the products of Kombucha fermentation on molasses. Food Chem. (2008). doi:10.1016/j.foodchem.2007.11.069

60. Yavari, N., Mazaheri-Assadi, M., Mazhari, Z. H., Moghadam, M. B. & Larijani, K. Glucuronic Acid Rich Kombucha-fermented Pomegranate Juice. J. Food Res. (2017). doi:10.5539/jfr.v7n1p61

61. Leff, J. W. & Fierer, N. Bacterial Communities Associated with the Surfaces of Fresh Fruits and Vegetables. PLoS One (2013). doi:10.1371/journal.pone.0059310

62. Wassermann, B., Müller, H. & Berg, G. An Apple a Day: Which Bacteria Do We Eat With Organic and Conventional Apples? Front. Microbiol. (2019). doi:10.3389/fmicb.2019.01629

63. Raghuvanshi, R. et al. Microbial Transformations of Organically Fermented Foods. Metabolites (2019). doi:10.3390/metabo9080165

64. Kazimierczak, R. et al. Beetroot (Beta vulgaris L.) and naturally fermented beetroot juices from organic and conventional production: Metabolomics, antioxidant levels and anticancer activity. J. Sci. Food Agric. (2014). doi:10.1002/jsfa.6722

65. Hallmann, E. et al. The Nutritive Value of Organic and Conventional White Cabbage (Brassica Oleracea L. Var. Capitata) and Anti-Apoptotic Activity in Gastric Adenocarcinoma Cells of Sauerkraut Juice Produced

Therof. J. Agric. Food Chem. (2017). doi:10.1021/acs.jafc.7b01078

[66.] Ren, H., Endo, H. & Hayashi, T. The superiority of organically cultivated vegetables to general ones regarding antimutagenic activities. Mutat. Res. – Genet. Toxicol. Environ. Mutagen. (2001). doi:10.1016/S1383-5718(01)00229-7

[67.] Wunderlich, S. M., Feldman, C., Kane, S. & Hazhin, T. Nutritional quality of organic, conventional, and seasonally grown broccoli using vitamin C as a marker. Int. J. Food Sci. Nutr. (2008). doi:10.1080/09637480701453637

[68.] Peñas, E., Martinez-Villaluenga, C. & Frias, J. Sauerkraut: Production, Composition, and Health Benefits. in Fermented Foods in Health and Disease Prevention (2016). doi:10.1016/B978-0-12-802309-9.00024-8

[69.] Podsedek, A. Natural antioxidants and antioxidant capacity of Brassica vegetables: A review. LWT – Food Science and Technology (2007). doi:10.1016/j.lwt.2005.07.023

[70.] Ellulu, M. S., Rahmat, A., Patimah, I., Khaza'Ai, H. & Abed, Y. Effect of vitamin C on inflammation and metabolic markers in hypertensive and/or diabetic obese adults: A randomized controlled trial. Drug Des. Devel. Ther. (2015). doi:10.2147/DDDT.S83144

[71.] Krajka-Kuźniak, V., Szaefer, H., Bartoszek, A. & Baer-Dubowska, W. Modulation of rat hepatic and kidney phase II enzymes by cabbage juices: Comparison with the effects of indole-3-carbinol and phenethyl isothiocyanate. Br. J. Nutr. (2011). doi:10.1017/S0007114510004526

[72.] Nelson, N. J. Migrant studies aid the search for factors linked to breast cancer risk. J. Natl. Cancer Inst. (2006). doi:10.1093/jnci/djj147

[73.] Martinez-Villaluenga, C. et al. White cabbage fermentation improves ascorbigen content, antioxidant and nitric oxide production inhibitory activity in LPS-induced macrophages. LWT – Food Sci. Technol. (2012). doi:10.1016/j.lwt.2011.10.023

[74.] Zabat, M., Sano, W., Wurster, J., Cabral, D. & Belenky, P. Microbial Community Analysis of Sauerkraut Fermentation Reveals a Stable and Rapidly Established Community. Foods (2018). doi:10.3390/foods7050077

[75.] Bousmaha, L., Ouhssine, M. & El Yachioua, M.

Fermentation du citron par inoculation microbienne. Afrique Sci. Rev. Int. des Sci. Technol. (2010). doi:10.4314/afsci.v2i1.61136

[76.] Aayah, H. et al. Characterisation of the dry salted process for the production of the msayer, a traditional lemon aromatising condiment. LWT – Food Sci. Technol. (2010). doi:10.1016/j.lwt.2009.09.005

[77.] Sanati, S., Razavi, B. M. & Hosseinzadeh, H. A review of the effects of Capsicum annuum L. and its constituent, capsaicin, in metabolic syndrome. Iranian Journal of Basic Medical Sciences (2018). doi:10.22038/IJBMS.2018.25200.6238

[78.] Jargin, S. V. Kvass: A possible contributor to chronic alcoholism in the former Soviet Union – alcohol content should be indicated on labels and in advertising. Alcohol and Alcoholism (2009). doi:10.1093/alcalc/agp055

[79.] Clifford, T., Howatson, G., West, D. J. & Stevenson, E. J. The potential benefits of red beetroot supplementation in health and disease. Nutrients (2015). doi:10.3390/nu7042801

[80.] Jang, D. J., Chung, K. R., Yang, H. J., Kim, K. S. & Kwon, D. Y. Discussion on the origin of kimchi, representative of Korean unique fermented vegetables. J. Ethn. Foods (2015). doi:10.1016/j.jef.2015.08.005

[81.] Kang, B. K., Cho, M. S., Ahn, T. Y., Lee, E. S. & Park, D. S. The influence of red pepper powder on the density of Weissella koreensis during kimchi fermentation. Sci. Rep. (2015). doi:10.1038/srep15445

[82.] Kim, E. K. et al. Fermented kimchi reduces body weight and improves metabolic parameters in overweight and obese patients. Nutr. Res. (2011). doi:10.1016/j.nutres.2011.05.011

[83.] Moon, Y. J. et al. Intracellular lipid accumulation inhibitory effect of Weissella koreensis OK1-6 isolated from Kimchi on differentiating adipocyte. J. Appl. Microbiol. (2012). doi:10.1111/j.1365-2672.2012.05348.x

[84.] Zheng, J., Zheng, S., Feng, Q., Zhang, Q. & Xiao, X. Dietary capsaicin and its anti-obesity potency: From mechanism to clinical implications. Bioscience Reports (2017). doi:10.1042/BSR20170286

[85.] Park, K. Y., Jeong, J. K., Lee, Y. E. & Daily, J. W. Health benefits of kimchi (Korean fermented vegetables) as a probiotic food. Journal of Medicinal Food (2014). doi:10.1089/jmf.2013.3083

INDEX